MISSING

FROM

THE

VILLAGE

MISSING FROM THE VILLAGE

The Story of Serial Killer Bruce McArthur, the Search for Justice,
and the System That Failed Toronto's Queer Community

JUSTIN LING

McCLELLAND & STEWART

McClelland & Stewart and colophon are registered trademarks of Penguin Random House Canada Limited.

Library and Archives Canada Cataloguing in Publication

Title: Missing from the village / Justin Ling
Names: Ling, Justin, author.
Identifiers: Canadiana (print) 20200197045 | Canadiana (ebook) 20200197061 |
     ISBN 9780771048647 (hardcover) | ISBN 9780771048654 (EPUB)
Subjects: LCSH: McArthur, Bruce, 1951- | LCSH: Serial murders—Ontario—Toronto. |
     LCSH: Serial murder investigation—Ontario—Toronto. | LCSH: Gays—Ontario—
     Toronto—Social conditions.
Classification: LCC HV6535.C33 T67 2020 | DDC 364.152/3209713541—dc23

Illustrations copyright © 2020 by Lochlan Donald
Book design by Lisa Jager
Cover art: Ryan Allan / EyeEm / Getty Images

Typeset in Lyon by M&S, Toronto
Printed and bound in the United States of America

McClelland & Stewart,
a division of Penguin Random House Canada Limited,
a Penguin Random House Company
www.penguinrandomhouse.ca

1 2 3 4 5   24 23 22 21 20

Penguin
Random House
McCLELLAND & STEWART

CONTENTS

AUTHOR'S NOTE

THERE are two words I use in this book that may be controversial.

The first is the word *queer*. While, once, it was exclusively a slur, the word has been reappropriated to serve a very important function. As the acronym used to represent the broader spectrum of sexuality has expanded, from the simple LGBT to the more complicated LGBTQIA2+ (Lesbian, Gay, Bisexual, Trans, Queer, Questioning, Intersex, Asexual, Two-Spirit, and everything else), many have, rightly, pointed to how fraught it can be to encapsulate the incredibly diverse range of non-heterosexual and non-cisgender identities in a handful of letters. It feels that, no matter how many letters are added, entire parts of that spectrum are captured under broad catch-alls, like *trans*; or must otherwise be happy being relegated to the plus-sign. I have opted to simply use the word *queer* to represent every point along that spectrum. There are drawbacks in trying to use a single word, much less a word that once went hand-in-hand with discrimination and violence. There is beauty in that, too. As a word we have reclaimed, we can define it as widely and expansively as we choose. A word that used to mean exclusion can be inverted to be inclusive.

The second word that will appear throughout this book, perhaps to some chagrin, is *community*. There is a very good argument to be made that, even if there are communities of queer people, there is no queer community. I think this book is both evidence of what a broader queer community looks like, and where exactly that lack of community is so painfully evident. To that end, the use of those two words together—*queer community*—may be more aspirational than actual. A community is not a utopia, but it should be a space where outside prejudices are unwelcome, and where solidarity is a default. Unfortunately, that is not yet a reality.

This book sits at an uneasy crossroads of these problems. I am a journalist, and I am a member of that community. This book is not an academic work, it is not an activist manifesto, nor is it a true crime book which spectates from afar. This book is an investigation of a tragedy of enormous proportions, which works to explain why it happened, and to learn lessons on how to stop it from happening again.

There is blame to go around in this story. But there is credit to be given, too.

This book is dedicated to the friends and family of the men who went missing from Toronto's Village, for whom this tragedy has been a daily reality for years. I have tried to tell their story as honestly, accurately, and empathetically as possible, and can only hope that this book doesn't compound the pain. Many have, over the years, chosen to speak to me and continue reliving that trauma, sometimes at great personal expense, and I hope this book does that sacrifice justice. I specifically want to thank Meaghan Marian, who is both a key figure in this story and was instrumental in helping me navigate how to report this story properly. To her, and all the families, biological and chosen, I'm eternally grateful.

I also want to dedicate it to the investigators who worked these cases. The system of policing itself is desperately in need of repair, and we shouldn't blink in the face of that challenge. While it is critical we hold the police, as an institution, accountable for the failures that led to this story, it is also important we recognize the hard work and dedication of the officers assigned to these cases. Figuring out how to untangle the complicated relationship between queer people and the police, and indeed how we improve policing more broadly, involves recognizing where police get it right. In my years of working on this story, I have found a real desire on the part of those officers to engage in critical self-reflection. So while this book is dedicated to the officers and investigators, I also hope it sparks more introspection about their relationship with the queer community.

And, finally, this book is dedicated to the queer community itself. A community which has been ridiculed, gaslighted, surveilled, targeted, and killed. It has been marginalized by police, government, and society at large. But, through it all, it has survived with a culture and community that exists despite attempts to extinguish its uniqueness, and in spite of those attempts.

MISSING

FROM

THE

VILLAGE

PROLOGUE

AT the foot of Toronto's Gay Village is a bronze statue of a tall, thin man, facing east but looking south. His ankle-length coat appears to be billowing in a gust of wind. His right hand grips his hat and gloves, and his left a walking stick. In his lapel is a rose. The statue is covered in a green patina, giving the young monument an artificial age. It stands on the corner of Alexander and Church streets. A block south is Wood Street. At times the man has been clad in colourful bandanas and rainbow bouquets. Other times he's stood below balloon banners.

A plaque sits at his feet. It reads: "Alexander Wood, 1772-1844. Militia Officer, Businessman, Public Servant, Justice of the Peace, Gay Pioneer." There's a bit of a longer biography, but one line sticks out: "He was involved in a homophobic scandal in 1810 and fled to Scotland."

You have to do some research to learn Wood's whole story. It's a wild one—an early entry in how law enforcement and homosexuality interacted.

Born a Scot, Wood travelled to the new world at the end of the eighteenth century, settling in the city of York, later known as Toronto. A noted bachelor but well-reputed merchant and magistrate, Wood occupied the early colonial role as both investigator and judge. In 1810, he brought a worrying story to the court. A Miss Bailey had been sexually assaulted. She couldn't identify her assailant, but she had, however, wounded her attacker in the struggle. She had scratched his penis.

To find the assailant, Wood conducted a series of interviews with local men. The rumour around town was that Wood's investigation involved an inspection of whether the man sported the wound Miss Bailey described. That rumour, whether it was true or not, earned him the mocking title of "inspector general of private accounts." Another version of the tale goes that there was, in fact, no Miss Bailey. Wood had invented it as a pretext. It's impossible to know what's true, but it's fair to assume there's some fiction in these accounts. Even with all his good regard in the community, Wood was outed and humiliated, and fled to Scotland to avoid charges of sodomy.

Wood returned two years later and seemed to outlive the accusations against him. Nevertheless, he earned a nickname: Molly Wood. A molly house, in English slang, was a bar or tavern where men could gather and seek the company of other men, where cross-dressing was common, and where police would often show up in force. In 1827, Wood purchased a tract of relatively barren land in York. It, too, earned a particular nickname: Molly Wood's Bush.

Despite the nineteenth-century homophobia, a century and a half on, Molly Wood's Bush became a bustling microcosm of queerness. The undeveloped expanse that Wood purchased northeast of the city's downtown became, appropriately, the hotbed of queer life in Toronto and one of the busiest queer districts in the world. Wood's statue was erected in 2005, to commemorate his posthumous role in creating a safe space for queer people.

Today, the Village sits in the middle of a crossroads. To the north are upscale shops and sprawling office towers housing the headquarters of corporate Canada. West is Queen's Park, seat of Ontario's provincial government. South and east, however, is a mix of new condo developments, historic properties, single-family homes, social housing, and shelters. The neighbourhood is a fault line for the stark class divide in Canada's largest city.

The Village itself has changed drastically over the years. In the late 1960s and early 1970s, the so-called gay ghetto was a constellation of repurposed beer halls and chi-chi supper clubs. Over time, as the community began collectively coming out, the Village took on a more permanent shape. Much of it congregated around the intersection of Church Street and Wellesley Street. Queer-owned clubs sprang up, trimmed with rainbow flags. Queer people across North America and beyond began flocking to the Village, moving into the towering co-operative apartment blocks that sat on Church Street or into the quaint Victorian-style detached homes in neighbouring Cabbagetown.

It has been a long process. Walking through the Village, for a time, meant looking over your shoulder to make sure you weren't being followed by a would-be queer-basher. Nightlife did well, with those in the closet preferring the anonymous cover of night to the identifying daylight. Hardware stores, clothing shops, and restaurants eventually followed, as the neighbourhood found security in numbers. Queer candidates would run for office, pulling the vote from the Village—coming tantalizingly close to political power, but never quite getting there.

For decades, the Toronto Police service homed in on the Village. Fixated on it. Even as some cops walked the beat, trying to make ties to the community, others were notorious for picking up drag queens, sex workers, anyone who looked different, and giving them the "starlight tour." They would be driven to an inhospitable spit of land in the desolate portlands, beaten, and left to walk home without their shoes.

There were the periodic raids on queer establishments. Puritanical morality laws still on the books let officers shut down drag shows. Antiprostitution criminal charges were laid against the patrons and owners of gay and lesbian bathhouses. Queer civil servants were interrogated and fired if undercover officers spotted them walking into a queer bar.

But things improved. What was once a refuge became a community.

With every legal milestone, the Village would cement itself a little further. Homosexuality was decriminalized in 1969. Sexual orientation became a protected class from discrimination under the Ontario Human Rights Code in 1986—it was added to the federal code a decade later. The pink purge of civil servants largely ended in the early 1990s. Gay marriage came about in some provinces in the early 2000s, before becoming law across Canada in 2005. A push to enshrine human rights protections for trans and nonbinary people in the early 2010s was fought at every turn by the political order, and wouldn't become law across the country until 2017.

The Village, through it all, became a victim of its own success. Fast-food chains and banks moved in, rents went up, the deluge of partygoers and bachelorette parties became too much for many. Many lamented the corporate floats and throngs of politicians marching in the annual Pride parade. Queer people moved out of the Village, to more affordable neighbourhoods. Queer bars sprang up in other parts of the city. The 2008 global recession hit the Village hard, throwing some long-running establishments underwater.

It was very much an open question, at that point, about just what it meant to be in and of the queer community—whether there was really a sort of broader queer community, or whether each of the letters in the LGBTQ acronym was just as divided as Toronto itself.

This story begins not long after, in 2010, during the dying days of summer.

ALEXANDER WOOD

1

THE VILLAGE

FOR a long time, Alexander Wood's cocked head was pointing, roughly, towards Zipperz.

Zipperz was an institution. For many years its facade was a pale pink, but its paint job ended about halfway up the two-storey building. Above that was drab concrete. When pink fell out of fashion, it was painted a bright aquamarine. And then it was black. The bar changed colour like a drag queen trying on new shades of lipstick. The contrast between the bright paint and the rest of the dour building gave Zipperz the particular quality of being a portal into another world, a secret passageway. Dating back to the 1970s, that's exactly what those doors, in various shapes, forms, under different names and ownership of past incarnations, promised to the city's queer community.

When you walked into Zipperz, you saw a grand piano sitting in one corner. It wasn't just a decoration. On any given night, a music student or an old crooner might be sitting at the keys, belting out a standard. Harry Singh, the owner, would often be found

floating around the place, talking to the regulars. Jody Becker, one
of the affable bartenders, would be behind the main bar, which
sat in the middle of the front room. Further inside, there were
pool tables, and a dance floor surrounded by black walls draped
in chains—that was Cellblock. To an interloper, the bar might have
looked dark, even gritty. But for anyone who went often, they
would know the chains disguised what was about as friendly a
spot as you can find in Toronto.

There were, of course, clues that the bar was a little friendlier
than its decor let on. There were the rainbow letters on the front
window, proclaiming: WELCOME WORLD. There was the back
patio, a leafy oasis with a tiny wading pool. There was an actual
throne—Singh told a local media outlet that it was a recovered
prop from the 1987 film *The Last Emperor*.

I'd been inside Zipperz before. I remember a much younger
version of myself thinking the inside was exactly how I always
imagined the quintessential gay bar would look. But I never made
it to retro night. Retro nights were famous at Zipperz. They happened every Sunday, but on long weekends, they were blowouts.

Friends who used to be frequent patrons look a bit wistful,
their eyes a bit glassy, when they remember the place, retro night
in particular. The best music, the best crowd, the best atmosphere.

One warm late summer night in 2010, one of those regulars
disappeared. Later that year, another vanished. A little more than
a year later, a third went missing.

It would become one of the Village's most enduring, and frustrating, mysteries.

* * *

Skandaraj Navaratnam's friends just called him Skanda. Born in
Sri Lanka in 1970, as the second eldest of four brothers, Skanda
was the live wire of his family. He grew up in the 1980s, in Sri

Lanka's north, where a vicious civil war was in its infancy. Young men in the Tamil-majority north, like Skanda, had limited options. They could fight for the army or join the rebel Liberation Tigers of Tamil Eelam—the Tamil Tigers—refusing those options could mean death. Skanda had earned a particular reputation as an ecological activist who had fought to preserve his country's jungles and forests from the emergent threat of deforestation. Activists don't fare well in civil wars. Skanda was arrested for his activism, and was tortured while in custody. It's something he would spend the rest of his life grappling with. "He was making a movie of his experiences and playing them over in his head," a friend and colleague would later remark.

In the early 1990s, Skanda fled. Not that he had much choice. He hoped that, as his siblings struggled to take care of their aging parents, he would be able to send money to support the rest of his family. So he came to Canada, where, like thousands of other Tamils, he was granted asylum.

I don't know Skanda's mindset when he stepped off a plane to start a new life in Toronto. A mix of anxiety and relief, I imagine. What I do know for sure is how quickly he became a fixture of the Village. He found an apartment not too far off Church Street, and the gaybourhood became his well-trodden stomping ground. For more than a decade, Toronto, the Village in particular, was home.

Skanda was like a magnet for friends—the bartenders and regulars at Zipperz, vendors at a farmer's market, neighbours. People gravitated towards him. No wonder. His charm was infectious. He could walk up to a stranger on the street and strike up a conversation without difficulty. His charm wasn't aggressive or cloying, it was earnest and genuine. It was his superpower. But like all superpowers, it originated from a dark place: he was lonely. In leaving Sri Lanka, he had left behind his whole life. "He missed his family. A lot," one friend told me. And so, arriving in Toronto alone, he set out to find a chosen family.

The concept of chosen family is integral to the queer community. Many queer people find themselves cut off or isolated from their biological family. Some queer people don't feel ready to come out to their family as their true self. Some families, still, can't accept a queer child. Sometimes queer people need to leave home to feel accepted in a bigger city. Building a network of friends and community to form a new family is a queer strategy that seems to span culture, era, and age. How that family is built is unique to each person. Some make friends at the bars, some use dating apps, others have standing brunches or meet at queer book clubs. Skanda worked to build a chosen family when he came to North America. Despite it all, or maybe because of it, he was social, outgoing, even flirty.

The queer community, sometimes forgetting its own struggle, can be cold towards racialized folks. For Skanda, as the millennium came and went, as he reached his thirties, and as the world began to look with suspicion on dark-skinned men after the terror attacks of 9/11, things didn't get easier. The world, in many ways, became a smaller, less trusting place—and the queer community wasn't immune. Skanda had his own trauma to grapple with. All that may have been hard to see from the outside.

Sarrah Becker met Skanda through her mother, Jody, the Zipperz bartender. Soon, she joined his chosen family. He was an uncle to her. "The first time we met was at the Zipperz's back patio," she recalled. "He had extra big hearts in his eyes for me." She grins when she remembers Skanda's dance moves.

Joel Walker met him at a pool bar on Church Street, a few years after he arrived in Toronto. "We hit it off immediately, and it was love at first break," Walker recalled. "He was kind of a loud character. And so am I, I guess, so that's kind of where our energies drew together." Even though Joel was younger, the two became fast friends, and Joel still gushes over finding a friend like Skanda.

"My fondest memory was him being at my birthday. There was a bunch of people who showed up—and I appreciate every one of them and everything like that—but he was my present," Joel remembered. "He was my favourite part of that day and he was all the time. I'm not used to having a friend like him in my life."

Skanda's love life had its ups and downs. For years, he was seeing a stoic man, more than a decade his senior, and they moved in together. While Skanda may have been loudly out of the closet, his partner wasn't. When guests came over, he insisted that Skanda was just a roommate. It was plain to anyone who walked around the apartment, however, that the spare bedroom was immaculate and untouched—doilies, undisturbed, everywhere—and that Skanda's affairs were in the master bedroom. Nevertheless, they kept up the ruse. There were other partners. One relationship was marred by physical abuse. Other relationships just weren't quite the right fit.

Like many others in the community, Skanda occasionally visited one of the Village's many bathhouses—he favoured one in particular: The Cellar. The clientele was older, more of Skanda's type. While Skanda generally dated men, he didn't hide that he occasionally saw women, too, identifying as bisexual.

He was just naturally a larger-than-life figure. "He wore jewellery—rings on every finger," Joel remembered. "Multiple rings, like two to three, sometimes on each finger. It normally sounds way over the top, gaudy, but for him, it worked." A gold ring in his left ear. Hulking pendants around his neck. Loud T-shirts. A lot of his clothing, you could tell, were finds at vintage stores—brilliant finds. His whole style was eccentric, but it fit together. If he was walking down the street in a crowd, Joel said, "you would see him first."

Skanda had a habit of calling everyone he met, regardless of gender, "girl," Joel recalled. "But with his accent he'd always say 'girl' like it's almost with no *I* at all. It's just *G-R* and a lot of *R*s and then an *L* at the end. And so when he thinks that something was malarkey or full of crap, he'd be like 'Girl, please.'"

Skanda was a master of Scrabble and a pool shark. He had an interest in tropical fish and gardening. He worked at the University of Toronto, as a research assistant. Over the summer of 2010, Skanda had adopted a husky puppy. He loved that puppy so much, Joel told me, it made him jealous—just a joke, he said a beat later, though I wasn't entirely convinced.

That puppy is how Mita Hans met Skanda. She was browsing scarves at a vendor's stall outside the St. Lawrence Market, near downtown, when her German shepherd dragged her over to meet Skanda's husky.

"When you see another brown queer person, as a brown queer person, you get really excited going 'Oh my god! Look there's one more!'" she told me. Given Mita's habit of introducing herself to others like her is so similar to Skanda's superpower, it's no surprise they hit it off.

I first met Mita at a coffee shop not far from Cabbagetown, where Skanda lived. When I walked in, she was chatting up another woman of colour, making friendly small talk. I figured the woman must be a friend, but Mita told me, no, she was a complete stranger. I asked her about it. With a warm smile, she explained that it's just something she does: introduce herself to other queer people, to other brown people, whom she sees on the street. With a hint of sadness, she dropped a maxim: "It's lonely at the intersection of otherness."

Mita figures that every time a friendly woman with a cute dog and a mop of grey hair introduces herself and gives you a tractor beam of a hug, that intersection feels a little less lonely. "There's that level of connection that's instantaneous of knowing each other's struggles," she added.

So there's Mita and her German shepherd bumping into Skanda and his husky, outside a scarf stall. "We all know each other and recognize each other and watch out for each other."

Both Mita and Skanda knew the man who owned the stall, himself a queer man from afar. He was planning a buying trip back to his home country. "They were talking about, you know, the impossibility of going home," she said of Skanda and their mutual friend. They talked about Skanda's longing to go back, to see his family. "That just wasn't possible for him," Mita said.

• • •

On the last day of August 2010, Skanda had a date. To judge by the messages they exchanged, it went pretty well. "Thank you for a wonderful eve," his date texted.

The first Sunday that September was warm, but fall was on the way. The next day was Labour Day. It was the last long weekend of summer. Skanda had been at a friend's cottage earlier that weekend in Bancroft, a small town in the expanse of picturesque Ontario wilderness between Toronto and Ottawa. There was a leak in the cabin roof, and he had jimmy-rigged a temporary solution—*I'll fix it in the spring,* he told his friend, Jean-Guy Cloutier.

Because it was a long weekend, the Village was buzzing. Skanda hit up a barbeque on the spacious patio of the Black Eagle, one of his favourite Church Street bars. After that, he headed to Zipperz for what would be a particularly busy retro night. Everyone was partying late, and why not? The next day was a holiday. In the wee hours of the morning, before last call, a friend saw Skanda leave through the back door and said goodnight—Skanda was with two friends, but didn't introduce them. Skanda may have, as he often did, smoked a joint before disappearing in the warm September air.

The next day, Skanda wasn't around. And he was not around the day after that. On Wednesday, his date from the week earlier, having not heard back from Skanda, texted again: "Did I pass or fail the audition?" He didn't get a reply. At the same time, an unsettled feeling crept across his circle of friends.

Skanda had a habit of skipping town for brief periods. One time when he'd vanished, he'd turned up at a Buddhist monastery in Niagara Falls. He liked the outdoors, so taking off to the cottage or to go camping wasn't unusual for Skanda. But since he'd adopted the puppy, he wouldn't leave it home alone for more than two nights in a row, let alone for days at a time.

And this was 2010. Cell phones existed, but leaving yours at home was pretty normal. Or maybe you'd headed out of the city and lost reception entirely. Or, perhaps, you spent a little too long eating pixelated apples in the snack game and drained your battery.

Jody hadn't heard from Skanda, but she couldn't reach Jean-Guy, either. She figured maybe Skanda had gone back to the cottage Monday morning. But that week, Jean-Guy came back into town—without Skanda. Suddenly, there was worry. Skanda was prone to flights of fancy, but he wasn't irresponsible. If nothing else, he wouldn't abandon the puppy.

Jean-Guy reported Skanda missing on September 13, 2010. That same day, he sent a text to Skanda's phone, letting him know his friends were worried enough to contact the police.

Within days, Zipperz turned into a sort of command centre. Friends poured in to grab posters with Skanda's face on them. A Facebook group was set up to coordinate searches of nearby parks. Jody spoke to queer newspaper *Xtra* in the days after he was reported missing: "Even if somebody is pissed off at the whole world, and they want to go disappear, you take your dog."

• • •

Abdulbasir Faizi, Basir to his friends, was, by his own admission, not a happy man.

He was born in Herat, Afghanistan, in the 1970s, at a time when the country appeared on the cusp of joining a club of prosperous Middle Eastern nations. Economic opportunity and democratic stability, with time, promised to create a country where conservative customs could co-exist with social freedoms and sexual liberation. It was a dream crushed when the Soviets invaded in 1979.

Many fled. Basir stayed and soldiered on. He hung on through a civil war and the rise of the Taliban. He married his wife, Kareema, in Kabul in 1999, but their lives, like the hope and prosperity of Afghanistan itself, had been spoiled by outside forces. They did their best to live through it, but the situation wasn't improving. Basir once remarked to a friend: "You do not know the things I have seen." Basir and Kareema decided that their growing family needed to find greener pastures.

Like many others fleeing the tumult of the early 2000s, Basir came to Canada with his wife. Together, they had two daughters. They moved into a home in Brampton, just west of Toronto and a popular destination for new immigrants like the Faizis. He found a job at a printing and label company not far from the family home. The couple did well for themselves, enough to try to venture into their own business. Basir bought two rental properties with a friend and looked forward to earning enough money to retire. But Basir was always cursed with rotten luck or maybe an overly trusting nature. The friend he had gone into business with double-crossed him—he took the money and fled. To top it off, he had been laid off for a time. In early 2010, Basir was forced to declare bankruptcy.

It was a breaking point. Basir confessed to his wife around that time that he was unhappy. He hated his job and wanted to move—if not back to his native Afghanistan, then somewhere else. Maybe to Ottawa, the nation's capital. He felt alienated from his life. What he didn't tell his wife was the other part of his disenchantment, the real root of his malaise. He was unhappy in another way that so many closeted people understand painfully well. He didn't confess to Kareema that, when he often called her after work to inform her that he would be working late or seeing friends, he was lying. He didn't tell her about the drive he took many evenings after work.

I've driven the route Basir would have taken. I can't help but imagine it was lonely. He would get into his modest sedan and fight the rush hour traffic and merge onto the Highway 401 east, leaving behind his suburb. Then Highway 427 south, towards downtown. Then the Gardiner Expressway east, driving past the illuminated CN Tower and the office lights of the skyscrapers of the financial district, empty but for cleaning staff. Then up the Don Valley Parkway, following the commuters driving home from work. He would take the Bloor Street exit and drive west to Church Street. He would park his car in the Village and head into one of his usual haunts. The drive is a little over forty kilometres but can take more than an hour and a half in after-work traffic.

Basir was a regular at Zipperz, where he may have sat across from Skanda, but he would also sidle up to the horseshoe bar at Woody's, with its reliably friendly post-work crowd. Later in the evening, he would often be seen at the Black Eagle, a more dimly lit establishment that was, just the same, a friendly spot, especially for men looking for discretion. It was a leather bar, popular with a crowd of gay men—almost, uniformly, men—who wanted something different than the other bars that lined the gay strip. They were generally older, hairier, heavier.

Sometimes, at the end of the night, Basir would head to one of the Village's men-only bathhouses: Steamworks or The Cellar. Those bathhouses are familiar to many men in the Village—particularly, but not exclusively, those venturing to Church Street unbeknownst to their wife. Inside their labyrinthian corridors are reams of men looking for discreet and unconventional encounters. Gay bathhouses are a tradition that goes back to a time when queer sexuality lived only behind closed doors. They remain popular today for plenty of men seeking men.

Basir had made friends in the Village, and he was open with them that he was bisexual. He confessed that he wanted to come out to his family, but not until his children were older. Many in the community know how hard that internal struggle is—the bargaining, trying to convince yourself it is a phase or a curiosity. Basir's cultural background, his religion, and his wife and two kids must have only complicated that internal monologue. He didn't want to hurt his family. Basir sought support, though. From time to time, he would go to the Salaam Canada, a community group for queer Muslims, for advice and counsel.

One night in 2010, in the sleepy chasm between Christmas and New Year's, he trod a well-worn path. First, the Eagle. Then, Steamworks, to meet a friend. A half-hour before midnight, Basir told his friend he was heading home, but the two made plans to meet two days later, on New Year's Eve. Basir's debit card transactions confirmed he had walked across the street to a burger joint for a late-night snack. The door to the condo he shared with his wife didn't open that night. He never took the long drive home.

It took very little time for Basir's wife, Kareema, to get worried. She tried calling him that night, but his phone was off. The next day, her sister filed a report with the Peel Regional Police.

• • •

Majeed Kayhan was ten years older than Basir, but like him grew up in Afghanistan, not far from the border with Iran. He was raised in a strict, traditional family, of which he was the baby. His father was a Muslim cleric, and the household was ruled by a particularly conservative order—devoutness of any stripe has a habit of doing that. Majeed was different. He was creative, musical. He had a wonderful habit of breaking into song, sometimes in Dari, but his lexicon of foreign music proved impressive later in life.

Majeed married in Kabul in 1983, amid the same war that hung over Basir. His two children were born in Afghanistan, before he fled with his family to Canada, settling into a suburb of Toronto. His extended family followed, but their marriage didn't last long in their new lives. They divorced in 2002, after nineteen years together, and Majeed headed to downtown Toronto. He started using his middle name, Hamid.

He began spending time at a Turkish bathhouse in the city's west end, the Oak Leaf, a mecca for men of all types—straight, closeted, questioning, coming-out, gay, queer. Some went there for a schvitz. Others went to hook up. It was there that Hamid fully discovered his sexuality.

When Hamid had filed for divorce, he'd listed his home address as a shopfront in the posh Yorkville neighbourhood—though that's not where he lived. His friends remember him moving into the City Park Co-op apartments, with his lover. The imposing apartment blocks stood just across the way from the patina-covered statue of Alexander Wood. He was out, at least in the Village, but his extended family was in the dark. He stayed close with them, just the same, but there was still some separation between his two lives. To his family, he was Majeed. In the Village, he was Hamid.

Living on the block kept Hamid close to the myriad bars and pubs of Church Street. Bartenders and barflies remember him, often, in fond terms: a friendly, smiling, grandfatherly type who would have a few drinks and serenade locals with Bollywood tunes. He would head out to gay-friendly campgrounds in the summer to unwind. He spent his days chatting with friends at some of the coffee shops on Church Street. He showed up to Pride events in traditional Pashtun garb, happily walking through the mess of partygoers, dressed like nobody else in the crowd.

Kyle Andrews and Hamid had met at the Eagle and got on well, though they were a study in contrasts. Hamid's endearing salt-and-pepper good looks were set in an older but friendly face with high cheekbones. Kyle is a big guy—huge red beard down to his chest, goofy smile. They just happened to be each other's types. Kyle and Hamid talked a lot about home. For Kyle, that was Nova Scotia. For Hamid, Afghanistan.

"When he was a young man he had always yearned for, not necessarily the Western world, but what was . . . out *there*," Kyle said.

Hamid first discovered the world beyond his sheltered life through cassettes. "Family and friends who went abroad, they would record things from their own collection, or from the radio, and they mailed them [back to Afghanistan]." When Hamid or his friends would receive the tape ration, it was a party. "They'd take over a warehouse, and they'd have a disco." Kyle giggled a bit. "Even though you think: Afghanistan, you don't think . . . there's a disco scene. But there was!"

Learning music through osmosis, through bootleg tapes as Hamid had, leaves you with a spotty knowledge of pop. Kyle and Hamid would be sitting around, listening to the radio. "He'd be like 'Oh, I know this song.' And he knew all the words but he wouldn't know the artist." The best thing was that he could actually sing. Kyle recorded a video of Hamid, staring off at the city over the railing of the balcony on which they sat. He crooned in Farsi, grinning, through tokes of a joint. Sometimes at Zipperz, to the amusement of owner Harry Singh, he'd break into old Bollywood tunes, and sometimes he would even dance. The songs betrayed a homesickness. Kyle said, "I think a lot of that was hard for him because, you know, around that there'd be some tears because he'd be remembering, and saying that he would always want to go back."

Behind the singing and the laughter, there was darkness. Hamid had a drinking problem. Especially on the second floor of the Black Eagle, which features a dimly lit bar and a busy dark room, he was known to get stumbly and handsy. Acquaintances describe him as lonely and looking for a connection, but lacking the social skills necessary to build a rapport with strangers. He could swing wildly from happy to sad, depending on how drunk he was. When he did talk to others at the bar, he openly talked about how much he wanted to go home, to Afghanistan. Some nights he would meander from his regular haunts to the Cellar—a clerk there remembers Hamid would hit on him relentlessly. That is, until Hamid learned he had a boyfriend, then he let up.

The Oak Leaf Spa was an important meeting place for queer and questioning men, but—like many bathhouses—it was a spot where drugs were used liberally. It's probably there that Hamid found crack. He spent years struggling with it, off and on. He would stop using for long stretches, then fall back into it.

That summer of 2012, Kyle had gotten into a fight with Hamid before he had gone home to Nova Scotia on vacation. "The last time I'd seen Hamid, I was a little pissy with him, and then I'd left him a shitty voicemail," Kyle remembered. The two had been on the outs that whole summer.

On October 14 that year, Hamid boarded the subway and headed just north of downtown to hitch a ride to a family wedding with his son. Coming from a large family, Hamid had an array of siblings, nieces, nephews, cousins—even three grandkids. A relative recounts seeing Hamid at the ceremony, recalling that he was always equipped with a smile and pockets full of candy for the kids. When his family dropped him back at the subway station after the wedding, he said his goodbyes. He wasn't around them often, but he still managed to see them now and then. He left the wedding with a big smile on.

Hamid did stay in contact with his son. When there was radio silence for a week after the wedding, his son got worried. He picked up the phone and tried one of Hamid's friends from the Village—he hadn't seen Hamid, either, since the eighteenth. Hamid's son filed a missing persons report on October 28. When he checked on Hamid's apartment, the birds his father kept lay dead at the bottom of their cages.

Kyle kept calling Hamid that fall, but his friend would never pick up. Eventually, the number came back as disconnected. "I was kind of worried he got into the drugs."

SKANDA NAVARATNAM

2

THE VOID WHERE
EACH MAN WAS

WHEN Skanda, Basir, and Hamid disappeared, they truly vanished. Joel Walker, Skanda's friend, likened Skanda's disappearance to an alien abduction. One second these men were sitting at the bar at Zipperz, the next they were gone.

Police did the requisite checks: their debt and credit cards hadn't been accessed, their cell phones hadn't pinged a cell tower, their emails hadn't been opened. It felt like there was not so much as an indent in the grass where they had been standing.

The only piece of evidence that appeared in the weeks that followed their disappearances came in Basir's case. He disappeared on December 29, 2010. In the first few days of 2011, someone called the city to report a decade-old Nissan that had been parked on their street since before the new year had rolled over. It's the kind of neighbourhood where someone would notice a car out of place. A necklace of bright yellow parking tickets was strung across its windshield. A tow truck was dispatched and police ran the plates: the car was registered to an Abdulbasir Faizi, forty-four years old, of Brampton.

Of all the places within Toronto city limits for his car to be, Moore Avenue was one of the least likely. It was a ten-minute drive northeast of the Village, and the opposite direction from his home. On that stretch of the street, there were only single-family homes and a small park—you wouldn't end up there unless there was something specific you were looking for. When I did that drive for the first time, it was not an intuitive route. From a home in the west end or from downtown, you'd need to drive east to Jarvis Street, head north, and take the Mount Pleasant exit, then drive along the winding street, passing dozens of residential streets, before finally taking a sharp right onto Moore Avenue.

It was an inflection point on the mystery. Why would Basir stop there?

There would be ample speculation in the months and years to follow. A local newspaper opined that Moore Avenue, flanked by Mount Pleasant Cemetery on one side and a park on the other, was an opportune spot to dump a car. That would compel internet sleuths, who may have read one too many Agatha Christie mysteries, to suggest Basir had been buried in the cemetery. When they found the car in early 2011, however, a search turned up no evidence of foul play. They guessed Basir had simply taken off and left his car somewhere it wouldn't be immediately found—his family tended to agree. Police even have a phrase for those sorts of cases: the missing person simply *vacated their life*. Just the same, police knocked on some doors in the neighbourhood. Nobody knew anything.

At the time, nothing quite fit. If Basir had been robbed, a criminal would likely know better than to dump a car on a well-lit residential street. Toronto is not lacking for deserted areas to hide an automobile. If Basir had wanted to run away, it would make more sense to ditch his car within walking distance of a train station or the airport—though, to do that, Basir would have needed to bring cash or his passport, and he had neither. And, despite some active imaginations, hiding a body in a locked-up cemetery in a residential neighbourhood isn't as easy as it seems.

Of the three disappearances, it was the most glaring piece of evidence to suggest something was desperately wrong.

There is another red flag, though. As a journalist, when I first began working on this story, it's what struck me most. It's that Skanda, Basir, and Hamid looked so similar. Here were three men who disappeared from the Village over just two years. If you walked into a room and saw the three sitting side by side, you could reasonably infer you had walked into a casting call. *Middle Eastern or South Asian male. Forties or fifties. Beard.*

Each family, each set of friends, toiled over these disappearances in their own way. Skanda's friends put up posters, searched ravines and parks. Basir's family took it upon themselves to search his email and computer for clues about his disappearance. Hamid's friends and family worked with police to try and find him.

I have lots of theories as to why, after three men of colour disappeared in fairly quick succession, nobody in the broader city seemed to notice or care. Why this had not set off some kind of tripwire. When I began working on this story, I would argue at length about those theories. Sometimes I've even argued with myself. Sometimes I think, maybe their cases had too many differences to reveal their similarities. Skanda, openly queer. Basir, in the closet. Hamid, somewhere in between. It seemed that, despite drinking at the same watering holes, they didn't even know each other.

But that is a poor explanation. I get angry about it. If three white women had vanished from the wealthy neighbourhood of Rosedale, just adjacent to the Village, their disappearances would have been national news. If three bankers had disappeared from the financial district, alarms would be going off immediately.

Why not these three?

• • •

While evidence of the men's whereabouts was scant, the ripple effects of their disappearances were obvious. Skanda's puppy was adopted. Basir's wife had to go on without him. Hamid's kids would never get to see their father again.

When Skanda disappeared, Sarrah Becker joined the search. She remembered one day in particular, trudging through the rain, trying to shield the missing persons posters in her hands. She remembered thinking that the cops had just skimmed over his case. "He was an easy write-off," she said. There was a prevailing theory held by investigators, she says: "Oh, he wasn't murdered, he just went into hiding." Sarrah couldn't figure out how to feel. She would get pangs of anger at her friend, buying into the idea that he had picked up and run off, selfishly, without telling anyone. But then she shook her head, convincing herself all over that he wouldn't do that. I suspect most of Skanda's friends felt similar frustration. They were powerless to bring him back, but putting up those posters was one thing they could do. So they pushed the nagging doubt aside and walked to the next pole. They strode to the next bus shelter. The next shop. And the next one. And the next one.

On her way home from work one day, Sarrah began walking up the leafy Don Valley ravine, which cuts through the east end of the city. The ravine is a natural marker that the city grew around. Sarrah walked up the pathways of the ravine where they begin, near Cabbagetown, and wandered through until she came out around Greektown, where she lived. It was a grim walk. She took the long route, along the walking paths, her eyes to the ground, looking for something. She might have picked up a water bottle, or a discarded T-shirt, wondering if it was his, wondering if her friend's body was somewhere in that ravine. The next day, she did it again. She found herself walking that route for eight years.

In early 2011, in the weeks after Basir went missing, his niece managed to get into her uncle's email account. In there, she found his dating profiles and the conversations he had had with other men. This was all a revelation to his family. Even through the shock, his wife, Kareema, drove to the Village in hopes of discovering something about his disappearance. It had been so sudden, so absolute, that his family was left to conclude that it was a deliberate vanishing act.

Hamid's friends and family, meanwhile, reached out to police to tell them as much as possible about him. His friends were open and blunt about his sexuality, his drug and alcohol use, his sexual habits. Opening your personal life like that is awkward and painful, but his friends hoped they could give police the information they needed to track him down.

At the time of each man's disappearance, his face wound up on the list of news releases on the Toronto Police website. Their name, age, where they were last seen. But without evidence, the cases soon lost priority. Skanda's and Hamid's disappearances were the responsibility of the Toronto Police Service's 51 Division. Because Basir technically lived outside of Toronto proper, his case was originally the responsibility of the neighbouring Peel Regional Police. As his car was found in Toronto, however, investigators from the city's 42 Division conducted the search. Given Basir was last seen in the Village, Peel called up 51 Division, so it was detectives from that detachment who interviewed his friends in the Village, and spoke to patrons of Steamworks. But his case seemed to get lost in the shuffle, the responsibility of three different police silos and none at the same time.

The rituals that each group of friends and family performed are ones that will become increasingly common and incredibly frustrating in this story. There is the early rationalizing—that there is an innocent explanation for their friend's or loved one's disappearance. Later, the sliver of optimism—that some extraordinary circumstances led to their disappearance, but that they will come back some day. Then, the nightmares of them sitting at the bottom of a lake. The campaign to find a missing loved one sits exactly between hope and dread.

No answers come.

Nobody calls in a hushed tone from a payphone. His shoe isn't found, sitting on a riverbed. A message doesn't pop up on Facebook, from their new profile, promising they're fine. Police don't call every other day with an update.

Television and movies prepare us for the eleventh-hour rescue. It doesn't happen. Friends and family live in the dark, fearing the worst, hoping for the best, but knowing that the worst might not even begin to cover it. They lie in bed and think through every scenario, optimistic and grisly. Sometimes an email comes in, from the missing person—just an automated spam message. A Facebook notification pops up, with a reminder of happier times, when they were still around. Someone sees their profile pop up on Grindr, but it turns out that the cops have logged into his dating app to search for clues.

Even with all that crushing dread, the people missing these men woke up every day trying their best. They put up posters, searched parks, called the investigators, spoke to the media, re-read their loved one's text messages for clues. But eventually, there's nothing more to do. That doesn't mean the nightmares or anxiety go away. Journalists still call, strangers still reach out to ask about the case, other missing persons cases drive speculation of a connection.

The void where each man once was looked different for each family and group of friends, but their experiences were similar in many ways. They were left bereft of answers, struggling to cope. The homemade posters asking for information about Skanda yellowed and got postered over. Friends continued trudging through city parks. Kareema filed for divorce, writing in the application that her husband had left for another life. Hamid's friends hoped that he was safe, wherever he was.

• • •

It was June 6, 2013—less than three years after Skanda disappeared, two and a half after Basir vanished, and nine months after Hamid's disappearance was reported to police—that the three cases were suddenly thrust into the public consciousness.

With little explanation, police took to Church Street with freshly printed missing persons posters in hand, one page for each of the three men. "Investigators have concluded there are a number of similarities between the three men and they have not been seen since they were reported missing," the police wrote in a press release. Suddenly, the three faces were everywhere in the Village.

Police had opened a full investigation into these three disappearances, assigning a dedicated task force—involving officers from 51 Division working out of headquarters—to get to the bottom of the mystery. Detective Deb Harris, a longtime veteran of the service, was tapped to head it up.

A reporter stood on Church Street, staring into the camera. "Those three men disappeared over a two-year span, but it's only now investigators are making a connection."

An officer stood in the polished atrium of police headquarters. "It's quite unusual. Look at the circumstances surrounding this case—we've not heard or seen from them for several years now." He goes through each missing man, underscoring the troubling details. "Is foul play suspected? That's unclear."

Sarrah Becker continued trudging through the Don Valley. Every day on her walk home from work, she detoured through the winding dirt tracks that lie beneath an overpass. Seeing the news that Skanda's case was back on the radar of officers pushed her to redouble her efforts, staring more intently into the overgrown weeds and plants, behind concrete pillars and into gurgling streams. She had dreams, nightmares, about Skanda.

An activist, a racialized queer man, spoke to a reporter in the street. "There seems to be a thread in these three disappearances. It is unsettling."

Kyle Andrews had been living in rural Nova Scotia for months, sitting in a tent. He didn't even know Hamid was missing until he returned to Toronto. When he did, the missing persons posters bearing his friend's face were on every telephone pole in the Village. Kyle was jolted into reality. He dialled a mutual friend: "What the fuck?" When he saw Skanda's and Basir's faces, he had one thought. Kyle asked his friend a question that rang out as more of a statement: "Serial killer?"

BASIR FAIZI

3

BRUCE MCARTHUR

THE first time I went looking for Palestine Road, I drove right past it. I had been bumping along a paved rural highway that stretches, without a twist or a bend, for kilometres through an expanse of rural Ontario between Lake Simcoe and the Kawartha Lakes. A grid of nondescript roads and numbered rural highways connect the farmland and the communities that make up the township of Eldon. I only caught the dark opening to the gravel road from the corner of my eye. I threw the car into reverse and backed up to the tree-shaded entrance.

Eldon, like the small townships around it, was founded in the early nineteenth century, with shops and markets congregating around local churches, forming little town hubs amid the sea of farms and fields. This was Ontario's breadbasket, for a time. At the Old Stone Church in Beaverton, just a few kilometres outside of Eldon, dozens of old Irish and Scottish names are set into stone gravestones, many of whom were the settlers of the area. The McArthur name is etched into many of them.

The churches are quieter now. The Old Stone Church itself is a national historic site. Some of the farms are still active, but many have fallen into disrepair. Where once there was farmland, now arrays of brilliant new solar panels glisten. Just west of Eldon, on the other side of Lake Simcoe, is the rapidly growing city of Barrie. Even so, Eldon is a world away from urban life.

As I eased off the pavement onto the gravel of Palestine Road, the sunny day disappeared amid an umbrella of trees. I bounced along the quiet street in the cool shade for a half kilometre. Eventually, the trees thinned out, letting in the sun and revealing rolling farmland. The little lane curves and twists around the fields—still far off from harvest time when I drove through it— intersected occasionally by the straight roads that connect this spiderweb of rough lanes. The nearest town to these farms is Argyle, a one-traffic-light community with a farmers' grocery, an antique store, and not much else.

Along the rough road, nearing the intersection of Highway 46, "No Trespassing" signs are nailed to trees that line the path. At first I suspected the homeowners, including the ones living in Bruce McArthur's childhood home, would be tired of the attention. But on one sign, there is a graphic of a man with binoculars up to his eyes, staring at a heron. It dawned on me that, on quiet Palestine Road, in the heart of the Kawartha Lakes, ornithologists are probably more of a nuisance than true crime enthusiasts or tourists obsessed with the macabre.

Just beyond the signs, on the McArthur property, sits a dilapidated barn, its red paint peeling off, listing slightly to one side, a chunk of the wooden structure missing, as though someone had fired a cannonball through it. It was there, on that farm, that Bruce McArthur grew up.

Born on October 8, 1951, to an Irish mother and a Scottish father, he had one older sister, but he wound up with plenty of foster siblings. In nineteenth-century Ontario, agricultural productivity tracked closely with the size of your family, and children were expected to work. Many farms would welcome destitute children from industrial London during the later half of the century. The English government figured life on the farm beat life on the shop floor—often, they were wrong. The government called them "home children." And, from 1869 to 1932, more than a hundred thousand were sent from the British Isles to Canada to work the fields. The conditions they lived in were a scandal and a blight on a fledgling colonial Canada, but the practice wasn't phased out altogether. Farms in the area pivoted, instead welcoming troubled children from Toronto and elsewhere whose parents believed they could learn some lessons from physical labour.

That's what McArthur's parents did. As the freewheeling 1960s opened up a new generation to sexual liberation and drug culture, some parents were keen to get their children out of the city. The McArthur farm was an ad hoc foster home, a boarding school, and a work camp, all in one. Throughout his childhood, McArthur was convinced the workload fell more squarely on his shoulders than others' in the family. That belief engendered a simmering resentment against his father. As a teenager, he was square-shouldered and stocky, but soft-faced and effeminate. He later told a therapist that he suspected his father had sniffed out a latent homosexuality and used manual labour as a misplaced tool to quash those desires.

In the McArthur household, religion was a point of tension—his Catholic mother pitted against his Presbyterian father. In those domestic disputes, McArthur would side with his mother, earning scorn from his father. He felt that he could never please his dad.

McArthur attended high school a few towns over, in Fenelon Falls, the industrial heart of the Kawartha Lakes. The city's eponymous falls powered the lumber mills, and the small hub was connected to the economic centre of Canada through the expansive Grand Trunk Railway, which sent trains through the quiet farmland nearby, on to Whitby, Toronto, straight down the eastern seaboard. The trains were still running when McArthur graduated in 1969—it wasn't until the 1970s that the line was abandoned and the tracks removed.

McArthur's graduation yearbook is, like anyone's, an inscrutable window into his teenage years. His nickname, according to the book, was "Snoppy." His favourite pastime: "a good argument." His "p.f," or "probable future"—"your guess is as good as mine," he wrote. His ambition: "To be successful." In his yearbook photos, he sports a crooked smile, with a wavy head of dark hair. By his own admission, he was shy and a poor student, likely labouring under some unrecognized learning disability. His schoolmates remember him as teacher's pet.

In high school he met his wife, who appears in the same yearbook. Her pastime, "daydreaming"; her probable future, "die young"; her pet peeve, "someone who can't decide what they want"; and her ambition, "if the world thinks its prepared—a nurse." McArthur, adrift and awkward, married his wife five years after they started dating, when he was twenty-three. Around the same time, he earned a two-year business diploma at a college in nearby Barrie. They fell into a haze of suburban normalcy.

The couple relocated to a high-rise apartment building in Toronto in the late 1970s. McArthur got a job at Eaton's, an iconic Canadian department store. He worked at the flagship downtown store, right on Yonge Street, just a few blocks down from a fledgling Village—a ramshackle neighbourhood of seedy beer halls reclaimed as gay haunts. The Village was only starting its tectonic shift from Yonge Street to Church Street. Since they left rural Ontario, McArthur's father was diagnosed with a brain tumour, and placed in a nursing home. His mother, meanwhile, started a relationship with a new man. McArthur, hurt by what he viewed as his mother's infidelity, cut off ties with her. He would spend the last few years of the 1970s travelling back and forth to the Kawartha Lakes to look after his father and the farm—McArthur and his father would finally forge a real relationship. McArthur's father, in the end, would outlive his mother. She died just two weeks after being diagnosed with terminal cancer, when McArthur was just twenty-six.

McArthur and his wife didn't stick around Toronto for long. By 1979, they were in Oshawa, a car manufacturing hub about an hour outside Toronto. There, McArthur found work as a salesman for the McGregor Sock Company. Initially, he hawked his wares—underwear as well as socks—on the road, before stepping up to become an account manager for a men's clothing company. McArthur's father passed on in 1981, but not before finally telling his son he loved him.

As the older generation died, McArthur and his wife started their own family in their home just outside Oshawa's downtown core. Nearly a decade after they'd left the Kawartha Lakes behind, they had their first child, a baby girl. A boy arrived two years later. Family life unfolded predictably: the kids started school, while McArthur advanced at work. McArthur was an active Presbyterian, just like his father. The church he attended sat just off the city's main drag, a skinny red brick chapel with long arched windows. He sang in the choir, and the congregation made up his social circle in the city.

But behind the facade of a rosy, happy family life, problems were mounting. Both children struggled socially. Friends of McArthur's son remember him as shy and not particularly good at school. Looking back, it was probably a case of an undiagnosed learning disorder, one of them suggested, just like his father. A friend recalls that McArthur was hard on his son, just like his father had been on him. His son confessed to a girlfriend, years later, that McArthur was physically abusive.

By the early 1990s, more serious problems were percolating. McArthur's son began exhibiting behavioural problems. Early on, there was some hope that his son would just grow out of it. He didn't.

Despite spending more and more time at work, financial problems were stacking atop each other. McArthur was also devoting more time to the church, struggling to prevent feelings from bubbling to the surface.

It didn't work. McArthur had, unbeknownst to his wife, been carrying on an affair with another man in the early 1990s. He began to recognize what he had always known about himself: he was gay. Not ready to blow up his family life, he stopped having sex with his wife, terrified of passing on a sexually transmitted infection.

For many men of that era who were exploring their sexuality, the World Wide Web, then in its infancy, was a saving grace. A whining dial-up noise still greeted every user. The internet was made up, mostly, of bare-bones usenet groups and rudimentary chat rooms. But for many, the new technology was like a wrecking ball, knocking down the walls that constrained their daily lives. For men wrestling with their sexuality, suddenly a whole new world was to be found inside the soft glow of a computer monitor. The mainstays of a discreet gay life—cruising public parks or visiting gay bars—were still too risky, too open, for many men. These free online chats were anonymous, and they left no trail. At least, that's what many of their users thought. That's where McArthur began to grapple with his own sexuality.

Eventually, McArthur told his wife and, not long after, his children. Despite the initial shock, his whole family took the news of McArthur's sexuality about as well as could be expected. The couple stayed together for a year before McArthur packed up and moved to Toronto. Even so, they remained a family. At forty-six, McArthur entered into his first gay relationship—with another middle-aged man who had come out later in life. The two moved in together in the Thorncliffe Park neighbourhood, a population-dense area of towering apartment buildings which sits sandwiched between railroad tracks and the Don Valley Parkway.

McArthur's departure from the marriage wasn't a clean break. The couple had money problems they had to deal with together; the two children were still in school. McArthur sought a psychiatrist to help him cope with everything, and admitted feelings of depression. He was prescribed Prozac. Even so, it all seemed manageable. Maybe it seemed more manageable than a life in the closet.

McArthur rejoined his social circle in Oshawa, although not the church. His son would come to stay at his father's apartment for stretches of time, even bringing friends over. McArthur eventually squared his accounts. By 1999, he was reporting a monthly income of $5,855, with expenses of almost the same amount. He was $130,000 in debt. He declared bankruptcy in January of 1999, but, with the help of a bankruptcy court, found a payment plan that worked. He left creditor protection by 2001, the year he turned fifty.

The romance he'd landed in, through his divorce, didn't last. After four years, during which he was navigating the relationship with his family and dealing with his financial woes, they broke up. McArthur wanted commitment, his partner didn't. Just the same, they remained friends and roommates.

The previous years had been incredibly stressful, but McArthur seemed to make it through. He even stopped his Prozac prescription, feeling as though he had gotten through the worst of it. The rumour-mill in Oshawa speculated McArthur had had a "nervous breakdown." But, on the surface, McArthur seemed to be coping.

• • •

Halloween has a special significance in Toronto's Gay Village. In the early 1970s, as the gay liberation movement began to get rolling, a small strip of rundown bars, tucked in among the body-rub parlours and arcades, had become, as it was called back then, the gay ghetto. Two bars in particular stuck out: the Parkside Tavern and the St. Charles Tavern. Inside you could find a mix of drug deal-ers, bikers, outcasts, and gays. Over time, the gay clientele became the majority, and never was that more obvious than on Halloween.

Patrons would don full gowns, flowing wigs, and ostentatious jewellery and make the trek down the bustling and seedy Yonge Street, in drag, from the Parkside to St. Charles, blowing kisses and waving to onlookers and gawkers. I've watched old newsreels of those nights, down in the sub-basement of our national broad-caster, the CBC, on an archaic grey-green machine the size of a chest freezer. Through grainy footage and intermittent sound, I could see scenes of partying and revelling, not entirely unlike what happens now, on Church Street, on October 31.

Back then, though, what began as a curious oddity for the city soon got ugly. Crowds formed. Maybe *mobs* is a better word. Many jeering spectators would launch eggs and insults at the drag queens as police stood idly by. It got so bad that, by the late 1970s, many patrons would sneak in the back doors of the St. Charles, fearing for their lives. Only the fiercest drag queens would risk the stroll to the front door. Some were so bold as to strut down the yellow paint on the centre of the street. Some kept extra outfits prepared, in case theirs was ruined by egg yolk. One would put razor blades in their wig, lest some poor soul try to snatch it. Eventually, police got hold of the situation, but only after well-connected gay activists dragged the police chief down to witness the unruly scene. Finally, barricades went up and police kept the violence from the crowd down to hurled slurs.

And, as acceptance of the community grew and as the commu-nity occupied its own space, not far off, on Church Street, the parade passed from simple tolerance to acceptance and, eventu-ally, celebration. The irate protesters were replaced with revellers looking to join the party. Now, every year, Church Street shuts down for the night, with a cavalcade of costumed partygoers min-gling in the street, popping in and out of the bars.

On Halloween evening 2001, before the festivities started, David, a well-known face in the Village, returned to his Church Street apartment building to finish putting together his costume for the evening. David was one of the Village's many escorts. He advertised in *Xtra*, and even handed out business cards. That evening, when David unlocked his building's back door and saw a familiar face jogging behind him, he held it open. He recognized the man as a former client but couldn't remember his name—even if the man had given it, it may well have been a pseudonym. But those apartment buildings, the City Park Co-op apartments, were full of local queers—Hamid Kayhan would move in just a few years later. The man must live in the building as well, David decided, and was therefore a neighbour. David, wanting to show off his costume, invited his former client upstairs to see what he had put together—it was a genuine offer, as he had no plan to turn a trick that evening. The man followed but seemed to think differently. A minute after David had unlocked and opened his door, the man pulled out a pipe and swung it into David's skull.

Bruce McArthur stood over David's body, metal pipe in hand, and continued the assault. Once was not enough. As McArthur rained blows down on him, David lunged for a candlestick and wielded it in self-defence. McArthur relented. There was a brief stand-off before David moved to call the police. McArthur begged him not to, even trying to rip the phone cord out of the wall. When David got an operator on the line, McArthur bolted.

David regained consciousness and dialled 911. Almost at the same time, McArthur was walking into a police detachment a few blocks away. "I don't know why I did it," he told officers.

David needed five stitches in his head. McArthur, charged with two counts of assault, confessed. The metal pipe he had been carrying, he said, was for self-protection from street hustlers—an antiquated term to refer to sex workers—who he feared could rob him. Police found David's business card in his wallet. And yet the attack, he said, was not premeditated. The court ordered a psychiatric evaluation.

Recounting the attack to the psychologist, McArthur claimed he lost consciousness. When he came to, he claimed, David was on the floor, bleeding. McArthur told the doctor he had had an epileptic seizure at twenty-five years old, and had been taking medication since then—he'd reduced his dose just months before the attack. He also explained his history with depression, and his prescription for Prozac, but offered no clear explanation of why he had done what he did.

"There is no trace of psychosis, no trace of hallucinations or delusions, no trace of mood disorder and no trace of any personality disorder or antisocial behavior," wrote the court-ordered psychologist in a 2003 report. "As a matter of fact, Mr. McArthur is well oriented in space, time and toward people. He is articulate and coherent."

By and large, the report appears at a loss to explain McArthur's sudden attack. Personality tests showed no evidence of personality disorders. It does say, however, that "Mr. McArthur's results suggest that he is characteristically passive and indecisive, but he may possess underlying resentments. His profile portrays an exaggerated striving to be liked as well as a rigid and tense compliance to social conventions." The report continues, summarizing McArthur's self-effacing habits, his strive to perfect his own self-image, to hide his personal quirks and unusual feelings from others. "He seems to dread making public mistakes or taking risks lest these provoke humiliation and disapproval from authorities."

Anxiety is a bedrock of modern life. To that end, the diagnosis feels almost relatable. The report paints a picture of a man as taut as a stretched elastic who simply snapped. And yet his unprovoked assault feels so disproportionate, so extreme. At the time, the assessment found McArthur's risk for further violence "very minimal."

McArthur didn't serve any jail time for the assault. He was ordered to attend anger management counselling and perform one hundred hours of community service. He was slapped with one year of house arrest, under which he could leave only for work and pre-cleared appointments, and another year when he was forbidden from visiting the Village entirely. During that time he was also ordered to stay away from the victim, stop visiting sex workers, and stay away from poppers—amyl nitrite, a chemical normally used to clean VHS tapes that, when inhaled through the nostril, acts as a sexual aid and muscle relaxant. The tiny brown bottles are a well-known sight in the queer community. McArthur had confessed to using poppers regularly. The court added three more years of probation on top of these other restrictions, ordering him to stay away from the apartment complex where David lived during that time—the City Park Co-op apartments. Not hard, as McArthur was still living in Thorncliffe Park, a few kilometres away from the epicentre of queer life in the city.

"It sounds to me like you're a pretty good person and it sounds to me like you're not going to be back here anyway," the judge told him. As he was getting set to dismiss the lawyers and McArthur, the judge offhandedly wished McArthur a good time at his daughter's wedding—his lawyer had mentioned the engagement during sentencing.

"Unfortunately, he won't be able to attend," McArthur's lawyer piped up. His house arrest would forbid it.

The judge considered for a moment, then said, "I would specifically exempt it to allow you to go."

Michael Leshner, the prosecutor, didn't object. "I'm in the Court of Appeal trying to get married next week, Your Honour, so I'm all in favour of marriage," he told the judge.

"Good luck to you," the judge said, to either McArthur or the Crown attorney. Maybe both.

McArthur never went to that wedding—his daughter called off the engagement sometime before the big day. He served his house arrest, finished his probation, and eventually applied for a pardon for his assault, scrubbing his criminal record clean. The prosecutor in that case did, however, succeed in convincing the Court of Appeal to recognize his right to get married.

On June 10, 2003, two months after McArthur was sentenced, Michael Leshner and his husband, Michael Stark, were the first same-sex couple to be married in Canada.

• • •

Just as McArthur was brought before the criminal justice system for the first time, he found himself without a job. He had gone to work for a new clothing company in 2001, only to be laid off. He found a new job in the same field, but left it about a year-and-a-half later. He was relying on his roommate, his ex-boyfriend, for financial support.

Then a new opportunity was dropped at his feet. A friend, Roger Horan, was looking for a business partner in his landscaping business—Roger was a designer and a consultant, not a gardener. McArthur had a green thumb, so it was a good fit. It helped that Roger, too, was gay. Together, he and Roger made up Artistic Design Ltd.

McArthur was the workhorse of the operation. Roger found clients and took care of the business side of things, but McArthur dove right in to the handiwork. He conscripted an array of friends, family, and acquaintances to help him. His list of clients grew quickly, largely through word of mouth. He built a reputation for incredible arrangements, with flowers you were unlikely to find elsewhere. He began before dawn, going to a flower auction in the city's west end, and would be planting by the time the sun rose. Eventually, he bought Roger out and took over the business himself.

Karen Fraser, who had known McArthur's family for decades, hired him to landscape her leafy backyard in the well-to-do Leaside neighbourhood in the mid-2000s. "We got a call from Bruce's sister saying that her brother had just purchased a gardening business," Karen told me. "He got caught in the apartment elevator taking one of his lawnmowers up to store it in the apartment and the landlord wasn't pleased. So he needed a place really fast and she said I understand you have a double garage and you're not using it. So, a simple arrangement." The arrangement was that McArthur could use her property to store his equipment and offload his flowers, and in exchange he would landscape her yard.

It seems the new work was a good fit for McArthur. Karen remembered, "When we met him he seemed like a man very pleased with his life. Loved his family, loved his kids, took care of his sister . . . and was really interested in his new occupation and he was good at it." Though, she recalled, he never quite got her dry sense of humour.

"My God, we never thought he was that sharp."

• • •

When his probation was over, in 2006, McArthur re-emerged in the Village. He joined a small club of gay dads who would grab breakfast or coffee on occasion. During the day he might be sitting inside the Second Cup coffee shop on Church Street. One barista recalls he would walk in, grab his regular seat. Sometimes he would be social, other times he would stare off into the distance for hours, until he left.

At night, McArthur would visit his regular haunts—Zipperz, the Black Eagle, Woody's. Joel Walker, Skanda's friend, recalls seeing McArthur hanging about the bars where he used to shoot pool.

Cameron Rennie, a bartender and manager at Woody's Pub, remembers him sitting at the bar, just a regular fixture.

Just as he was coming back to the community, he found himself playing host to his son, as part of a court mandate. A criminal conviction for harassment left McArthur's son remanded to his dad's custody. McArthur pressed his son into work. Clients recall seeing the father–son team carrying trays of plants together throughout the summer. Karen would invite the pair inside for lunch, but they were content to sit in the backyard, eating their sandwiches.

In addition to his son, McArthur had other helpers. Some were recent immigrants, often South Asian or Arab.

"Skanda was so shy," Karen remembered. "He'd just stand there, staring at the ground." She remembers her usual repartee with McArthur—he'd say something half-baked, she would make a wisecrack. This time, they had an audience. "Skanda looked at me and started grinning, and Bruce would keep going, perfect straight man. He had a lack of ability to take in information."

Joel Walker recalled that McArthur was more than Skanda's boss. Skanda liked an older, bigger man, and the two dated off and on. McArthur demanded commitment, though, and that wasn't Skanda's speed. They had broken things off on a number of occasions, only to wind up back together. Of all the men Skanda dated, Joel remembers, McArthur stood out.

"Every one of them I ever met was fine," he said. "Except for one." And that someone was Bruce McArthur. "Obsessive and controlling" is how Joel describes him. McArthur and Skanda generally spent time together in the dark recesses of the Black Eagle, the leather bar on Church Street, or at McArthur's apartment.

In the week before Skanda went missing, Joel became fed up with his friend's toxic relationship. Skanda had been distant for weeks, as he fell in again with McArthur. The night before his disappearance, Skanda had popped in to one of their usual haunts to grab a beer, shoot a quick game of pool, and say hi. Then his phone rang—McArthur, Joel thinks—and Skanda said his goodbyes and rushed out. When Skanda went missing, McArthur was quick to lend a hand in the search for him. He would ask Skanda's friends what the newest update was, whether police were making progress. He may have even helped put up missing persons posters.

"Bruce was very focused on asking me, 'Did the cops say they heard anything? Are they getting leads?'" Joel remembered.

Karen remembers McArthur seemed to have a revolving door of workers whom he brought to her property. One, she knows now, was Hamid Kayhan. McArthur and Hamid would have met after McArthur's probation, as his release conditions specifically forbade him from setting foot inside Hamid's apartment complex. Karen never even got Hamid's name, nor had she seen the posters put up after his disappearance. If she had, she might have recalled his face. She had met him only once, when McArthur brought him to her house. "Bruce was peeved with him," she recalled. "He said: 'He's not going to work out.'"

Kyle Andrews did see those missing persons posters when they went up in the summer of 2013. When he called the police tip line featured on the missing persons posters, he volunteered to come in to talk to investigators.

"I talked about sex and marijuana and booze in the gay village and they didn't bat an eye," Kyle remembered of his interview at the police station. Investigators asked about Hamid's ex-boyfriends. Kyle told them Hamid's former partner had died and couldn't say much more about his other flings. So Kyle started telling the cops about the last night he had seen Hamid.

"We're hanging out and I came over with some booze and marijuana and we're having a little bit of a good time, listening to the radio and being intimate," Kyle remembered. There's a knock at the door, and Hamid answers: it's Bruce.

Kyle, recounting the story to investigators, says Bruce is one of Hamid's friends, and sometimes they would hook up. "I gave them, you know, not really enough details to track him down," he admits. Kyle couldn't remember his last name.

In that 2013 interview, investigators had already heard of Bruce, however. "They even tried to lead me on, like, 'Well, do you know what kind of work did he do? Like outside with flowers or did he mow lawns or, you know, was he an arborist?'" Kyle remembered.

Like Karen, Joel Walker also did not see the posters. He had long since left Toronto for Winnipeg. But when police started asking about the disappearances, again, in 2013, Joel was called in to the local police station to give a statement. He is sure McArthur came up in that conversation.

The task force assigned to finding these three missing men kept hearing a name from friends of these missing men: Bruce McArthur.

4

REVIVING A COLD CASE

OTTAWA is quiet in the summer. Though it is normally a vibrating hive of journalists, politicians, and staffers, the city settles in the doldrums of summer. Legislators empty the nation's capital around June, migrating back to their home ridings, to see and be seen with constituents at barbecues and block parties. Staffers take long-awaited vacations or hole up in air-conditioned offices to prepare war plans. Reporters, who usually scramble about to chase down government ministers through the ornate stone hallways of Parliament, relish the tranquillity and spend the summer trying to catch up on forgotten work and passion projects.

But this year—2015—there's an election underway, which many expect would set Ottawa alight. Not so. Unlike American races, Canadian elections don't generally last for more than a month and a half. Election day, now, is still five months away, meaning the pacing is absolutely glacial. There's also some conventional wisdom: the best place in the country to be if you want to avoid politics during an election is Ottawa. My title says I'm Parliamentary

Reporter for VICE News, but there's not much politics to be reporting on.

So on a languid, humid Thursday in July, I swivel in my chair. I stare out at the grey cubicles that line my office space, on the third floor of the capital's Parliament buildings. My desk is the one closest to the window, on the aisle second from the left. The surrounding desks look more or less as mine does—piled high with papers, books, newspapers. The room is tucked off a long marble hallway. A few doors down, to the left, is the well-adorned Senate chamber. To the right, farther down the hall, is the House of Commons. The well-placed office space is set aside for reporters in the Parliamentary Press Gallery. It's commonly referred to as the Hot Room, a name inherited from a time when the building was so replete with journalists that you'd have to loosen your tie and dab the sweat off your brow. It was so packed that tables had to be set up in the hallway to accommodate the reporters.

On this summer day, it is anything but packed. Hot, though, it is. I'm practically hugging the air conditioner next to my desk. I zone out, my gaze focusing somewhere beyond the yellowing framed photos of political journalists who worked here decades before, out through the tall windows, overlooking the waterfall that feeds into the Ottawa River.

With the political world hibernating, I'm racking my brain for a new project.

And then, a thought jumps into my head. It's a sudden shock, like being jolted awake at night with the sudden realization you've left the oven on. I can picture the headline, one I saw years prior. A story about men who had been disappeared from the Gay Village in Toronto.

On this quiet afternoon, I grope around in the dark, trying to recall details. All three were brown-skinned, right? They were in the closet—or, maybe not all of them. Were they last seen at the Black Eagle?

I can see the outlines of three portraits of the men. Brown-skinned. Bearded. Middle-aged. But the portraits are a little too far away, and it's a little too dark, to really make out their faces. But I can tell just how similar all three looked. I remember a gut feeling, from when I read that story: serial killer.

I snap back to reality and open up the best memory aid for our collective psyche: Google. I try some vague search terms—*missing men Toronto*. Too broad. *Missing gay men*. Still too broad. *Missing men Toronto Gay Village*.

The second hit is the story I'm thinking of. "Piecing together the story of three missing men from Toronto's gay village," the headline reads. June 8, 2013. It's on *Xtra*, Canada's main gay news outlet. Underneath the main photo is the smiling face of Andrea Houston. Her bright pink hair matches the brilliant rose hue of the website's banner. I wrote for *Xtra* for years and got to know Andrea very well.

> More details are emerging about three missing men who vanished from the Church-Wellesley Village.
>
> Toronto Police Service investigators say the three missing-persons cases are connected through "similar ethnicities." Detective Deb Harris, who is leading the investigation, says the three men were not all openly gay. "They frequented the Church and Wellesley area and lived similar lifestyles."

That word, *lifestyle*, always makes me cringe when it's applied to queer folk. As though it were describing a love for crochet or Caribbean cruises. It strikes me that collapsing such a core part of someone's identity into a signifier as fleeting as a lifestyle also robs police and the public of a vital piece of the picture. A detail that could help tie cases together and expose trends.

But here were the personal details of all three men. Skandaraj "Skanda" Navaratnam: Last seen, September 6, 2010. Abdulbasir

"Basir" Faizi: Last seen, December 29, 2010. Majeed "Hamid" Kayhan: Last seen, October 14, 2012.

Skanda "left a new puppy," a police spokesperson said. Basir had called his wife to say "I'm coming home late tonight," his sister reported. Hamid "just disappeared off the face of the Earth," recalled a drinking buddy.

I hit Back and scroll through the search results again, reading through a dozen other news stories.

Navaratnam was last seen leaving a bar on Church Street. . . .

Faizi's car was found in the Leaside neighbourhood. . . .

Kayhan was last seen at a family wedding. . . .

Those stories are all from 2013.

I start poring over the stories: had police made an arrest?

In the two years since, there has been almost nothing. No triumphant police press conference, announcing they had caught a serial killer. Alternatively, no quiet announcement that any of the three men had been found.

A local newspaper in Mississauga, near where Basir lived, followed up on his story in 2015 reiterating his family's plea to see Basir come home. *The South Bayview Bulldog*, a community paper serving the Leaside neighbourhood, published a story some months later, wondering why Basir's car had wound up where it did. No other media—not one of Canada's major newspapers or television stations—had revisited the incredibly troubling story of the missing men. Nor would they, until years later.

There's a web forum I'm familiar with, always buzzing with amateur sleuths looking to shed light on missing persons cases or unearth clues to unsolved murders. These armchair detectives put their various skill sets to work to bring attention to cases, swap theories, and comb through online histories to trace digital footprints. There are many forums like this. At their worst, these online communities can be a rubbernecking flat-footed investigator, engaging in detective cosplay. At their best, however, they are sympathetic allies. Many members of these forums have experienced loss in their own lives, and know how heartbreaking it can be for the families left without answers.

The forum I log on to is more the latter than the former, more altruistic than a meeting place for looky loos. And there is a thread about the three men. Users have posted other missing persons files that seemed similar. They attached news stories of serial killers targeting gay men in other cities worldwide. "Where have these men gone?" wrote one user in 2014.

Other than that, there is very little. I puzzle over the silence. Surely someone else finds it odd that these cases have gone unsolved for so long. I fumble for a pen and a pad of paper. I'm lucky to find them. My desk is barely visible through strewn paper, stacks of reports, books, notes, fading Christmas cards, and other debris.

With a burst of energy, I'm firing off emails and messages. First, to Andrea, to ask if there are any details from the story that she neglected to include or updates she's learned since. She responds nearly immediately: "Nothing new," she writes. She apologizes that she hasn't even kept contact information for friends and family of the missing men. While I was stuck in Ottawa, she had a great network in the Village. She suggests a few names to reach out to, but is as bewildered by the lack of answers as, it seems, anyone. It becomes pretty clear from the outset that if Andrea has had trouble shaking things loose in this story, I will too.

I'm on my own.

I find a 2013 press release, listing Detective Deb Harris as the officer responsible for the cases. Her office number goes to someone else's voicemail, so I try her email. It bounces back immediately: she retired a year prior, heading to the city's fire service. I try her there—*What can you tell me about the missing men?* As I wait for a reply, I have a go at the byzantine network of phonelines and automated directories at the Toronto Police Service. I leave some messages and hope for a reply.

I reach out to friends of Skanda, but they're far from chatty. The stress of organizing publicity about his disappearance in 2010, only to have it all brought back in 2013, had been a major strain. They don't want to relive it. They suspect the worst. They want answers more than anyone, I figure, but I can't blame them. If his disappearance hasn't been solved yet, what are the chances it ever will be?

I have little luck in finding friends or acquaintances of Basir or Hamid.

Two weeks after I first reach out to Andrea, I head to Toronto. The election has finally begun to heat up. The four leaders of Canada's major political parties are getting set to square off in the first election debate, and I'm tapped to provide post-game analysis. I check into a hotel not far from the Village. I head into the VICE Canada office and give my editor the rundown of what I'm working on—*I think there's a serial killer,* I say. I get arched eyebrows, but a nod.

Finally a voicemail gets returned. I hear from Detective-Sergeant Mike Richmond, who's sympathetic. I give the officer a pitch: Let me come in, let me talk with some of the investigators, let me look at some of the old case files. Surely some renewed public attention could be helpful?

He says it's possible. He passes me off to the detective who, technically, remains the head of the case: Detective Constable Josh McKenzie. He's on vacation. More time goes by, as the summer turns to fall.

Finally a reply. "Any attention on a missing persons case can be useful. Sometimes even the smallest detail can trigger a memory

and move the investigation forward," McKenzie writes to me in
early September. Despite that, he says, there's not much more
the service can release. He promises to look into it. I promise him
I'll keep following up. Tenacity and a willingness to be incredibly
annoying are both golden skills for journalists.

I'm outside a strip mall, just off the highway connecting Ottawa
and Montreal, leaving another message for McKenzie. Coopera-
tion, I say, is better than the alternative. I iterate that his voicemail
will be full of my voice if I don't hear back. It's a friendly threat.

I'm sitting in a rental car in the interior of British Columbia,
penning an email, doing my best movie cop impression: *We can do
this the easy way or the hard way.* I raise the spectre of filing a freedom of information request to compel the police to release some
documents to me.

I'm in Toronto, checking in with the detective. *Could I meet you
at police HQ. Or, maybe, for a beer?* Maybe honey catches more flies.

McKenzie isn't unresponsive. We go back and forth. He's obviously an officer with a workload that extends beyond a task force
that ended a year before, so I'm hardly his first priority. There are
periods of silence, and there are flurries of emails. We keep in touch.

Election day, October 19, comes and goes. Incumbent Conservative Stephen Harper is ousted, progressively branded Liberal
Justin Trudeau romps to victory. A particular rallying cry for his
party is to hold a national inquiry into murdered and missing
Indigenous women and girls, something his predecessor resisted
as unnecessary. Hundreds of outstanding cases of vanished Indigenous women remain unsolved, and Trudeau promises to try to
bring closure, especially for the families of those women who
disappeared without answers. He pledges to investigate the systemic racism and indifference that have played a role in the lack
of answers. I can't help but feel the parallels.

It's November 2015. McKenzie and I finally speak over the phone.

I was expecting the cop archetype I'm used to dealing with. Gruff, disdainful of media, wary of reporters. That's not what I get. McKenzie is young, that's clear right away. I thought, prior to our call, he may have had the case dropped on his lap after it was designated unsolvable. Not so. He has worked the case virtually from the beginning. He says that, while his hands are tied as to what he can release, he'll investigate the art of the possible and get back to me. He does tell me that while the investigation has been expansive, without going into too much detail of what that means, it is currently "suspended." I hang up more optimistic than I was before dialling his number.

In early December:

Any news, Josh?

Two weeks later, an email, 3:49 a.m.:

Justin, this is taking longer than expected to put together for you. I've attached the missing persons posters that we put up around the Church and Wellesley area. I'll have more information for you by the end of the month.

Below the message are the photos of Skanda, Basir, Hamid. The same posters I've seen, now, a thousand times.

I send an email the next morning:

Do you think I could pop into the TPS HQ for us to have a chat?

No reply. New Year's goes by. I'm in Toronto.

I'm in town this week. Can we set up a meeting? Happy to do it in your office any day this week, or over the weekend. We can do it over a coffee, lunch, beer, dinner. On a plane, on a train, in the rain, etc. Just let me know.

Next day.

Hey, just following up again.

I hear back January 7:

> I have submitted a document to my boss for approval, then I'll send it your way. If and when you have follow up questions give me a call and I'll do my best to answer them. I wish I could give you more to go on, but with it still being an open investigation my hands are tied. I'm in court today and tomorrow and not back to work again until Thursday January 14th. I like your use of Dr. Seuss. Thanks.

In the ensuing months, I send some more check-ins and queries, all unanswered. It's March 2016 before McKenzie finally gets the sign-off and sends the documents.

As I open the document McKenzie has emailed to me, I'm quite literally holding my breath. I scroll down to the bottom and exhale sharply.

It's two pages. Not even. It's a page and a half. I scroll back to the top. It's just a summary. A plain-language wrap-up of what's happened. It concludes: "There is still no concrete evidence to explain what happened to these missing men, or where they may be located today. At this time, the investigation is still open. Anyone with information as to the whereabouts of these missing men, or who may have information to provide, are asked to call the Criminal Investigation Bureau of 51 Division."

The investigation is still open.

That line sticks out like a thorn. As McKenzie explained to me over the phone earlier, Canadian missing persons cases will never be declared "cold." So, yes, they're technically "open," but police use some weaselly language to keep them as such: "Suspended."

Open, but suspended.

. . .

For two years, and my former editor can attest to this, this story made me insufferable. I would bring up the story in meetings. I would email her at odd hours with new theories. When I was in the office, I would roll my chair over to her desk and start rambling about the story. When I moved from Ottawa to Toronto, my fixation became only more intense.

On multiple occasions, I sifted through missing persons databases, both official and volunteer. I plugged in the pertinent variables. Gender: Male. City: Toronto. On the RCMP database, there's a category for "bio group"—that means race, I gathered—but the options are limited. I try "Asian," "east Indian," and "other." There's no search field for "lifestyle," and no category on any of these sites for "gay." No matter the combination I searched, few of the results looked similar to the three men I worried about. I tried all sorts of searches. Each different permutation gave me a different list of faces. I clicked on them, one at a time.

There's Mohmud "Moe" Jiwani, a businessman who parked his car just south of the Village in 2006 and vanished, not far from a gay strip club. I get hold of a private investigator hired by his family to try to solve his disappearance. He picks up the phone, and I start rambling. I'm spewing out everything I know about my three cases, suggesting there could be more victims, asking whether the man he was hired to find was maybe, just maybe, gay.

There's a long pause on the other end of the line. Then a soft chuckle. "Wow," he says. "That's a really good theory."

A sharp intake of breath on my end.

"But it's entirely wrong."

Turns out Moe had business troubles that may have explained his disappearance. He wasn't gay. Dead end.

I look into Sahil Sharma, an Indian exchange student living in Surrey, British Columbia. He disappeared in 2008 after he went to his university with $4,000 in cash to pay his tuition. That led many to write off his case as a robbery. But then I learn that he deposited the money with the bursar before his disappearance. He left campus without the cash in his pocket. Police found no evidence that he was suicidal, and no drug or money issues.

I call the local detachment of Crime Stoppers to ask about Sahil. I reach someone familiar with the case, and we chat about the seeming similarities, but there are more differences—he was brown, yes, but he disappeared from the other end of the country, Sahil was considerably younger than the three Toronto men, and there was no indication he was gay.

I end the conversation with the Crime Stoppers detachment with a promise that either side will follow up if we find anything relevant.

As I go case by case, something hits me hard: it is not easy to find open missing persons cases in Canada. When I plug in my search to the RCMP database—the database that was supposed to be the central repository for all open, unsolved missing persons cases in the country—Skanda's name does pop up. Trouble is, Basir's and Hamid's don't. I'm puzzled by that.

So as I sift through photo after photo, name after name, I start to become very aware that there are so many people who aren't listed. People who live in police filing cabinets and in frames on loved ones' bedside tables.

Thousands of people who have vanished twice.

HAMID KAYHAN

5

ANDREW AND SELIM

ON a late spring afternoon in 2017, I was the only one on Moore Avenue, which looked more like a quiet suburb than an enclave of Canada's largest city. On Monday mornings, the traffic that snakes down the road is a pretty clear reminder that you're still well within the city boundaries. There's no parking on the street during the morning rush. But when I was there, it was dead quiet.

I drove up there on a hunch and parked roughly where I believed Basir's car had been found. I got out of my car and paced up and down the street. I even tried parking in different spots on the stretch of road, just to see if that improved my perspective. I walked up to the cemetery and rattled the locked gates. I walked towards the ravine, to peer down. It was only then that I noticed the path. A sign next to it read: The Beltline Trail. I started down the path, which stretched some distance into the woods. It connects Moore Avenue to the larger Don Valley. It struck me that this, as much as anywhere in this sleepy neighbourhood, might make for a half-decent destination for a man in the closet looking for some privacy.

I opened my phone and plugged in an address. A landing page popped up, complete with half-naked men, arm-in-arm. The site offers detailed and methodical listings on cruising sites around the world where men, especially men in the closet, can find other men looking for the same. The closest result? The Beltline Trail, exactly where I was standing. "This is a tree covered jogging trail and is very secluded," the listing advertised. "Beltline is very busy at night."

I remembered: Basir disappeared just after Christmas. Would anyone be braving the cold to climb down the steep entrance to the trail, especially as there are plenty of indoor venues for men to meet discreet men? But, sure enough, one review of the Beltline offered some sage advice: "It is worth the visit, even in the winter."

I walked down the trail, with no aim in particular. It had been some six years since Basir had disappeared, and I was not quite sure what I was hoping to find. And yet I walked down one path, doubled back, tried another, all the while eyeing the leafy banks that lined the trail. I stared up at the million-dollar homes perched along the Beltline, wondering whether the owners knew what went on in this park after dark.

Had Basir been in the Beltline Trail the night he disappeared?

I drove around a bit longer, weaving through the quiet streets and cul-de-sacs. I pulled into Mallory Crescent, a well-to-do lane of million-dollar townhouses and high-end apartment buildings, and parked the car. I stepped onto a small patch of grass that over-looked the Don Valley, with the Beltline lying in the distance.

It's entirely possible that, on that warm day in May, Bruce McArthur was working a few feet away, at one stately but modern-looking home with huge garden planters sitting out front. I could well have parked right behind his silver Dodge Caravan. I may have even made eye contact with him, as he carried boxes of flowers to the backyard.

• • •

It's a few weeks later, in June, and I'm sitting in the VICE Canada offices. The story I have written stares back at me from my computer screen and is one that asks more questions than it answers.

I've exhausted my leads with the Toronto Police. They promised to let me know if there were any updates, but I correctly guessed there would be none. I've messaged, emailed, called so many friends of the missing men, but with little success. I did learn that the task force set up to investigate these disappearances in 2013 even had a formal name: Project Houston—as in, *Houston, we have a problem*, I learned later.

I have compiled as much detail about Project Houston as I could confirm. Here's what I wrote:

> It has now been four-and-a-half years since Kayhan went missing. The lead detective has since retired. Zipperz has closed. The Black Eagle is still there, a popular outlier in the neighbourhood. Faizi's company in Mississauga has since been bought up, then bought up again, existing under a different name. But we are no closer to learning what happened to the three men.

This kind of story can feel like Chekhov's gun. You can toil for two years, working, digging, and tinkering, and that story just sits on your desk. But, eventually, it has to go off. Eventually, you need to publish that story, even if there is no satisfying conclusion. Even if there are nothing but new questions.

> Many, including the police, tried to make sense of the Toronto disappearances, or connect them to a larger trend. As is increasingly the case for the most puzzling of real-world mysteries, armchair detectives on the internet joined the hunt. Some drew a correlation to the fact that all three men went missing around major holidays—Navaratnam, on Labour Day;

Faizi, just after Christmas; and Kayhan, a few days after Thanksgiving. That theory didn't exactly crack the case.

I'm sitting across from my editor, Natalie Alcoba, at a long wood table in VICE's warehouse of an office in Liberty Village, all glass and metal. She highlights one passage in particular.

> One theory that seems to connect the dots—the fact that three men, of similar skin tone, age, and sexual orientation went missing without a trace within two years—in any satisfying, albeit disquieting way, is that Toronto's gay village had a serial killer.

She gets to the last line. "Serial killer?" she asks, an eyebrow arched.

"I don't know how we can avoid saying it," I reply.

She frowns a bit. I go on. "Listen, we can take it out, but everybody is going to be thinking it. So let's just say it."

I've already agonized internally about that line a dozen times. It feels fantastical to suggest someone has committed three murders when not even a single body has been found.

At the time, we didn't even know these men were dead.

Honestly, Natalie *was* right. To suggest, in print, that Toronto had a serial killer was brassy. We should've cut the line or, at least, couched it. Natalie, like most good editors, was almost always right. But that didn't mean I was about to listen to her.

"If we don't say it," I assert with some put-on aplomb, "what's the point of the story?" Neither the media nor the police, to this point, has come out and said the words. Right or wrong, I felt like it was time someone did. Because, if I was right, there was a real likelihood that there were other victims, and other men vulnerable.

So we ask the question:

Did Toronto have a serial killer?

Which leads to an even more unnerving question.

Does it still?

We publish the story on June 9, two weeks before Toronto's annual Pride festival weekend. Pride technically goes on for the whole month of June, but the final weekend is the crescendo of the festivities—there's the parade, and a constellation of parties, shows, drag spectacles, and marches.

The suggestion that a serial killer looms over the city amid the revelling does attract some attention. Some local Toronto radio stations call to talk about the story. The story bounces through social media. Many in the city had either never heard about the missing men or had forgotten it entirely. Some in the queer community harboured the same simmering curiosity—the same anxiety—about the story I had. This story only rekindled that sense that something was amiss and had never been rectified.

The quiet voice of optimism in my head, hoping desperately that publishing the story will knock loose some bit of information, is let down. There is no out-of-the-blue phone call or some anonymous email with details I have missed. I am no closer to learning what happened to Skanda, Basir, and Hamid. My phone doesn't light up, with a timid voice on the other end offering a crucial puzzle piece. There is no source inside the Toronto Police Service looking to dump details from within the investigation— not yet, anyway.

Pride comes around, washing everything in a crest of food-dyed rainbows and glitter. Again, there's that optimistic internal monologue, hoping that someone is going to tug on my sleeve, pull me to a corner of the bar, and reveal some lead in a hushed tone.

But it doesn't happen.

As throngs of people shuffle their way through the cordoned-off festival area, I stare at every telephone pole and bus shelter I wander past. I start seeing posters—with photos of middle-aged, brown-skinned men on them. Facial hair. Big red letters: MISSING. I blink and they're gone. Just imagined. It has been nearly seven years since Skanda disappeared. Over six since Basir went missing. Four and a half since Hamid was last seen. Four since the police reopened these cases. Two since I started working on the story. I can't stop counting that time.

There isn't much more I can do. Journalism, a lot of times, is the art of moving on, as frustrating as that is.

I guess there's a bit of hypocrisy there. I've spent two years poking the cops, asking for accountability for their decision to move this investigation to "open, but suspended." But here I am, stuck at the foot of the same stone wall they were in front of. And I can understand some of what they must have felt.

So I go out and revel, as is Pride tradition. I party, I drink too much. I wake up Monday with a hangover.

• • •

If you set foot in Toronto in the summer of 2017, or even if you didn't, there's a decent chance you've seen Andrew Kinsman's face. A close-cropped haircut, a beard with a life of its own—huge, bushy, a mix of dark brown, grey, tan. His missing persons poster was ubiquitous.

Andrew was last seen June 26, and was reported missing two days later. A day later, on June 29, he was listed as a missing person by Toronto Police. On June 30, I got a message on Facebook. At this point, Andrew had been missing for four days. "I'm sure you've heard, but a friend of mine went missing," read the message. "Not sure if any connection but thought I would let you know." If he's not found in a few days, I thought, maybe I'll dig into it some more.

My gut said they weren't connected, simply because he was white. But something did seem off.

A few days later, he was still missing. And while I waited, it seemed the posters had multiplied. Where once there had been one on every fourth telephone pole, in some neighbourhoods there was one on every second pole. Then every telephone pole. Everywhere in the city. When one poster came down, two new ones replaced it. That, I would later learn, was an official policy of the ad hoc committee to find Andrew.

I scoured Kinsman's Facebook page. He wasn't friends with any of the other missing men. But we had some people in common, so I reached out to them. Andrew had been missing for three weeks when I walked into a Starbucks in Cabbagetown, scanning the coffee shop for Ted Healey, consulting a Facebook profile picture on my phone for reference. A middle-aged man with a goatee waved at me from a corner of the room. I introduced myself, and he, in turn, introduced me to his husband. As I rummaged for my notebook in my bag, I awkwardly tried to explain that I still didn't know whether Andrew's disappearance could be connected to the other three cases, but it was worth investigating. It was an odd thing to say to the friend of a missing man. It felt simultaneously callous, indifferent, and reassuring.

Ted was cautious, too. "My concern is that I'm not adding to any hysteria that is already happening online," he wrote to me when I first contacted him. I promised him that I wasn't aiming for hysteria.

The details Ted provided over coffee were the usual details of a person's life. Andrew had a wide circle of friends. It wasn't like him to disappear. He lived in Cabbagetown, just east of the Village. He wasn't much of a drinker, but he went out. The three—Ted, his husband, and Andrew—met for tea every two weeks.

It wasn't hard to get hold of Andrew's friends, and they were eager to get the media to pay attention to his case. A Facebook group had been set up to publicize his disappearance and organize the search effort. In speaking to Andrew's chosen family, they were more than happy to paint a picture of a man who sounded hard not to love. They painted a portrait of a sharp-witted guy with a dark sense of humour, but who had a sweetness to him, too. He had an intense drive, and didn't suffer fools gladly. Around him, he had built an incredibly tight-knit family. He was the superintendent for his building, and was everything you could want from a neighbour. The others in the house adored him. "He's uncommonly decent," Meaghan Marian, a close friend, told me then. Dwight Ferguson was a longtime friend of Andrew, they had crossed paths many times, but met again on a dating app in the early 2010s. It became clear they were meant to be more like brothers than partners. Andrew loved baking, so he and Dwight worked on new recipes, whiling away hours canning jams and sauces.

Andrew worked at the Toronto People With AIDS Foundation, part-time. It wasn't a job, one friend told me, it was a calling. He was responsible for the Essentials Market—a food bank for the foundation's clients in need. He recruited just about everyone he knew into lending a hand, pressing them into service for the greater good. His mission in life was to build resilient communities, and this market was a means to that end. Andrew was hoping his contract with the foundation would be turned into a full-time job. "He was optimistic about it," Ted told me.

Andrew was outspoken about his politics. In 2016, a year before he disappeared, twenty-nine-year-old Omar Mateen walked into the Pulse nightclub in Orlando, Florida, carrying an assault-style rifle and a handgun. He methodically went through the gay club and executed the patrons. By the time police intervened and killed Mateen, some three hours after the attack began, forty-nine members of the queer community were dead. Not long after, Andrew wrote an essay: "On the murder of LGBTQ+ persons, after Orlando." In it, Andrew wrote that passivity and indifference,

coupled with a lack of solidarity, has made the community painfully vulnerable. "They're going to get away with it, because we
let them," he wrote. "And they are us."

I questioned Andrew's friends, searching for possible ties to the
other three missing men. One detail jumps out. Years ago, Andrew
had worked at the Black Eagle. It felt like an awful coincidence that
four missing men had been regulars at the same bar. But, then
again, the Eagle was a popular hangout. If the regulars of the Black
Eagle were being targeted, I was about as likely a victim as Andrew.
Maybe it was just that, a coincidence—but other than their being
gay, it was the only thing I'd found that all four had in common.

Given everything we knew, Andrew's disappearance didn't
look like a suicide, nor was there any sign of drugs involved. And I
had a hard time accepting that Andrew had just picked up and left.
The Monday morning he disappeared, he fed his cat, Oom (Moo,
backwards), took his morning pills, and packed his satchel—with
enough stuff, a friend told me, for a day, not a week. He also sent
off a text to a friend, arranging a time to go together for his driving
test. I knew that he had returned a set of keys his neighbour had
absentmindedly left in her mailbox, and the two chatted about
Pride weekend. "We shared a good laugh," she told me. I know he
told her he was heading off to meet a friend for coffee. And I know
that was the last time his friends and neighbours saw him.

You don't schedule a driving test if you're about to pick up and
leave. His friends had the same feeling. "It very much looked like
he left—not left for good, but just left for the day," his housemate
told me.

"It's not like him to just disappear," Dwight said. He had spoken
to Andrew the Thursday before Pride, but hadn't seen him the
whole weekend—Dwight had gotten sick and skipped the festivities. "It wasn't till I got a call Wednesday . . . that I knew he was
missing," Dwight said, recalling the day he was reported missing to police. Immediately, it was "fear. Worry. Concern." Friends

organized a meeting on the front lawn of Andrew's building, to begin organizing the search. As Dwight walked to the Cabbagetown apartment building, with the summer sun dipping in the sky, he peered into every alleyway on the way, looking for the unthinkable.

At the front-lawn meeting, Andrew's constellation of friends, co-workers, and neighbours turned into an organizing committee. This collective was the one responsible for blanketing the city with posters—not just in Toronto, but in other parts of the province and the country. Some even put up posters as far away as South Africa and Australia, in solidarity. Friends organized searches of parks and ravines. They pushed reporters into paying attention. And it was working. TV cameras returned to Church Street. Reporters wondered if something was, again, wrong in the Gay Village.

When it came to the police, his friends were unrelenting. The full court press by his friends to convince the investigating officers that something was quite wrong is what led detectives to assign so many resources to the case as early as they did. When police searched Andrew's apartment, everything pointed to what his friends had been saying—it wouldn't be like Andrew to just up and leave. The only thing missing was Andrew's satchel. And there was no evidence that Andrew had any money troubles. In fact, owing to his distrust for banks, Andrew had stashed wads of cash throughout his apartment. Convinced that Andrew hadn't simply vacated his life, as they assumed for other missing persons, they got to work. In the first week of the investigation, police conducted dozens of interviews, checked every hospital, shelter, and coroner's office in the city and beyond, and had filed requests to his phone company and bank. They searched parks and sent marine units into Lake Ontario. They held a press conference with his friends, imploring the public for information.

That languid July, I kept checking in with his friends. I called the cops. "Suspects? No," Detective-Sergeant Mike Richmond told me. He promised that "we're ramping this investigation up."

Police made requests to Facebook and Andrew's email providers, asking for details of his last login but, as I know, getting tangible information from those companies is exceedingly difficult. Police need to file what are called Mutual Legal Assistance Treaty requests—known almost exclusively by their acronym, MLAT. Because Google, Facebook, and other social media and email providers are located in the United States, requests need to go through the Canadian courts before being served to the foreign companies. Richmond told me that getting information can take six to ten weeks—that is, if the company opts to send anything back at all. MLAT requests are just that, requests, and can be hard to enforce. By the time those details finally came in, they were hardly illuminating. Andrew hadn't accessed any of his accounts since he had disappeared, and his phone did not respond to pings from his cell company.

While that work went on, investigators checked every hospital, shelter, and coroner's office in Toronto for a sign of Andrew.

The most stark similarity between Andrew's disappearance and the other cases was the total lack of leads: the incredibly odd feeling that Andrew has simply vanished. The community picked up on that. The missing persons posters I was imagined were now back, for real. Not just Andrew's face, but he was joined by Skanda, Basir, and Hamid.

• • •

When police discovered they had another unsolved case of a missing queer person, they started Project Prism, on July 28, 2017. It was announced in a press release shortly after. The release explained that Prism was dedicated to investigating Andrew's disappearance. But there was a new name attached: Selim Esen.

If Andrew didn't quite fit the profile established by the first three missing men, Selim couldn't have matched it more perfectly.

Forty-four years old, 5'10", 150 pounds, brown eyes, brown hair, full beard. He was, as police put it, "quite familiar with the Church Street and Wellesley Street area." But it was the date that jumped out the most. Selim had disappeared on April 15. Two full months before Andrew.

I searched through the Toronto Police website to find the original release about his disappearance. It's short. There are the basic details about Selim, where he was last seen. It mentions he frequently has a silver rolling suitcase with him. The last sentence: "Police are concerned for his safety."

Having read hundreds of these public posts at this point, I knew that line often belied a belief that the odds of the person being found alive are low. Even as they publicly tied Selim's and Andrew's cases, one officer I spoke to played down the possibility of foul play. Selim was "transient," the officer stressed. He pointed out the small wheelie suitcase as evidence that he had no fixed address.

When I spoke with friends of Selim, it was clear he struggled with drug use. He moved around a lot and didn't always have a permanent place to stay. But they also told me that just before his disappearance, Selim had completed a peer-counselling course. He was working on recovery. He had locked down an apartment, a friend told me. He had a place to stay.

I couldn't square it. I knew that the cops, especially the ones who cover the Village, deal with a lot of missing persons cases and drug use is a commonality in many of those cases. But how they hadn't seen the connections between Selim and the men from Project Houston baffled me.

From the moment police announced that they would be investigating more mysterious disappearances from the Village, panic set in. There's not really another word for it. Social media was alight with queer people warning each other to stay safe. In the bars of Church Street, every TV was turned to the news. Soon, the paranoia ramped up. Someone mocked up a poster with the missing men's faces—the three men from Project Houston, the two from Project Prism, and a collection of faces that I didn't recognize. I started looking up the unfamiliar names. Some of them had already been found, some alive, some dead—men who had seemingly no ties to the Village. The fear had started feeding itself.

As the fear grew, police downplayed the similarities between Selim and Andrew, and then further tamped down speculation that there were ties to Skanda, Basir, and Hamid. "There has been some suggestion, within the Church/Wellesley community, that the disappearances of Andrew Kinsman and Selim Esen are linked as well with three other men reported missing from the same area from 2010 to 2012," read a Toronto Police statement. "Detailed investigation and evidence obtained, thus far, in the course of both investigations, has not confirmed a link although, as part of the police investigation, this is being considered."

The police jargon didn't dispel the belief that these cases were linked. Far from it. Consensus started to emerge in the Village: this was a serial killer. And the disappearances weren't going to stop.

Police leadership weren't saying so publicly, but based on investigative documents filed by detectives, the cops who searched Andrew's apartment noted that between the cash savings he had stashed and his hungry cat, the indication was that "he had no intention of leaving."

They concluded, as far back as mid-August, "Given that none of the other males who went missing from The Village have turned up, it is reasonable to believe the worst."

• • •

On August 3, 2017, I was sitting off to the side of the room on the second floor of the 519 Community Centre, a modern-looking hub inside a classic-looking brick building right on Church Street.

Perched on a radiator, I was trying my best to be a fly on the wall at a town hall meeting that the community centre had called to discuss the disappearances, responding to the widespread anxiety. In front of me were two hundred scared, pissed-off queer people, assembled around large round tables.

There was no clear purpose for the meeting—just a collective worry and belief that something had to be done. Pat solutions were presented that felt obvious but nevertheless useful: tell a friend if you're meeting someone you don't know, keep track of your friends, call the police if you know anything.

The cops were there, including several officers from Project Prism. Inspector Peter Code got up to address the room, looking very much the odd man out.

"Sadly, I do not have a lot of information for you at this time," he began. "I can say right now I have no evidence of criminality. There's a lot of speculation in relation to that. I also have no evidence at this time to link throughout the cases of disappearance of Mr. Kinsman and also the disappearance of Mr. Esen. I can say that cases of disappearances that have not been solved do not get closed. But they do wait for additional information to come in. So for us, even though we don't have a linkage now, we are certainly looking at previous cases."

It was obvious that Code's stock answer would allay no fears. And he seemed to anticipate it.

"If there are going to be questions tonight like 'What have you uncovered?' or 'What techniques are you using?' or 'Where are you looking?' I'm so sorry because I know it's not satisfying but I'm not able to give you that information."

Nicki Ward was there that evening.

"I actually made a point of grabbing a few of the officers there, some of them I knew, some of them I didn't, and literally pulled them out. They were sort of cloistered, if you remember, at one table," she said later. "Like the unpopular relatives at a wedding, all at one table. And I physically got them up and said, 'Go out and mingle.'"

That sort of bluntness is Nicki's style. She's a longtime trans activist and has never been accused of being shy.

"Everybody in the room was saying, 'Is there a serial killer?'" Nicki remembered. "Not just me, not just anybody, but all of us would say so. And in fact many of the people I talked to after were saying, 'Is there a serial killer and was he in the room with us?'"

It's hard to describe the atmosphere in that room. This was a battle-worn crowd. There were older guys, men who likely remembered the riots and protests of the 1980s. There were younger queer people who had been active in recent years, advocating for justice for marginalized groups. There were transgender and poverty advocates, who had spent years shining a light on police brutality, poverty, transphobia. It was a wealth of experience and activism. Riches of frustration and anger.

Overall, though, there was a rare consensus: paranoia. But it was well-placed paranoia. The community knew the score. Someone was targeting gay men—mostly racialized queer men.

A facilitator tapped by the 519 to run the event asked the room: "Have you ever felt unsafe?" A second question: "Have you ever been assaulted?"

When I mentioned it later, Nicki barked out a laugh as she explained her reaction. "It was actually a laugh—*like that one*—it just went around the room. Everybody raised their hands, right? Everybody in the room has experienced physical and/or sexual assault—and not just *some time in the past,* but in the recent past."

I hadn't put my hand up, but of course I fit into that group.

There was another display of hands that night. The moderator asked for people to indicate whether they knew any of the missing men.

Andrew Kinsman. Dozens of hands shot up, across the room.

Skandaraj Navaratnam. Maybe eight or nine.

Majeed Kayhan. A few.

Abdulbasir Faizi. No hands.

Selim Esen. One hand.

While the roll call was going on, I looked around the room. Organizers had taped up missing persons posters on all four walls. The five faces looked out onto the crowd. Smiling. Peering. It was an eerie reminder of the threat. One poster read: "Look out for each other."

Another question: "Are you worried?" The whole room stands up this time. "Are you confident enough is being done?" The whole room sits down.

After the event wrapped up, I apprehensively approached the lone hand that had risen for Selim. It was easy to miss, but I was standing nearby. The hand belonged to a friendly looking man sitting on a mobile scooter.

"Can I ask you a few questions?" I said.

"Sure," he said with a smile.

His name was Richard Harrop, and he told me about a time when he had come to the park next to the 519 to read. That's where he met Selim. Over time, the two started chatting. Richard would talk about what he was reading. Selim would talk about his struggles with drug use, and how he was working on recovery. "He missed his family," Richard told me. "He was really trying to get his life back together so he could face his family. He wanted to go back to Turkey."

The two became close enough that, when Richard went for a doctor's appointment, Selim would pick him up from the hospital. Selim was supposed to pick Richard up one day in April.

He never showed up.

• • •

It took me a long time to put together Selim's back story. I was perplexed. Of the five men who had disappeared, Selim was one of the most recent immigrants to Canada. And yet I couldn't seem to find good accounting for his past, prior to Canada, or even his time here. I knew he was Turkish but not much else. I learned that entwined in his addiction was a difficult relationship with his on-again, off-again partner, Sammy.

Beyond that, I had very little on Selim. It took months, but on one particular search for background on Selim, I found a LinkedIn profile, which gave me a list of Selim's past employers. That's what led me to Earl Everett.

Earl and his husband, American expats living in Turkey, had opened the Denizen Café, which sat in the shadow of Istanbul's historic Blue Mosque. For years, he employed Selim at the café. When I reached him, he was still heartbroken over Selim's disappearance. He and some former staff had been trading messages about it.

Selim, I learned, had been working for a time in Australia but had returned to Turkey. Earl had recently opened up the café and was asking around, looking for staff. A friend of Selim said: *Hey, we know someone.*

"He was a natural at it," Earl told me over Skype. Selim was eager. He knew which spices the café needed without being told and would head out to the market, returning with bags of them. They were spices that Earl didn't even recognize. Like many gay-owned establishments, the Denizen Café attracted a fair number of gay staff—they seemed to join through osmosis. Selim helped that process along.

"He fit right in. He was one of the family."

Of course, a de facto gay coffee shop in Istanbul, even in 2012, wasn't common. Earl knew it. "You had to be very careful with all sorts of things. You couldn't be out. You couldn't be *out* out."

But Selim was out. He was *out* out. He had told his parents he was gay. And, tough as it may have been, they accepted it. Selim's brother had struggled with drug use, and they'd nearly lost him. The idea of cutting off Selim because of his sexuality was inconceivable. They still loved him—in fact, it sounds like it was hard not to.

"It was amazing how loved he was. And how gentle. He had a beautiful soul," Earl remembered.

Selim and Sammy made the move to Toronto. Selim would fall into drug use and, like his brother, he struggled.

Earl lost touch with Selim after he returned to Canada for good. Earl was facing his own issues. As a more socially conservative political culture took hold in Turkey, he packed up and left the country. But when Selim went missing, he remembers the shock and concern of all the ex-employees of the café.

When Selim disappeared, Sammy took the search into his own hands. He prepared a list of every hospital, clinic, prison, and mental health facility he could find. "I called them one by one," he told me. Sammy reported him missing. But police came to a quick conclusion as to what had happened to Selim: the partner did it. There was reason for it—police had previously been called to the apartment they shared. While the incident was more complicated than it had appeared, it turned police attention to Sammy. Years later, sitting across from Sammy over lunch, tears streaming down his face, I could tell that allegation still hurt. "My love for him and his love for me is undeniable," Sammy told me. As officers investigated him, Sammy tried to convince them someone else was responsible for Selim's disappearance. It took weeks before they believed him.

I didn't know any of that at the time. What I did know at the time was that Selim was not simply "transient."

SELIM ESEN

6

PARANOIA

A paranoid energy covered the Village that summer. It blanketed Church Street like a thick fog. With Andrew's disappearance, old fears descended on the community and settled, hanging around the bars and restaurants. I would hear it at the bar as I would sit and eavesdrop.

I heard that . . .

There's no way it's not connected . . .

Serial killer . . .

When Selim's face was splashed across the TV, it seemed to render absurd the idea that Andrew's disappearance was a dark coincidence. It was no longer a question of whether a serial killer was stalking the Village, but why he hadn't been caught yet.

Each person found a different way of dealing with the fear. Some stayed away from dating apps. Some steered clear of the Village. Many became more diligent about telling their friends before venturing out for a hookup. New networks were popping up—networks of people in the community who promised to look out for one another. Who would check in on each other. Who would make sure that, if they didn't come back from a date, their absence wouldn't go unnoticed. It wouldn't get overlooked.

It was all a feeling of *Am I next?* "A friend of mine had a date with somebody that he met on Grindr," Mita Hans remembered. "He found himself in a panic attack ten minutes before it was time for them to meet. Because *what if?* It's just, you know, those activities that seemed so normal such a short time ago, that they didn't think twice about. Their biggest fear [then] was that you wouldn't hit it off, for whatever reason. Now it's suddenly: *Am I inviting a serial killer into my home?*"

Mita, like so many in the Village, began adopting defence mechanisms. "You start cataloguing, mentally, who else have I not seen?" She described the concentric circles, rippling outwards, as she thought of her close friends, her wider circle, her old friends, her acquaintances, taking mental stock of who she had seen at the grocery store. Who she had seen at Pride. "Is there anybody that we haven't seen in a while? Has anybody reached out to them? Did they say that they were leaving? Drugs and mental health crises can push people to the very edges of the map. It's more difficult to reach them," she said.

These concerns were part of why Mita helped set up a buddy system, encouraging her own friends and acquaintances to tell a friend before heading out on a date. Or posting to Facebook where they were, who they were with. She sighed. "Those precautions were useless."

For me, there were limits to what I could do. I kept on the Toronto Police Service for updates. I annoyed whichever detective would answer my emails. My conversations with the Project Prism detectives were more useful and transparent than a normal call with an investigator, but I always hung up the phone feeling frustrated.

Meanwhile, as summer turned to fall, Andrew's friends didn't let up the pressure. They had, at that point, put up more than eight thousand posters. "It was really hard not knowing," Dwight Ferguson, Andrew's long-time friend, told me. The helplessness. The hopelessness. Dwight and the others channelled that energy into those posters, the 9-by-11 pieces of paper that refused to let the city forget. "By that point we knew Halloween was going to be the last big chance we could do it, because we were all burning out." And so, that Halloween, the Village was blanketed in those posters all over again.

It still wasn't enough for Dwight. "You go to bed, and even an hour or so after that, you're still going through your head, what else could I do? Where else can I look? What else?"

Andrew's sister, Karen Cole, would post updates to a Facebook group for the volunteers. One summer day Karen and Pat, another sister, explored a viaduct along Bloor Street. "Very overgrown," Karen noted. As the fall came and the overgrowth had receded, "we have a window of opportunity here," Karen wrote. "Now we can see through to the ground much more easily," she wrote, calling everyone to join her in searching. The whole group was that driven. Constantly searching.

The fear that hung over the community never left those closest to these disappearances, as the temperature dropped and the Village turned cold, grey, and empty. The unnerving feeling that a serial killer stalked the street remained, but its veil was thinner. Or maybe we just got used to it.

Life went on. What else was there to do?

I left VICE News in October of that year, but I found this story hard to shake. Every time I would take a lunch meeting or head to a job interview, I found myself bringing up the missing men. *There's this story I've been working on . . .* I'd start. Maybe it would be a podcast. Maybe a documentary. But the interest just wasn't there. The story didn't have an ending. Just a gap where an ending should be.

Whenever the topic came up in conversation with friends, my answer was always the same: *It's a serial killer, and the Toronto police don't seem to believe it. I don't think they're going to catch him. Andrew and Selim are going to go unsolved, just like the other cases.*

• • •

That same summer that Andrew disappeared, friends of Alloura Wells started to worry. Just twenty-seven, she was street-involved, struggling through a difficult relationship, and would occasionally turn to sex work for some extra money. It wasn't an easy life. She had, for a time, been on a provincial support system and put together enough money to rent an apartment. But she couldn't keep up and was evicted. She spent long stretches of time sleeping in a tent in the Rosedale ravine.

Alloura was transgender. For many trans people, the economics of everyday life can be tough. Basic interactions, like a job interview or a lease-signing, are riddled with landmines and pitfalls. There's no telling how a prospective employer or landlord will react when the gender of the person sitting across from them at the table doesn't match their ID. Often, even getting a so-called regular job means swallowing the daily microaggressions—inappropriate questions, constant misgendering, outright hatred. This was a daily reality for many trans people, even in 2017. Even today.

The fight to extend basic human rights protections to transgender people had been a long one. Politicians across the country fought bitterly against basic protections from discrimination based on gender identity or expression. Activism led to the adoption of legislation that protected gender expression and gender identity in the province of Ontario in 2012, which forbade firing or evicting someone for being trans. Similar legislation was debated federally, which would cover hate crimes and other federally regulated matters, but it was defeated. It didn't become law until June 2017—the same month Alloura disappeared.

In spite of Alloura's precarious situation, she wasn't totally alone. She had a network of friends and family who loved her, a father who accepted her, a sister who would give her a place to stay when Alloura turned up on her doorstep, friends who looked out for her.

One of those friends was Monica Forrester. And Monica knew something was up when she hadn't seen her friend in a while. Monica was an outreach worker with Maggie's Sex Work Action Project, which organizes and advocates for sex workers in Toronto. She knew that radio silence could mean a handful of things. First, Monica and the others at Maggie's called around to see if she could have been in prison. Sex work is criminalized in Canada. While the law and enforcement have lurched to-and-fro over the years—it is currently legal to offer sexual services, but it is criminal to pay for them—it's common for sex workers to be arrested just the same, sometimes on flimsy drug charges, or even on a traffic violation.

They picked up the phone and called a prison where Alloura had been locked up before, the Vanier Centre for Women in Milton, a Toronto bedroom community. Her friends provided Alloura's legal surname and the prison told them, *yup, a person with that name is here.* A sigh of relief. In prison is better than dead. And too often, sex workers, particularly those who must resort to survival sex work, end up dead. That word, *survival,* carries a darker double meaning.

A friend of Alloura bought a greeting card and sent it to Vanier, addressed to Alloura. A kind of *get out soon* card.

Weeks went by. While the Village's panic over the disappearance of Andrew Kinsman simmered into a lingering unease, Alloura's friends and family still thought she was in prison.

On August 5, a real estate agent named Rebecca Price was hiking with a friend in the Rosedale ravine, the leafy valley that winds through Toronto, just north of the Village. As they walked along a secluded path, the two stumbled upon a tent. Next to it was the body of a transgender woman. The spot was unnervingly close to where Abdulbasir Faizi's car had been found. Less than a kilometre, as the crow flies. Rebecca likely didn't know that, but later it was a fact that wasn't lost on many in the community.

The body had been there for nearly a month, exposed to the elements—when police performed an autopsy, they couldn't identify the body nor the cause of death. Incredibly, police did not even issue a news release about the discovery or tell the public that a body had been found. Months later, police tried to justify that failure. "Based on the state of the body, there were no details that the police could release to the public," police spokesperson Meaghan Gray said in November.

Rebecca Price never stopped trying to put a name to that body. Her actions showed an incredible level of empathy. She was bewildered at the lack of coverage on the news, at the thought of the dead woman whose family deserved to know. She took it upon herself to call up the detective responsible for the unidentified body for updates. "I think he just couldn't wait to get me off the phone," she told *Xtra*. She even tried reaching out to the 519 Community Centre for help, but that went nowhere, too.

Rebecca even bought flowers and laid them where she had found the body. As she tried to get answers for a woman she had never met, friends of Alloura checked back in with the Vanier Centre for Women. The story had changed: Alloura wasn't there. She hadn't been there at all that summer. Her friends called Alloura's father, Mike. In early November, he went to 51 Division, which covers the Village, to file a missing persons report, but he was told bluntly that Alloura was itinerant and her disappearance wouldn't be considered an emergency or made a high priority. They provided him with a non-emergency phone number to call.

Police finally considered Alloura a missing person on November 6. Two days later, 51 Division put out a press release, asking for help in finding Alloura. Later that day, officers there reached out to the neighbouring division to alert them to the possibility that the unidentified remains found in the ravine were Alloura.

Rebecca Price saw the report on the news. She knew immediately that the woman she'd found was the same transgender woman who had gone missing. "If it wasn't for Rebecca Price . . . we would never have known there was a body," Monica told the *Globe and Mail*.

On November 30 police confirmed the body was Alloura's. Five months after she died, nearly four months after her body was found, Alloura Wells's friends finally had some answers. Police, however, didn't have a cause of death. The state of her body made it nearly impossible to determine what had happened.

• • •

Tess Richey stepped out onto Church Street on a Friday night in late November with an old friend. While the Village may be a refuge for queer folks, it has also become a safe haven for women leery of the downtown clubs. That has brought an influx of straight women to these gay bars—something that is, generally, welcomed by the community.

Tess was one of many women at Crews & Tangos that night. The two-storey bar has set itself up as a Toronto mecca for drag queen shows, packing in patrons so tightly on most weekends that it can be hard to see the performances through a sea of twenty-somethings. Tess had come to Toronto from North Bay, a four-hour drive north of the city. In school, she'd studied counselling for victims of intimate partner violence. But, in Toronto, like many people her age—she was a week away from her twenty-third birthday—she was bouncing between part-time jobs while she tried to land something permanent, either with an airline or a hotel. She had been contemplating heading to Italy to take a job as an au pair.

Tess and an old high school friend walked out of the drag bar around 1:30 in the morning, but they weren't ready to call it a night. The pair stood in the melee outside the bar for a bit. They wandered up Church Street, chatting with a couple who were drinking on their front porch on a side street, and joined in. It was 4 a.m. before Tess's friend finally had to throw in the towel and ran to catch the streetcar home. Tess called an Uber, but she wasn't there when he arrived. The driver waited for a bit, then left.

When Tess's family woke up the next morning and couldn't reach her, it didn't take long for them to know something was amiss. They filed a missing persons report the next day, and police did canvas the neighbourhood and put out calls for help. But two days after her disappearance, police appeared to be no closer to figuring out what had happened to her. Unsatisfied with that response, Tess's mother, Christine, arrived in Toronto with a crew of family. They began their own foot patrols of the Village, searching for clues or witnesses.

Four days after Tess was reported missing, her mother and a friend investigated a building just two blocks north of where Tess had last been seen. The family friend peered around the edges of an imposing mansion—a former bar that had shut down and was now under renovation. She investigated a stairwell along the side of the building, and called out for Christine. It was there that they found her daughter's body, at the bottom of the stairwell.

Tess's body showed no obvious signs of trauma, and police ruled it an accident. It wasn't until the autopsy came back that they realized their mistake. It was a homicide: Tess Richey had died of "neck compression." She had been strangled.

On December 4, 2017, police announced they had footage of a suspect: a wiry young man who had been seen with Tess in the wee hours of the morning.

• • •

Four days later the Toronto Police Service held a press conference to address the successes and failures of the waning year. These end-of-the-year briefings are designed to let police set their spin on the ups and downs of the year—to, in a good year, boast of a reduction in crime and a high clearance rate of solved cases. This year, however, Chief of Police Mark Saunders could best be described as embattled. He stepped to the podium to address a room full of journalists and defend against accusations that the service had not done enough in the cases that centred on the Village. Saunders had ordered a review of how the police force handles all missing persons cases, but he refused to speak in specifics about any of those unsolved cases that had rattled the community. In his own understated way, he told reporters: "I do think there are things we could have done better."

The community felt hunted. Five disappearances. One murder. An unexplained death. And there was a pervasive belief that police were indifferent to these cases. They couldn't figure out who was missing, let alone who had taken them.

Saunders was flanked by officers responsible for various high-profile investigations. When it came to the cases of the missing men, it was Detective-Sergeant Mike Richmond who was tasked with updating the public on the progress of Project Prism.

"There has been a great deal of misinformation and speculation relating to the Project Prism investigation disseminated through the media and other mediums," he told the assembled journalists. And he was right, the paranoia had led some to start linking cases that, clearly, had no ties to the Village at all. But this felt like an attempt to gaslight the community and to insist that nothing was amiss. That everything possible was being done.

To their credit, some answers were coming. Two days after that press conference, police released more security footage of Tess's final moments. The footage showed her walking with a wiry young man, his blurry face obscured by the night. Days later, the man in the footage would turn himself in at a police station. "I'm the guy in the photo," he told officers.

Richmond specifically mentioned the investigation into the disappearances of Skanda, Basir, and Hamid. "This investigation was done under the title of Project Houston. The investigation was done over a period of roughly a year and a half. Unfortunately it failed to resolve the disappearance of these three missing males." That statement from Richmond was arguably the most specific the Toronto Police had been up until then about when Project Houston had actually begun and ended. Before this, they had been cagey about the exact time frame for the investigation.

Those assigned to Project Prism had reviewed the old files, he said. "There is no evidence at this point in time which in any way establishes [that] the disappearances of Selim Esen and Andrew Kinsman are linked to the disappearance of the males from the Project Houston investigation." More than that, he said, "There is also no evidence to support that the disappearance of Selim Esen or Andrew Kinsman are linked." There is no evidence of foul play, Richmond went on. "There is no evidence that a serial killer is responsible for the disappearance of any of the missing males."

One reporter followed up with the chief: "Is there any reason for you to say, definitively, that there is not a serial killer in that area?"

"The evidence, today, tells us that there is not a serial killer."

THE ROSEDALE RAVINE

7

"WHO'S BASHING WHOM?"

ZIPPERZ had closed on August 3, 2016. Once a de facto headquarters for the campaign to find three missing men, it had gone the way of many older buildings in Toronto: bought up, to be replaced with condos. Its bartenders, the ones who remembered Skanda, Basir, and Hamid sitting at the bar years earlier, scattered to other establishments, other jobs. Harry Singh opened other joints on Church Street, but he seemed cursed by bad luck, as none lasted more than a year or two.

Buildings don't have institutional memory, communities do. If they did, the squat concrete building on Carlton Street might have reminded the regulars of what had happened forty years before. Zipperz had occupied that spot for some sixteen years. But, going back to 1978, the building housed Studio II. Gay bars were not, at that point, a novelty to Toronto. But having queers own the bars definitely was. For years, most queer establishments were wink-and-nod affairs. Some bars required male patrons to enter with a woman—but that was mostly for show, as gays and lesbians would pair up to gain entry and split off once inside the doors. Other establishments, like the Parkside and St. Charles taverns, were shady beer halls. Bikers and criminals rubbed elbows with the movers and shakers in the queer community.

Norm Bolter, who owned the two taverns, once remarked that "a gay person shouldn't own a place like this, he'd get too emotionally involved." But the community was proving him wrong. There was The Manatee, a bar on the cutting edge of disco that boasted a motley crew of drag queens on its impossibly small stage. Then there was David's Discotheque, a club with ritzy airs, featuring a porcelain statue of Michelangelo's *David* in the middle of the club, bracketed on both sides by winding staircases to a raised dance floor.

David's was co-owned by Jay Cochrane, a larger-than-life tightrope walker, and Sandy LeBlanc, a bit more of a hard-nosed businessman.

Sandy became a stereotype-bucking icon in the community. He drove a motorcycle and dressed like a biker. Born to an English-speaking family in francophone New Brunswick, Sandy had, like many small-town queer youth, decamped for Toronto not long after graduating high school. He was 5'3" yet could be seen roughing up troublemakers at David's who needed evicting from the bar. But he also held fundraisers at the disco, held queer-focused all-candidates debates during provincial elections, and dipped his toe into some of the gay liberation groups. But those early days were hard going. Business was boom and bust. He and Jay had split, and the tightrope walker had opened a rival club: Studio II. When a mysterious fire wrecked David's on New Year's Eve, 1977, Sandy was out of work. Sandy and Jay buried the hatchet and Sandy wound up at Studio II.

It was a complex of a bar. There was a movie theatre downstairs, doubling, when needed, as a drag queen theatre—it even had a concessions stand. There was a myriad of bars, a dance floor, a café, a board games room, a jungle-themed room, even a make-up store for queens in search of a friendly place to shop.

On September 20, 1978, Sandy was standing at the doorway of the club, tuxedo on, pouring champagne to celebrate the club's second anniversary. He left around 3 a.m. A woman working the counter of a doughnut shop nearby remembers seeing him drive off in a station wagon.

The next day, friends started to get worried. He hadn't returned their phone calls. He wasn't answering the door. So they broke it down. They found him, naked and face down on the bed. The carpet was so wet with blood that it was squishy underfoot. He had been stabbed nearly one hundred times. "It was overkill," David Penny, the first cop on the scene, recalled.

An autopsy revealed that one wound in particular was probably the fatal blow. One stab wound had punctured the coronary artery in his neck, and he hemorrhaged into his neck cavity. The other wounds were largely superficial or appeared to have occurred after his death. His bedroom window was open, and a handkerchief was found in the alleyway below.

It was a jarring crime. *The Body Politic*, Canada's main gay newspaper that generally avoided crime stories, devoted a small article to Sandy's murder in its next issue. They quoted Detective Julian Fantino, asking for "assistance from anyone in the gay community who can help." The killing struck a chord in the community, not just because of the brutality of the killing, but because Sandy was one of a rash of killings that struck the community in the 1970s and 1980s. Local punk band the Forgotten Rebels, who played David's on occasion, even wrote a song about Sandy's killing, calling it "3rd Homosexual Murder." (Frontman Mickey De Sadist embodied the character of a serial killer on the loose, warning the city's gays they could be next.) Sandy was, in fact, the fourth queer person to be murdered over the course of a month.

There were few murders of queer people, closeted or otherwise, in Toronto in the 1960s. In 1963, a fifteen-year-old was arrested for the murder of married bank manager Ronald Grigor, whose wife was out of town when he was found, naked and blugeoned to death. He was convicted of murder, after a trial in which the teen-ager admitted to bludgeoning his victim "while defending himself against homosexual advances," as the *Toronto Star* put it. And there was the slaying of Bruno Seidel, a Greek-German émigré, who was found stabbed to death in his apartment in 1967. Seidel was "thought to have become homosexually involved with a youth who killed him to rob him of his wallet," the *Star* reported at the time. Seidel was one of three homicides that went unsolved in Toronto that year. Police managed to arrest a teenager who had been driving Seidel's car and using his credit cards, but the teen wasn't charged with his killing. Seidel's murder remains unsolved to this day, listed still on an online Toronto Police archive of the city's cold cases. There is no mention of his sexuality.

But it wasn't until the mid-1970s that the papers began to report on the upswing of "homosexual murders." By my research, there were 42 killings of queer people in Toronto from 1975 to 1985, making up some 7 per cent of the total murders in the city over that time. In the worst years, one in seven murder victims was queer—predominantly gay men and trans women. While they were more likely than a non-queer person to be a murder victim, a murder of a queer person was also less likely to get solved. One in five queer murders did not lead to an arrest, even at a time when solve rates were nearly 90 per cent. And those were only the cases that hit the newspapers, or where the victim's sexuality or gender were made public.

Killings of queer people tended to be more violent, more over the top. Overkill, like Penny said. "That was a common thread with my five years in the Homicide Squad," he said. He investigated about a half dozen murders of gay men around that time, in the late 1970s and early 1980s.

That decade was a crucial one. It served as the city's coming out. It also came at a time when police repression of the community was at a fever pitch, when it wasn't unusual to see headlines in the *Toronto Sun,* a tabloid with a hard conservative bent, like "Three faggots raped me: Teen," and "Who's bashing whom?"—the latter story quoted Paul Godfrey, head of the greater Toronto council, concluding that "police bashing" was the real concern.

Many queer people knew that Godfrey had it quite backwards.

In 1974, four women went to grab drinks at the Brunswick Tavern and found themselves attracting the unwanted attention of a male patron. They told him to piss off. When he wouldn't, one thing led to another, and beer was getting thrown in both directions. Things settled down, but a few of the women climbed onto the stage, which overlooked the bar, and grabbed the microphone. They had in hand a napkin containing some slightly tweaked lyrics to "I Enjoy Being a Girl," an old Rodgers and Hammerstein tune.

> *When I see a man who's sexist, and he does something I don't like*
> *I just tell him that he can fuck off, because I enjoy being a dyke.*
> *I won't dress up cute and frilly, in clothing that I don't like*
> *I'll just strut in my jeans and stompers*
> *Because I enjoy being a dyke.*
> *I'm a fully les-berated woman, I work for the revolution now*
> *I struggle and I cuddle with my sisters*
> *And I don't need a man to show me how.*
> *I've always been an uppity woman*
> *I refuse to run, I stand and strike.*
> *Because I'm gay and proud and angry,*
> *And I enjoy being a dyke.*

Pat Murphy, one of the lesbians who was singing onstage that night, said the audience cheered their performance, but the bar owner was less enthusiastic. "The next thing you know there's like ten cops walking towards the table," she recalled years later in an interview with the Egale Canada Human Rights Trust. The women were arrested and held for much of the evening. A cop struck one of the women in the face on their way out. That cop would later be acquitted of assault charges. But, just as they'd sung onstage that night, they were not ones to run away, so the women went back to the Brunswick Tavern to collect witnesses of their baseless arrest. The cops were waiting for them. They were arrested a second time, and three of the four were slapped with a slew of charges—only one of which stuck in court. The lot became known as the Brunswick Four.

In December 1977, police raided the offices of the *Body Politic,* seizing, among other things, the newspaper's subscriber list. Members of the paper's editorial collective were charged with criminal obscenity. The charges were, notionally, over a feature published in the paper written by Gerald Hannon, a member of the collective, exploring why adult gay men sought out relationships with younger boys. While it was not an endorsement of pedophilia, it nevertheless gave the *Sun* and the Toronto Police licence to go after the pesky queer paper. It took more than a year before a court finally acquitted the paper of the scurrilous charges. The provincial government appealed the decision—the legal saga went on for years, with new raids and new charges, but the paper and its staff won every case.

Bathhouse owner George Hislop remarked that the perpetual presence of the cops in gay bars and bathhouses led to a feeling that the community wasn't safe from the cops. "I'm constantly being asked: 'Is it safe to go to the baths? Is it safe to even go to a bar? Are the police in there?'" Hislop summed up the perpetual question queers have to ask themselves about the undue police attention: "Why? What are we doing?"

In 1978, Toronto elected a queer ally: Mayor John Sewell, a fierce critic of the Toronto Police. He joined a rally to support the

Body Politic, telling the crowd: "We know it's not illegal to be gay. We should take the next step and make it clearly legitimate to be gay." For his trouble, he was lambasted by the media and city council ("The chain of office for mayor is becoming a daisy chain," one alderman quipped). The establishment political class, in league with the police, wanted to make an example out of him. To show that politicians ought not get too close to the queer community.

Principled and defiant, Sewell later sat down for an interview with the paper a year into his term. "With the bigoted cop, you have to say: 'Sorry, you're bigoted and we don't want you,'" Sewell told the *Body Politic.* "If there was a general rule that said: 'No, you can't harass gays. You're not allowed to do that,' I think most cops would say: 'Okay, I can't do that. Maybe I'd like to, but . . .' And the world would change."

That may have gone a long way. A lack of diversity in their ranks left those young cops bewildered by the communities they policed. There were no openly gay officers back then, and few officers of colour—Penny recalls being paired up with Toronto's first Black cop.

The hatred for the community wasn't universal, however. Penny recalled walking the beat, poking his head into gay bars and coffee shops and getting to know the locals. He would take Hislop out for lunch to get the local gossip.

Sewell took direct aim at the Toronto Police Morality Department, the one known for targeting gay bars, bathhouses, and anywhere that queer people congregated. Toronto Police had been allowed to hide the squad's budget under other line items—Sewell tried to put an end to that, and force the cops to publish their full line-item budget. His attempt, over his short two-year term, to bring the Morality Department to heel had little success. In 1979, "a year when an increased police budget meant no decline in the incidence of either rape or murder," as the *Body Politic* put it, some 190 men were arrested for "sexual offences"—a euphemistic term for cruising.

Sewell's second term promised to pave the way for those kinds of reforms. When his re-election campaign kicked off in 1980, he forged an alliance with George Hislop, the queer activist and owner of a local bathhouse. Hislop announced he was running for a seat on city council to represent the growing queer community— the *Star* reported that the broader homosexual community in Toronto stood at some three hundred thousand, many of them living in the district Hislop hoped to represent. Political power seemed in reach.

As the campaign began, sexuality became a core issue. The Toronto Police openly campaigned against both Sewell and Hislop. An anti-gay campaigner asked Sewell, to his face, whether he was a "practising homosexual." ("The answer happens to be no," Sewell replied, the *Globe* reported.) Running against Sewell was Art Eggleton, who insisted he wasn't campaigning against the queer community—and yet blew dog whistles on the stump. At one point Eggleton baselessly accused Sewell of bussing in queer activists from San Francisco.

Eggleton beat Sewell by less than 1 per cent of the vote, while Hislop came third in a three-way race, about two thousand votes shy of winning a seat on council. It was a disappointing result for the city's queer community, but it was proof that the queers could organize, and that being slurred as a faggot wasn't, necessarily, politically toxic.

Emboldened by their win, however, Toronto Police ramped up the repression, even as murders went unsolved and attacks continued. Inside the force, there was a debate raging.

"A gulf began to open between the administration and rank and file officers," *Globe* columnist David Lewis Stein wrote in 1980. The beat cops, he reported, tended to be younger, and they wanted the force to demilitarize. They generally couldn't afford to live in the neighbourhoods they policed. "They work in shifts and feel like an occupying army." And yet they were being called in to mediate domestic conflicts and racial tensions, Stein wrote. It left the beat cops frustrated, both with their higher-ups and with the communities they were tasked with policing. "[City officials] leave the dirty work to the cops."

The dirty work left to the rank and file was a horrible business.

A March 1980 edition of *Body Politic* broke the story of Derek Grant, a patron of the St. Charles Tavern. Through police surveillance, he had been caught engaging in consensual sexual activity in the bar's bathroom. That's when two uniformed officers came crashing through the doors. They dragged him and the other man out through the bar to their squad car outside. Derek tried to wrest himself free, and the arresting officer put him in a chokehold. Derek was taken to nearby police headquarters, but not long after he was thrown into his cell he began to convulse and vomit. He was pronounced dead upon arrival at the hospital. A coroner's inquest into his death cleared the officers of any wrongdoing and commended their work. The officer had robbed his partner, John Robertson, of the man he loved. John was called to testify at the inquest, but it became clear that the goal was to clear the police of any wrongdoing, and to shift the blame onto Derek. "It was like he was on trial," John told me.

Derek was one of many to be arrested inside that bathroom. Police, it turned out, had been given the key to a supply closet in the bathroom—a ventilation grate in the door gave them a prime vantage point to spy on the goings-on at the urinals. Peter Maloney, a lawyer, bathhouse owner, and activist, decided to put a stop to it. Flanked by Hislop and Brent Hawkes, an openly gay ordained United Church pastor, he walked into the office of Norm Bolter, the owner of the St. Charles.

"I say to him: 'You're going to change the locks on that closet. You're going to close off that grille and you're not going to allow the police to use that anymore. And if you don't, I'm going to send a picket to the Parkside [Tavern] and I'm going to shut your business down,'" Peter told me. And it worked.

Police always found ways to make their arrests. They would go undercover into public washrooms known to be cruising hotspots and try to entice men into making a move—as soon as they did, the men would be arrested. Cops would respond to burglary calls and, upon learning the homeowners were gay, would arrest them on charges of running a brothel. Undercover officers were caught sabotaging a banner at a gay rights march, seemingly looking to cause strife and provoke a riot. (The agent saboteur trick didn't work.)

If the rank and file were ignorant, the brass was openly homophobic, and they didn't take kindly to anyone questioning their tactics.

Peter, then a law student, started attending public police board hearings to demand better accountability from the force, trying to finish the crusade that Sewell had started. "I was constantly going after the police budget: How much were they spending? Why were they getting increases? Why did they need any new officers, et cetera, et cetera?" he recalled.

Peter lived on Gerrard Street West, just past Yonge Street, which demarcates the east-west divide. One day, he got mail for an office that sat on Gerrard Street East; this continued for a while. "Someone calls me one day and said: 'Did you notice?' And I said: 'Yes, I did.'" The caller was a postal worker. He told Peter he was deliberately switching the letters. The Toronto Police had instructed him to report all letters sent to Peter's address. It's called cover surveillance, Peter explained. The postal worker was asked to "examine the envelopes and record who they came from—not to open the letters, but rather just to look to see where stuff was coming from—and to report back to the police." Because they were only reading the cover of the envelope, a warrant likely wasn't necessary. The cops wanted to know who Peter was associating with. The postal worker was switching the letters as his own little act of civil disobedience. It took decades for the reports to be unsealed, but the cops had been surveilling both Peter and Hislop, even tailing them as they travelled around the country. All because Peter had the audacity to question their tactics. The Toronto Police morality and intelligence units had the bathhouses under surveillance, too—Peter was a part owner of one of them. And, periodically, cops carrying sledgehammers would break through the doors at one of the neighbourhood steam baths, arresting the owners, staff, and patrons inside. The sauna-goers would be lined up against a wall, sometimes wearing a towel, sometimes naked, while they were being processed. A steady beat of the raids culminated in one huge set of raids on February 5, 1981, when two hundred officers from the city police force raided four bathhouses. They called it "Operation Soap."

"I remember a fat, ugly plainclothes cop rushed into my room and said 'Don't move. Just stay where you are,'" recalled one man, interviewed years later for an archival project. "God, the noise, the bedlam, the terrible confusion. He wouldn't let me put any clothes on. They herded us all into the room downstairs, and just as we were. And, of course, [they were] insulting us, and laughing, and just acting like pigs. And they were pigs."

"I heard some sort of commotion at the front foyer. I could see a bunch of people streaming into the building. This man still had me in a body grip of some sort. I was struggling with him, and I then yelled out for somebody to call the police. It was then that somebody yelled back: 'We are the police,'" one of the bathhouse patrons told the CBC back then.

"Police seemed to be enjoying themselves," a report from the time quoted one man. Another recalled, to a town hall meeting organized in the following days, that he was shoved into a shower room by the cops. One officer joked how much he would like to hook up the showers to lethal gas.

The day after the arrests, three thousand protesters streamed into the streets, demanding the charges be dropped. Thousands of pissed-off queers surrounded police headquarters, chanting "No more shit." Police in riot gear surrounded the police station. Thus far, the protesters had lit some trashcans on fire and vandalized some cop cars. "The reaction kept getting worse and worse and worse — on both sides," Brent remembered. Then the sound system, set up across the street, went live. "The crowd's attention turns away from the police officers and towards the speakers," Peter recalled. "So there's Lamonica Johnson."

Lamonica's husband, Albert, had been shot to death by Toronto Police two years earlier. He appeared to be in distress when police approached him outside his home in 1979. When he ran inside, police followed. Police said he was brandishing an axe. His daughter, who witnessed his killing, said he followed orders and was on his knees when police opened fire. As Lamonica spoke, telling of her own struggle against police brutality, the crowd drifted away from the line of cops to listen.

After some speeches, the crowd marched to Queen's Park, the seat of the provincial government, to continue the protest. Officers were already waiting. When some protesters tried to get through the front doors of the legislature, officers swung billy clubs with abandon. "The officer at the back grabbed the belt of one officer, so that he could lean forward without falling over," Peter recalled. "And he had a baton in his hand, and he whacked some guy over the head and the blood spurted onto me, because I was standing next to him." Peter looked the officer dead in the eyes, as he realized what he had done. "He was just horrified."

The queer community demanded an inquiry into the raids, wanting to know why they had been approved. Police Chief Jack

Ackroyd defended his officers, releasing a whitewashed internal report that downplayed the homophobia and the violence employed and threw prostitution allegations at the bathhouse owners. That report satisfied Eggleton, the mayor, and Godfrey, chairman of the broader Metro Toronto council. The police stooges at the *Sun* attempted a limp damage control, running stories with headlines like "Gay Link to Mob Suspected."

Police headquarters dumped a great deal of money into these morality raids. What of the homicide investigations? "They couldn't care less," longtime queer activist Dennis Findlay told me. Dennis was so convinced of the police's complete indifference to the safety of his community that he helped set up a community patrol, trained in self-defence, who walked the streets doing the cops' job for them.

When the numbers were finally dislodged from police headquarters, they backed up just how indifferent the cops were. In 1981, Homicide had a staff of just 22 and a little under $5 million in their budget. The Morality and Intelligence units had a combined staff of more than two hundred people with a budget of $7.5 million. (While Intelligence also investigated organized crime, the unit spent six months surveilling the bathhouses in preparation for the raids.) The raiding party that busted the bathhouses that night outsized the entire Homicide division by a factor of nearly ten to one. "I don't think even a raid on Hells Angels clubs would require that many policemen," a local politician noted at the time.

Harassing queers was more important for the Toronto Police Service than solving their murders throughout the 1970s and 1980s. That is a sentiment that rings true for many, even today.

Things would improve. The community got its public inquiry. Chief Ackroyd eventually, grudgingly, accepted the queer community as an integral part of the city in an official statement. Murders targeting queer people continued, but the rate slowed significantly. Those killings that did happen, generally, were solved at a

rate similar to other homicides. Gay and lesbian officers eventually joined Toronto Police. The raids didn't stop entirely, though.
Police found new excuses to bust up queer establishments, often
relying on liquor code violations as grounds to kick the door in.

Even if it felt like Toronto had learned its lesson, it always found
new ways to prove it had not. In 1991, Toronto Police surveilled
Peter Maloney all over again, according to documents obtained
by the CBC and the *Globe* decades later. The cops had tapped his
phone calls and spied on his dinner dates with Susan Eng, a close
friend of his who also chaired the Toronto Police Services Board.

A member of the top police brass was "extremely concerned"
that Peter was close to Eng, as he might be a "security risk,"
according to the report. The accusation was pretty scurrilous on its
face: Peter was a practising lawyer and had been involved politically throughout Ontario. The report seemed to focus on Peter's
"criminal background" from the 1980s—that is, his charges from
the bathhouse raids. The investigative file says the concern about
Peter came from Julian Fantino, superintendent of detectives.
That same year, 1991, as the spying on Peter began, Fantino was
appointed chief of police for London, Ontario.

Once a beat cop tasked with solving the murders of queer
people in the Village, Fantino would go on to run a special operation which seemed to conflate gay men with pedophiles. And he
would become infamous in the queer community for it.

In 1993, police in London fished dozens of cassettes from a
river in the city. A local teenager had found dozens more. The
homemade tapes were pornographic—mostly of men, some featuring women—and many involved underage participants. The
two men who had made them were responsible for a long-running
campaign of sexual exploitation of minors. They were arrested,
charged, convicted, and sentenced.

It could have ended there. But it didn't. One arrest led to
another. And another. A task force was established, promising

that the tapes found in that river were evidence of a larger problem. The face of this new crusade was Fantino. It was Fantino
who stood in front of a stack of tapes in 1994, vowing that his
work was only just beginning. He called it "Operation Scoop." The
tapes, he swore, were evidence of an organized child pornography
ring that existed beyond these two men. They weren't. One of
those tapes was *Abbott and Costello Go to Mars*. Others were perfectly legal pornography. In fact, even though Fantino's project
arrested more than sixty men, only the original two were convicted of possessing child pornography. A few were convicted of
statutory rape—even though it was consensual sex; the age of
consent for vaginal sex was fourteen in Canada, but eighteen for
anal sex. Others were convicted on sex work charges.

There were certainly complex legal questions at hand. Maybe an
investigation was even warranted. But Fantino concocted a story
that smeared much of the London queer community, enabling
a witch hunt and a moral panic in the process. When a young
investigative journalist began asking questions, police began
harassing his sources—the young sex workers who were supposedly the victims of this child porn ring, who had been cajoled into
testifying against the men. Gerald Hannon, the *Body Politic*
writer who had been targeted by the police for his writing in the
seventies, penned an extensive story for the *Globe,* detailing how
London Police had pressured many of those in the videos to testify against the older gay men. The project, which had grown to
include multiple agencies including the Toronto cops, ended up
being a prostitution bust, not a child pornography investigation.

In 2000, Fantino got a new job: Chief of the Toronto Police
Service. Just a year into his tenure, female undercover officers
slipped into the Pussy Palace, a lesbian party held at the Club
Toronto bathhouse. Once inside, the officers decided the party
had violated the city's liquor rules. A team of male officers raided
the party and charged the organizers with liquor code violations.

It was years before a judge threw out the charges, and the service didn't issue an apology until a decade and a half later.

The naughts were not the eighties, however. Fantino, seemingly recognizing the growing prevalence of the community, even volunteered to appear on the cover of a local gay magazine. I've spoken to Fantino—I even covered him when he was elected to Parliament in 2010—he is emblematic of a culture within policing, not uniquely responsible for it. Fantino was a product of a police force that did things a certain way and had no interest in doing better. I believe it was a police force that in 1978 genuinely wanted to solve Sandy LeBlanc's murder but did not want to do the hard work to build a relationship with the community that would make it possible. This was a force that threw the Brunswick Four into a jail cell for committing the crime of being lesbian in public, a militarized police force that campaigned against John Sewell and George Hislop because they wanted the force to modernize, a force that raided bathhouses and bars again, and again, and again, that tried to paint queer activists as pedophiles. It's not surprising, then, that people who lived in or visited the Village were loath to go down to police headquarters and sit in an interview room. In plenty of cases, speaking to the police wouldn't do much good. In some cases, speaking to the police could put you in jeopardy.

The community was alive to the broader problems of the Toronto Police, too. When the G20 summit came to the city in 2010, the force, led by then Chief Bill Blair, dispatched riot cops to break up peaceful protests, arbitrarily stop people on the streets, and arrest more than 1,000 people. They were held in makeshift detention camps, strip searched, and there were complaints of homophobic slurs being hurled at the detainees. When Blair showed up for a Pride brunch days later, a mob of pissed-off queers assembled outside the 519 Community Centre, where the brunch was being held. Inside, Blair asked the invited crowd: "how was your weekend?" A local filmmaker shot back: "I was detained."

Blair shrugged. "Well my weekend was better than yours I guess, my friend." Outside, after failed attempts to placate the crowd, the protesters made their way into the building, chanting through a bullhorn: "this is what community looks like! Show me what hypocrisy looks like!" The crowd jammed their fingers towards Blair. That all happened two months before Skanda disappeared.

Morality raids weren't ancient history, either. In the late summer of 2016, officers had been dispatched to Marie Curtis Park, in Toronto's west end. They were prowling for men cruising the park. Some cops went undercover to solicit sex from unwitting men. When they happened upon those men, rather than asking them to move on, the officers slapped handcuffs on them. There was no dialogue. No consultation. Just arrests and outings. In November 2016, Toronto Police announced that they would be laying eighty-nine charges against men arrested in the park. It took a full year of protest and legal action from the community for the police to drop the charges. The announcement came as Project Prism, a task force so named because of the rainbow created when light hits a prism, was in full swing. It felt like history repeating itself, all over again.

ANDREW KINSMAN

8

SURVEILLANCE

ANDREW Kinsman had terrible handwriting. It's a wonder that Toronto Police were even able to make out the details of his calendar. The month of July had entries that look, to me, like "WELCOME BUT," and "CHIRO JESSER."

The entry for June 26—which, in 2017, was Eid, the end of Ramadan, his calendar reminded him—contained two handwritten entries. "PAY FIDO" read one, reminding Andrew to pay his cell phone bill. The other, scrawled into the top-right corner of the calendar box, could've said many things. "bpm 3 lucks," maybe? Or "ipm Slacks," perhaps? Investigators, knowing that the entry could be the key to unlocking the mystery behind Andrew's disappearance, figured it out.

3pm: Bruce. Or maybe it was 2 p.m. Even they weren't sure. But it was, nevertheless, a solid lead in an investigation with far too few of them.

Investigators spent July and August perplexed. Even after

obtaining the IP logs from his phone and email providers, they were no closer to explaining where he had gone.

Unlike some of the other missing men, there were a huge number of friends and acquaintances ready to speak to police. "There was a lot more to go on with Andrew than Selim," Detective Dave Dickinson told me. Even though the disappearances of the two missing men were being handled under Project Prism, they were being treated as entirely separate cases, Dickinson said. Police, to that point, did not believe they were connected.

There was Rob, Andrew's ex-boyfriend. He and Andrew had an intense, tumultuous relationship that had ended some time before. Rob had left for Vancouver, but police dwelled on the possibility he had returned for Toronto Pride.

There were the other residents in Andrew's building. While Andrew was universally described by his friends as caring, they also remarked he had his limits. "He does not give people a third chance," one friend told cops. Andrew had feuded with some residents of the building whom he suspected of stealing—the arguments had, on one occasion, gotten physical.

There was Andrew's sex life. It was hardly a secret that he was into BDSM. Investigators seemed to hover over these facts as a possible explanation. But these acts are consensual, and serious injury from those kinds of sex acts—let alone death—are incredibly rare.

There were two Australians, who one friend suggested might know something. The two were go-go dancers, porn stars, and sex workers whom Andrew, supposedly, hooked up with. When police interviewed them, they recognized Andrew from around the Village but said they didn't know him personally.

There was the possibility that there was no foul play at all. Andrew had been upfront about his struggles with depression, and he had survived cancer some years earlier. At the same time, he was a health nut and took care of himself. Nobody seriously thought he was suicidal. He had previously talked about disappearing—heading into the woods and cutting off contact. But that would require planning, preparation. There was no evidence of that. Those comments seemed more like idle fantasy, not any sort of concrete desire or plan.

These were all theories. The calendar entry was a real clue that could point to where he had headed just before his disappearance. With that crucial piece of information in hand, in August, investigators started tracking down security footage from around the neighbourhood. One camera, in particular, pointed at the street just in front of Andrew's building. The angle wasn't friendly, but investigators got a copy of the tape anyway. The footage is in full colour, but it is tantalizingly incomplete. The camera is pointed directly at the building's yard, fixated on some shrubs and a stone pathway. The sidewalk, and part of the street, is visible, but only just barely so.

At 3:06 p.m., June 26, a red van can be seen driving up the street, pulling over to the side of the street farthest away from the camera's lens. Its wheels are visible, but little else. The driver's side door remains closed. There's the briefest glimpse that appears to be someone entering the passenger side door, but it's impossible to tell who entered the van. Another security camera, from the same street, captures a man of Kinsman's height and build exiting his building at the same minute, heading towards the intersection where the van is parked. He gets in. The wheels turn, the vehicle lurches forward and disappears from the frame.

Police widened the search. They sifted through more footage and caught the van driving away from Kinsman's address a couple of blocks away. But, frustratingly, the cameras fail to capture the licence plate. It was an older model Dodge minivan, decked out with roof racks, rain deflectors on the passenger-side window, a rounded back, and silver rims with five spokes. There are thousands of vans in Toronto that, roughly, match that description: 6,181 vans, to be exact.

Two months after Andrew's disappearance, Detective Charles Coffey visited a Dodge dealership and showed a manager the vehicle they were interested in. The manager identified it as a 2004 Dodge Caravan 20th Anniversary Edition—its particular chrome side trim and its lack of fog lights were unique to the specific edition of the van.

With this information, Detective Dave Dickinson sent a request to the Ontario Ministry of Transportation and asked for every Dodge Caravan registered in the province—give or take a couple of years on the make. A few days later, the ministry sent a spreadsheet with every such vehicle: there were 6,181. Finding a suspect in that pile would be impossible without something to weed them out.

That's where the calendar came in. How many, Detective Dickinson wondered, were registered to a Bruce? This was a fraught exercise. The van that picked up Andrew could have been registered under a different name. The list provided by the Ministry of Transportation wouldn't include vehicles registered in another province. Or rental vehicles. Never mind if the vehicle was stolen.

Dickinson's query was answered. There were five Bruces who owned that model of van, as it turns out. Only one Bruce owned a 2004 Dodge Caravan 20th Anniversary Edition. That Bruce also had a record in Versadex, the Toronto Police records management software—Versadex is the database of "all general occurrences, known offenders, street checks, radio calls for the Toronto Police Service and any other data by the service."

Bruce McArthur, born October 8, 1951, who owned a 2004 red Dodge Caravan.

For detectives Hank Idsinga, Josh McKenzie, Patrick Platte, and Charles Coffey, all of whom had worked Project Houston and were now on Project Prism, it must have been like seeing a ghost.

• • •

On Sunday September 15, 2013, McKenzie was poring over his notes. Police had compiled everything they could about Skanda Navaratnam, Basir Faizi, and Hamid Kayhan and were hunting for links. People's lives these days are full of so many data points: emails, texts, phone calls, dating profiles. Trying to find overlap between two men, never mind three, was a complex mission. Investigators knew they all went to the Eagle and the Cellar bathhouse. In some cases, they had dated the same men. But those few connections hadn't gotten them anywhere.

McKenzie found another link. In Skanda's email address book was a deleted contact for silverfoxx51@hotmail.com. That same email address was written on a notepad discovered in Basir's home. Coffey cross-referenced the address books of Skanda and Basir, and found only two email addresses that overlapped. Whoever owned that email address was a rare direct contact between these men.

McKenzie ran the cell phone number associated with the deleted contact entry in Skanda's email. It came back as Bruce McArthur, born 1951. McKenzie kept digging: on Silverdaddies.com, a dating site both Basir and Skanda used, Bruce McArthur had a profile. McKenzie jotted the details down, and investigators made note of the connection in their investigative record.

Four years later, in early September 2017, Dickinson reviewed the notes and told the other officers he might have identified, as the investigative files put it, "a possible person of interest in Kinsman's disappearance."

When the Project Prism team ran McArthur's name in the internal Toronto Police database, they saw his 2001 assault conviction. While McArthur had obtained a record suspension—a pardon, essentially—the arrest was still in the database. But there was something else: McArthur had been arrested in 2016.

• • •

It was an early evening in June 2016, and the sun was still hanging high in the sky, ushering in what was about to be Toronto's hottest summer on record. It was already an oppressive, damp heat.

Bruce McArthur was lingering outside the apartment building of an old friend—I'll call him Matt. McArthur knew he wasn't welcome inside, so when Matt arrived home, parking his vehicle on the street, McArthur said, "Let's go for dinner." In the past, the two had had sex on occasion, but Matt was very much in the closet—par for the course for many of McArthur's partners. It had been a few weeks since they had hooked up, but their arrangement had, at this point, been going on for years. Matt agreed to the dinner plan, but asked McArthur to stay downstairs as he went up to his apartment to shower and to feed his cats.

The two drove separately to a Tim Horton's parking lot in the north of the city, where the 401 highway meets Allen Road, an abandoned expressway project. They parked, and Matt suggested they hook up in his truck. McArthur refused: he liked his van better.

So Matt climbed through the sliding doors of McArthur's vehicle and settled into the back. That was McArthur's "little travelling playroom," as a former partner bitterly remembers it. The seats were removed, giving the two men lots of space. A tarp was laid out on the floor. A fur coat was laid out on top of the tarp. The two started hooking up, and, consensually, it got rough. But it kept escalating. More than rough, it became violent. McArthur wrapped his thick hands around Matt's neck. He squeezed, enough to activate Matt's fight-or-flight mechanism. But he was trapped under McArthur's weight, unable to reach the door—fleeing wasn't an option. So he fought. Matt rolled to his right, squirming out of McArthur's grip. He pushed back. Free from his grip, Matt lunged for McArthur's throat. He held McArthur there for a minute before making a break for the sliding door. The whole thing lasted less than five minutes.

Springing out into the parking lot, Matt rounded on his attacker, screaming. He pulled out his phone, threatening to dial 911. McArthur just sat there. As Matt ran back to his car, he began dialling, and McArthur climbed into the front seat and drove off. Matt recounted the whole affair to the operator. He considered giving chase, but he was talked out of it by the 911 dispatcher. Making this call meant Matt could soon be outing himself to his family, but even so, he took the risk.

Two officers from 41 Division arrived on the scene, met by a still-shaken Matt. He told them as much as he could: he and Bruce had never exchanged last names. He told them about how the man he had hooked up with for years had, quite suddenly, "freaked out." He complained his throat was sore, but he had no visible bruises. Since the police had a phone number, that was enough to get an address. The officers headed to McArthur's apartment complex.

He beat them to the punch. He walked through the front doors of 41 Division, went up to the counter, and told the desk sergeant he would like to make a statement. "I just want to tell my side of the story," McArthur told the officer. Just like he had done after assaulting David.

It was a busy night as officers bustled through the station. Sergeant Paul Gauthier was less busy than the rest, so he came out and placed McArthur under arrest, on the suspicion of domestic assault. McArthur declined a lawyer. The other officers, en route to McArthur's apartment building, turned around and headed back to the station. As McArthur sat in an interrogation room, facing Gauthier and another of the officers who had interviewed Matt and with a video camera rolling, he recounted how he earnestly believed that Matt wanted to be choked. It was a misunderstanding, he said. McArthur was, as Gauthier told investigators later, "genuine and credible."

Gauthier was no slouch. He had spent time in the Sex Crimes division—although his time there wasn't spotless. He had been rung up on administrative charges for, allegedly, failing to fully investigate a piece of DNA evidence that implicated a repeat sex offender in a 2010 assault. Even so, Gauthier conducted the interview alongside another officer, one who was specifically accredited to handle domestic violence cases. They didn't tape the interview—they didn't have to, they figured. The two of them concluded that there was not enough to file charges.

There were no grounds here to search McArthur's van or his apartment. A request to search his phone or computer had a scant chance of being approved by a judge. Police could have pursued a peace bond—which can impose release conditions, such as travel restrictions, in exchange for no criminal charges being laid—but even that felt unnecessary in the circumstances. A sexual assault charge would be a stretch, and the chances of conviction seemed slim—the initial sex, after all, was consensual. A domestic assault charge was more straightforward, but McArthur sat there and told officers that the encounter could be explained by some mixed messages and crossed wires.

An investigative report, prepared years later, summarized the incident: "It was determined that there were no grounds to lay charges and McArthur was released unconditionally." Nonetheless, it was protocol to enter all the investigative notes into the police database, Versadex.

Just over a year later, in September 2017, after McArthur became a "person of interest" in the disappearance of Andrew Kinsman, Detective Constable Charles Coffey pulled Gauthier aside to ask about the interview. Coffey had previously worked out of 41 Division and had been seconded to Project Prism. Gauthier recounted the incident, the interview, and the decision not to file charges. He promised to go back and check his notes, and Coffey thanked him for the help.

. . .

There would be plenty of scrutiny of the past interactions between the Toronto Police Service and Bruce McArthur. But, in the fall of 2017, investigators were more concerned with the task at hand. They began reviewing the notes from Project Houston. The detectives had obtained McArthur's email address and a number of his usernames for various dating apps. That gave them a starting point. They learned which bars he frequented, and which bathhouses he preferred. They found McArthur's address—a high-rise tower in the Thorncliffe neighbourhood surrounded on most sides by green, leafy ravines and parks. From McArthur's apartment, on the nineteenth floor, there's a clear view of the Mount Pleasant cemetery, near where Faizi's car was found; it overlooked the ravines of the Don Valley, where Sarrah Becker used to pace.

Officers got hold of security footage of the garage, where they saw McArthur park his red Dodge Caravan. They saw him open the driver-side door, climb out of the van, and turn towards the elevator. Portly, white hair, balding.

Investigators reviewed security footage, going back months. On August 19, 2017, they noticed something interesting. Just weeks after police had announced the creation of Project Prism, McArthur began driving a brand new minivan.

Police ran the vehicle registration, and it didn't take long to figure out the previous owner of the van. That August, McArthur had bought the 2017 Dodge Caravan from a dealership in Windsor, near the U.S. border. The dealership was initially hesitant to work with the police, but told them enough—the van was purchased over the phone. Colour didn't seem to matter to him, he only asked what the cheapest option was. The dealership told the police the whole transaction took some ten minutes.

Figuring out the provenance of McArthur's new van was something—but it didn't explain where the old van had gone.

Investigators fanned out to check known addresses associated with McArthur.

They found it sitting in his daughter's driveway in Bowmanville, a short drive outside Oshawa. Police knew they needed to search that van, and throughout September, McKenzie was dispatched to make the drive to McArthur's daughter's house to keep an eye on the red van.

Police stepped up surveillance of McArthur himself. They followed him from his apartment building to his coffee shop in the Village. Detective Constable Platte grabbed a coffee cup McArthur had discarded, so they could run his DNA. They observed him and his son doing yard work, including in Karen's backyard, on Mallory Crescent. They obtained surveillance video from his building, to help establish an exhaustive schedule of his daily routine. They investigated his friends and Roger Horan, his former business partner, searching for clues that he might have had accomplices. They installed a GPS tracker on his new minivan so they could keep tabs on him. They obtained his cell phone records, noticing he had not used his phone at all over the afternoon Andrew Kinsman had gone missing. They went back and reviewed Andrew's computer, finding photos of McArthur. Friends explained: McArthur and Andrew had known each other for years.

As McKenzie rolled down the street in Bowmanville on September 27, he realized the van was gone. Police found themselves scrambling to try to track down the missing van all over again. They had a hunch: maybe McArthur was trying to get rid of it, so they started checking in with the scrap yards nearby. Before long, in a small town just east of Oshawa, at Dom's Auto Parts, they found McArthur's van in the lot. The tires were gone, and the licence plates had been removed, but the VIN matched McArthur's van. Police impounded the van and turned it over to forensics. They found small patches of blood.

A DNA test confirmed some of it was Andrew Kinsman's blood. There were two other DNA profiles police couldn't yet match.

At this point, police had ample evidence McArthur had killed Andrew, which gave them enough to go to a judge and apply for new, more expansive, warrants. But only circumstantial evidence tied him to the other victims. The evidence of one homicide, however, was enough to get a warrant to search McArthur's apartment itself. Armed with a judicial authorization, they snuck into his building on December 5, while he was out. They had to quickly abandon the search, however, when Detective Dickinson called frantically: the GPS tracker on McArthur's car indicated he was coming home. The officers came back two days later, hoping they had more time. They paired off: officers from the Technological Crime unit began copying McArthur's hard drive, while Detective Constable Joel Manherz led another team in searching his bedroom. Opening the drawer of his bedside table, they found a thick metal bar—they snapped a picture, and took a DNA swab, just in case. They had less than an hour before the call came that McArthur was on his way home. They put everything in order and left.

Back at the station, investigators began reviewing what they had found. Even though they had downloaded less than half the contents of his computer, police found dozens of photos of the men from Project Houston, including their missing persons posters. Some photos were downloaded from their social media pages, while others McArthur had evidently taken himself. In one, Hamid Kayhan is posing in a fur coat. There were saved copies of news stories about the disappearances from the Village. Police had a wealth of evidence that connected McArthur to these missing men, but they wanted more before applying for an arrest warrant. They needed evidence of foul play. The next step was to obtain a wiretap for McArthur's phone—that would likely tell them if he had an accomplice.

It was a day later that Chief Saunders would stand in front of the news cameras to say there was no evidence that a serial killer was stalking the Village.

On January 17, 2018, Manherz analyzed the data from McArthur's computer again, looking for fragments or archived files. That's when he found the folder of photos McArthur had tried to delete. Some of the pictures were taken in McArthur's bedroom, others were clearly taken in his van. The fur coat is featured prominently in some. There are photos of Selim Esen, the metal bar from McArthur's bedside table squeezing against his neck. There are others of Andrew Kinsman, lying in the back of the van, plants sitting next to his head. It's clear from these photos that the men are dead. Other photos are of men whom investigators can't identify. It was in that moment that police realized they had a serial killer. They made plans to arrest Bruce McArthur on January 20, 2018.

9

THE ARREST

ON January 18, 2018, John was riding in the passenger seat of Bruce McArthur's new van. He had met McArthur on Growlr, a dating app for older, bigger, scruffier guys, and they had hooked up a couple of times. John had arrived in Canada only five years prior. McArthur had preferred discretion, refusing to give John his phone number. John understood discretion. After all, he was married to a woman, and he hadn't told anyone about the time he spent with men like McArthur.

A few things were different this time. One was that McArthur was driving a new van. McArthur started quizzing him: *Does anyone know you're here? Did you tell anyone where you were going this morning?*

John assured him it was their secret.

When McArthur returned to his apartment building with John, the officers watching him observed he didn't park in his usual spot underneath the apartment blocks in Thorncliffe Park. Someone else had parked there. McArthur shrugged it off as the two men headed upstairs in the elevator.

Once inside, McArthur ordered John into the bedroom, clothes off. *We have to hurry,* McArthur said, *my roommate or son could be home any minute.* McArthur joined him in the bedroom a minute later, brandishing handcuffs. *We're going to try something different,* McArthur said, before the unmistakable chink of handcuffs-on-metal told John he was affixed to the bed. McArthur left him there, alone, for a minute. When he returned he was carrying a black duffel bag, from which he pulled a black leather hood. He slipped it over John's head. The hood had no holes.

It's at this point that John started to panic. He asked McArthur to remove the hood. McArthur ignored him. He started to struggle, writhing until the hood slipped off his head. McArthur landed on him, taping his mouth shut.

It had been just over six months since Andrew Kinsman disappeared, and just weeks since police provided their most recent update on the case, still insisting there was no serial killer stalking the Village. It's hard to say whether John had seen those news reports.

McArthur certainly had. He knew that, despite a flurry of activity in the summer, Project Prism had largely gone quiet. The chief of police had just told the city that they did not believe a serial killer was active in the Village. From the outside, it seemed that Project Prism would end just like Project Houston had: Without catching Bruce McArthur. Then came the knock at the door.

Bruce McArthur walked to the entryway, opened the door, and was greeted by detectives Platte and Dickinson. Seconds later, he was the one in handcuffs against his will.

Police had had eyes on McArthur nearly constantly at this point. From the moment McArthur pulled into the parking garage and entered the elevator with John, a brown-skinned man whom they did not recognize, the investigators snapped into action. All the planning, all the preparation, had just gone out the window. They ran red lights, dispatched teams across the city, called urgently for the warrants they needed.

As two of the officers handcuffed McArthur and brought him outside, a detective made his way to the bedroom, evidently unsure of what he would find. The relief must have been palpable.

• • •

That same day, I'm at home, nursing a cold. I tried to get on my feet to head out to get some work done, but sagged back onto the sofa pretty quickly. It's freezing outside, with flurries blowing by my window. *I'll just stay in,* I think.

I get up to make myself some tea. I'm standing, waiting for the kettle to boil. It has been just weeks since Chief Saunders ruled out the idea of a serial killer. But my mind keeps flashing to the faces of Navaratnam, Faizi, Kayhan, Esen, Kinsman. And there are others. I picture a corkboard in my head, their missing persons posters pinned to it. Other faces hang from pins, on the periphery: Tess Richey. Alloura Wells. Cassandra Do, a trans woman who was strangled, assaulted, and left dead in her own bathtub in 2003—still unsolved. There are other faces just beyond the light that I can barely see.

Before the new year, I wrote an analysis piece for *Maclean's* magazine, asking: *Are police doing enough to find missing people in Toronto's Gay Village?* The responses on social media were depressing.

"Maybe they choose to not hang around there and go somewhere else?" posited one Twitter user. "To some extent I think people in the city's LGBT community want to feel marginalized even though they barely are nowadays," wrote someone on Reddit, themselves gay. "Since when does this become the police's problem?" wrote a Facebook commenter. That skepticism about an obvious problem was unsurprising. After all, the chief had down-played the existence of a serial killer just weeks prior.

Before the kettle boils, I hear my partner's voice from the other room. "Hey, come look at this," he says. I walk back to the living room. He turns his phone to show me a tweet.

BREAKING: Police announce an arrest in connection with missing men in Toronto's Village. News conference will be held at 1:15 p.m

My heart leaps into my throat. I turn on the TV just in time to see Detective-Sergeant Hank Idsinga step onto the podium. Tall, broad-shouldered, a short layer of hair on his head, he's had a con-sistent style for years: a boxy blue suit, a pale-coloured shirt, a wide loudly patterned tie. Idsinga is nearing his thirty-year anniversary on the force—more than a third of it on the Homicide squad. His former partner, now the chief, stands off to the side, out of frame, watching as Idsinga briefs the media on the investigation.

• • •

"This morning at approximately 10:25 a.m., police arrested sixty-six-year-old Bruce McArthur of the city of Toronto. He is self-employed as a landscaper using the company name Artistic Design and he lives in the Thorncliffe Park area. He has been charged with two counts of first-degree murder in relation to Mr. Kinsman and Mr. Esen. We believe he is responsible for the deaths of Mr. Esen and Mr. Kinsman and we believe he is responsible for the deaths of other men who have yet to be identified. In other words, we believe there are other victims. As of right now, interviews are taking place and police have secured five properties.

Four in Toronto and one in Madoc connected to Bruce McArthur in an effort to further investigate these occurrences. Investigators are asking for the continued assistance of the public in this investigation."

Have you found the bodies?

"We have not yet found the bodies. We're actively looking for them. We're conducting the search warrants in efforts to locate the bodies, but at this point in time, no, we have not located them."

We don't know the cause of death?

"We have a pretty good idea of what the cause of death is but I'm not ready to discuss that yet."

What led you to the man arrested?

"Specifically, some evidence was found yesterday. The investigation was going on for many months leading up to this and some new evidence was uncovered yesterday which pushed us over the edge and enabled us to develop our reasonable and probable grounds to arrest Mr. McArthur."

· · ·

Karen Fraser's home on Mallory Crescent sits at the end of a cul-de-sac. In the middle of the paved loop is a patch of green—a municipal sign announces it as the Mallory Green. If you stand on the teardrop-shaped island of grass or sit on the bench in the shade, Karen's house almost disappears behind a set of towering, leafy trees. The rest of the houses that line the end of the street are huddled together—a mix of small bungalows; low-rise brick apartment buildings; and modern, redesigned homes that are increasingly common in the well-to-do neighbourhood. Karen's looks more solitary than the others. It sits apart from the rest of the buildings, at the bottom of the loop, sort of like it's sliding away from the rest of the neighbourhood, down the hill just beyond, into the ravine.

Behind her house is a secluded backyard—once luscious with huge, ornate planters and a thicket of ever-changing flowers. After the police were done with it, it would be barren, spartan. Just beyond the edge of some flower beds, her yard drops off, sloping down. Below is the Don Valley, a serpentine chasm that stretches throughout the city's east end. Well off in the distance, to the southwest, is the city skyline, the CN Tower just barely visible, a reminder that the home is well within city limits. Train tracks and a highway ferry commuters to and from the city. Several times a day, a train runs through and interrupts polite conversation. Karen was in the middle of explaining the common interruption when a train ran by. "Around here, we just smile," she said, pursing her lips as the deafening roar drowned out the chatter. "I'll get more lemonade."

The first time I visited Mallory Crescent was in the spring of 2017, months before Andrew Kinsman went missing, long before Bruce McArthur's name had been connected to these missing men, as I was still writing my first story for VICE. Warnings of a serial killer in the Village had long since gone quiet. Project Houston had been mothballed three years earlier.

It soon became clear, in the hours and days following McArthur's arrest, that police would need to focus their attention on Mallory Crescent.

• • •

At nearly the same time that police were putting handcuffs on McArthur, there was a knock at Karen Fraser's door. Expecting a delivery, she opened the door of her neatly kept home and looked outside.

"There was no one there," she remembered. She poked her head of vibrant red hair out the door. "But I caught movement out the left side and I turned and there were two men in navy blue—didn't really look like police—and one of them said: 'Are you Karen Fraser? Are you Karen Fraser? You've got to get out now.'"

Karen was puzzled. She speaks slowly, deliberately, giving the cogs some time to churn. She asked to see their badges. She wondered if it was because of a break-in they had had at the house a few months before. But the urgency in the cops' voices didn't suggest it was a courtesy call. One of the cops said to her: "You've got five minutes to get out." That's when they told her that Bruce McArthur, her gardener, had been arrested. They didn't say what the charges were, just that it was a very serious matter.

Normally, police would be armed with a search warrant, so Karen asked where theirs was, stalling as she worked out her plan of action, not fully realizing how serious things were. Because of McArthur's impromptu arrest, the cops had had to call it in to a judge on the way. "It's coming," they told Karen.

Karen went inside to get her husband, Ron Smith. Between them, they had five minutes to put into a suitcase everything they might need, without knowing how long they would be gone, without even knowing where they would go. The officers ordered them to report to 51 Division for an interview. "Surreal is the word that kept coming up," Karen recalled of those long minutes. At that point, Ron said, they still had no idea why the cops had arrested McArthur, and whether they might be held responsible for whatever serious crime had been committed. "They were kind enough to let us know at least it wasn't us," he says, with some mirth.

At the station, Ron went into the interrogation room first. Karen sat outside, staring at her phone. That's when the news alert popped up: *Toronto police charge 66-year-old Bruce McArthur with first degree murder in connection to the disappearances of Selim Esen and Andrew Kinsman.*

She sat there in disbelief. Before she could digest the news, it was her turn to talk to the investigators. She tried to defend McArthur. "You know, he was just diagnosed with diabetes and he's ignoring it," she remembered telling them. "And my father did the same thing when he was diagnosed and my father became very violent." Even then, the little voice in her head began grappling with the news. "My brain is saying: *Nice try, Karen, but two people?* But that was the only explanation I could come up with."

Investigators were combing through Karen and Ron's home, top to bottom, just as they were doing in McArthur's apartment. Their search would include other homes McArthur worked at, as well as a property in Madoc, a community east of the city, owned by his friend and former business partner.

Their search continued outside, led by a K9 unit. They homed in on the spacious backyard, where Karen's well looked-after flower beds, colourful in the spring and summer but desiccated and grey in February, lined the edges of the yard. Where the concrete plateau, which holds a small patio set, gives way to the grass, frozen and dead, massive darkly coloured stone planters stood, barren of flowers. Only a thin layer of snow lay on top.

"They didn't know it was the planters. They brought the dogs in and—as they put it, in police jargon, the dogs *attended* the planters—they zeroed right in on them," Karen said.

Karen and Ron had lived in their quasi-suburban neighbourhood for decades but had made few friends there. After the police moved into their home, suddenly neighbours began reaching out with offers to help. Even amid the ordeal, Karen and Ron had a place to stay—and the cops took it upon themselves to feed the cats, who had been properly off-put by the disruption.

A day later, the cops called. "They told us what they had found in the planters."

The news hit like a thunderbolt. Canada has had serial killers before, but they have been few and far between. Police were faced with the enormous task of trying to figure out just how many victims there were. Police knew that Mallory Crescent was McArthur's staging ground for his landscaping business. They now suspected that he used the property to hide his crimes, as well. In McArthur's apartment, police got hold of a client list, and fanned out across the city and province to check those properties as well, while they appealed to the public for any information about other properties he may have worked on. There were more than a hundred residential properties throughout Toronto; a rural property in Madoc, north of the city; a farm in the Kawartha Lakes, near where McArthur grew up. Any of these properties might have had evidence of McArthur's crimes.

• • •

Once Idsinga reads out McArthur's name, I begin furiously typing it into Facebook, Twitter, Google, and countless other portals to mine information online. This is the first thing many journalists do in cases like these—time is of the essence, as the pages are now pulled offline relatively quickly, or earlier results get buried by news reports.

McArthur isn't hard to find.

While some accused criminals' social media pages are sparse or nonexistent, maybe spartan by design, McArthur's Facebook page is busy. The most recent post is a recording of bird calls. There is a trailer for the TV show *Designated Survivor*. A check-in to a bed and breakfast in Rome. His daughter has commented on his posts. There are photos of him and his family. Photos, ones that will soon be everywhere, of him dressed as a mall Santa. A photo of him on Church Street, during Pride.

I downloaded as much content as I could in the moment. I sifted through his photos, there's one face I keep seeing over and over. It was clear pretty quickly that the man and McArthur are together, in some way. They appeared often, arm-in-arm. He was there with McArthur's wife and kids. For dinner with friends. He's Persian, I gathered, as he and McArthur posed for selfies together with his family in Iran. He's mid-forties, maybe early fifties. Bearded. His face could have very easily been on one of those missing persons posters.

I rubbed my temples. *What are the chances this guy is still alive?* I thought to myself.

I scrolled through McArthur's friends and find the man—I'm going to call him Reza—hoping to see he had been posting stories about the arrest. No such luck. It looked like he'd been online in recent days, however.

I went back to the list of McArthur's friends, looking at each face. That's when I saw a familiar picture: a man with a dark goatee, sitting on a park bench, a large dog sitting to his right—the profile name was Skanda Nava. But I recognize him immediately. I'd stared at this Facebook profile for hours. It hadn't changed at all since September 2010. It's Skandaraj Navaratnam.

Skanda was Facebook friends with his killer. More than that, he was Facebook friends with his killer *and police couldn't catch him.*

I looked for the other missing men but don't see their faces on McArthur's list of friends. There were plenty of other men on there, many of whom fit the victims' profile to a T. As gently as possible, I sent messages asking how they knew McArthur—knowing full well there would already be a virtual army of journalists, online sleuths, and various busybodies doing the same.

"Never met the guy," responded one Facebook friend.

Most people just don't reply.

While I was trawling through McArthur's page, I started to fire off messages to old contacts I've acquired in years of reporting on this story. I went back and looked through the online missing persons cases just to see if there's something I've missed. A quote from Idsinga rung through my head. "We believe he is responsible for the deaths of other men who have yet to be identified. In other words: We believe there are other victims."

Then I started searching for McArthur on the gay dating web-sites, especially those preferred by men of a certain age. It didn't take long to find him.

McArthur went by silverfox—sometimes silverfoxtoronto or silverfoxx51.

"Hi! My name is Bruce," he wrote on one site. "Average guy looking to make friends."

"I am self employed with my own landscaping business so that keeps me busy most of the time. I can be a bit shy until I get to know you, but am a romantic at heart," read another profile. One said that he's looking for guys with a "kinky side." On yet another he wrote: "Like to give abuse to submissive men of all ages . . . like to find a guys buttons and push till you cant take anymore. Like to push a guys limits to [sic] they go over the edge . . . into long sessions to see how much you can take."

Each profile was accompanied by a photo of McArthur. Some of them showed him staring awkwardly into the camera. One with a mischievous grin. Another of him, clad in a leather jacket, leaning against a tree—Andrew Kinsman had taken that photo himself, police learned. McArthur last logged in to one account the day before his arrest.

It was unsettling on so many levels. McArthur looked like so many other men who use these sites. It was only knowing what he was accused of doing that gave all his words a second meaning, that made them seem so nefarious. These profiles would spark all sorts of moralizing in the media. The tone of the coverage suggested the network of online dating sites were seedy, dangerous, dark. Like a modern, digital version of Al Pacino's *Cruising*, the classic cop drama that has been reviled by the queer community for its hyperbolic depiction of homosexuality, for its insistence on marrying sex and violence.

But here was confirmation that Bruce McArthur, sixty-six, charged with two counts of first-degree murder was, in fact, the

Bruce McArthur who had partied on Church Street for Pride. Who was a known face in the Village. A guy who might have sent a Facebook friend request a few months before, and who you hadn't thought about since.

After the social media checks were done, I ran a thorough Google search—best done before the results were clogged with news stories on such a sensational case. Acting quickly can turn over some good leads. In this case, I found a listing from the *South Bayview Bulldog*, advertising a Halloween decorating contest, organized by a neighbourhood woman: Karen Fraser. The winner would receive a flower arrangement by Bruce McArthur. I called the number on the ad and left a message, only hinting at the reason for my call. Understandably, it took some time for her to call me back, but that's how I eventually met Karen.

Police had mentioned McArthur was a landscaper and owned his own company. I tried all manner of searches through a corporate registry database, but got no hits.

Within hours, McArthur's face was everywhere. His happy grin. His twinkling eyes poking out above a white Santa's beard. A shot of him standing at the precipice of Niagara Falls. A question arose immediately: Where was his mugshot? It's a question that still comes up, and the answer is unsatisfying. Although releasing a mugshot is a nearly automatic practice in the United States, in Canada, police generally refuse to hand the photos out, usually in an effort to avoid prejudicing the public against the suspect. It's true that they don't always hold themselves to that standard—police say they will release a mugshot only if spreading the suspect's face will aid in the investigation and no other photos are available, an exception that seems to be made more often for racialized suspects—there was no good reason to release McArthur's mugshot. There were, after all, an abundance of photos freely available right there on his Facebook page. The availability of those photos turned out to be something of a curse, as most of McArthur's photos were group shots, and Canadian news outlets religiously avoid publishing innocent folks' faces alongside suspected criminals, while yet other newsworthy photos were unusable because of their resolution. That left photo editors with few choices.

Columnists and writers of letters to the editor were furious that the newspapers were projecting that image he had made for himself. But that's the difficult tension in this story. The chilling nature of social media superficiality let McArthur cultivate a selective image of himself. A loving father, partner, member of the community. McArthur had the ability to present himself as well connected, well liked, normal. Normal, unassuming. Avuncular. But, in the real world, he was not quite that trope of the friendly serial killer next door. There had been so many warning signs.

• • •

It was the world's first real look at the real Bruce McArthur. The aging, sagging man trudges into the courtroom, his face drooping into a tired grimace. It has been only hours since he was arrested. The officer uncuffs his hands, and the man steps into the Plexiglas prisoner's box. Standing, he listens meekly to the charges against him: two counts of first-degree murder. He's handcuffed again and led out.

Bleary-eyed, I stumble out of the courtroom and bee-line to the clerk's counter, where I find myself behind another reporter, also looking to get a copy of McArthur's charge sheet, a perfunctory summary of the charges file. She's looking incredulously through the glass, asking through a speaker—"It costs *how much*?" The clerk shrugs. It's only a few quarters, but the reporter is obviously not carrying change. I reach into my pocket and tap her on the shoulder. I slip a five-dollar bill under the tray. This round of documents is on me.

There's scant details on the charge sheet. Address, date of birth. A list of the charges he's been arraigned on—two counts of first-degree murder, as read out in court.

Charge sheet in hand, I spin around to find myself making eye contact with Tu Thanh Ha, a reporter with the *Globe and Mail*. He is sitting on a bench, documents on his lap, peering at me over spectacles resting on his nose. Ha is one of the best reporters in the country. He is capable, he's thorough, and he's endlessly kind. He is able to grapple with the morbid with an unending sense of empathy.

We worked together on a strangely similar story, in Montreal. Now, we both find ourselves in Toronto. Ha, still with the *Globe*. I'm freelancing. I haven't even, at that point, figured out who I'll be covering this story for. An editor at VICE has agreed to take some reports from the courthouse, but I don't have much of a plan beyond that. It just felt wrong that I wouldn't be on this story somehow.

Ha pats the spot next to him on the bench and motions for me. "So," he says after I sit down.

"How is it that we only see each other in these kinds of circumstances, Ha?" I ask.

He chuckles. The situation was so morbidly absurd, so dark. What else is there to do?

· · ·

As I was grabbing court documents, two other VICE reporters flipped me an email: *We found some crazy shit on his son.* McArthur's son had been charged with harassment for targeting a Waterloo woman, over two months, with lewd and obscene phone calls. His behaviour bordered on stalking. It had even made news.

"He repeatedly made crude sexual remarks, referred to the woman's relationship with her wife and often whispered her name before she could hang up," reads a 2014 news report from the *Waterloo Regional Record*. The weirdest thing was, as his defence lawyer noted at the time, "They're absolute strangers." The son of an openly gay serial killer, who targeted queer men of colour, had embarked on a campaign to harass and intimidate a lesbian woman whom he had never met? It seemed a lead worth following. The court records concerning his arrest were in Waterloo.

That was tomorrow's problem. That night, I headed to the Village with no aim in particular. I had a few requests to do live hits for local and national TV. As I stood in front of different news cameras, shivering a bit, I tried to convey what was happening. I peered into the bars and coffee shops. I saw the city's homeless trying to stay comfortable in Barbara Hall Park, next to the 519 Community Centre. Mostly, I just trudged around. Maybe I was in shock; maybe more in awe that this neighbourhood had seen so much and was about to see so much more.

The next morning, three days after McArthur's arrest, I woke up, downed some coffee, got into the car, and began the hour-and-a-half drive to Waterloo. I was in a strange state, a state between crying and laughing, between professional enthrallment and humanitarian despair. Everything moves a mile a minute when you cover a story like this, and it can be difficult to stop and take stock. To be a reporter in this case will mean unearthing the intimate personal details of a man accused of multiple murders. You'll unearth fresh, painful memories for both accused and victims alike. It is voyeuristic and grotesque, but it is necessary. At least, we tell ourselves that.

I reached into the glovebox and pulled out the emergency pack of cigarettes, there for just that sort of occasion. I pulled one out, fumbled for a lighter, and lit it. Then I lit another. And soon found myself buying a pack at a roadside gas station for the first time in years.

I sat in an uncomfortable chair in a sterile waiting room in the modern Waterloo courthouse while the court records I had asked for were retrieved. I finally got called up to the counter. The documents on McArthur's son painted a picture of a man struggling with mental illness. I learned it even had a proper name: telephone scatalogia—the compulsion to harass people over the phone. As part of his court-ordered release program, McArthur's son was to live with his father, at the apartment that police were now combing through.

. . .

I had focused more on chasing the story than on figuring out my own professional logistics. Luckily, Ha had, with my blessing, mentioned my name to the *Globe*. That weekend, the paper's managing editor called to offer me some kind of gig. The deal was, in short: *Start reporting, we'll figure out the contract language later*. That worked for me.

Five days after McArthur's arrest, on Monday, I'm sitting in the bright offices of the *Globe*'s fifteenth-floor offices, across from Ha. I start getting the jitters. *What now?* I imagine myself standing at the base of a mountain, staring up. The peak is somewhere above, but the height of the mountain is shrouded by clouds. I know I need to climb it, but I have no idea how high it goes or what lies beyond.

But you climb a mountain one step at a time. So we began to piece together McArthur's various connections with the two victims he was accused of killing—Andrew and Selim—and the three men whose murders he had not been charged with—Skanda, Basir, Hamid. I was convinced McArthur was responsible for their disappearances as well, but police were still cagey. We had virtually nothing more from the police than the name and age of the accused and the names of the victims. The cops had figured out that the planters at Mallory Crescent contained the bodies of these missing men, but had not divulged that information yet. And while we knew the cops suspected there were more victims, we had no idea how many there could be.

We spent those initial days poring over McArthur's dating pro-files and social media accounts, looking for connections between him and the other missing men. Leads started popping up. Some-one recommended I talk to Joel Walker, a friend of Skanda. I reached him on Facebook.

"I wouldn't even look at the killer's picture for fear I would know him," Joel wrote. "Until recently."

"And?" I asked.

"And I was right not to. I had hung out with him and Skanda on multiple occasions."

The weekend Skanda went missing, Joel saw him only briefly. They may have played a round of pool, maybe not even that. Then Skanda was gone, off to see McArthur.

Kyle Andrews, Hamid's friend, recounted an eerily similar story. "The second last time I saw Hamid was with Bruce McArthur in his apartment," Kyle recalled. McArthur and Hamid had been friends and would hook up on occasion, but McArthur's posses-sive behaviour unsettled Kyle. Just like Joel.

We reached Andrew's friends, too. Not only had he and McArthur known each other, but they had been something—maybe friends, maybe old acquaintances, maybe partners, perhaps all three—for over a decade. Bartenders and Village denizens con-firm that McArthur hung out at the same bars as the victims—the Eagle, as well as popular pub Woody's, and Zipperz.

We had connected McArthur, one way or another, to several of the missing men. But we understood little about his motivations. I was sitting in the *Globe and Mail* offices when my phone rang. I answer it.

"Hi, my name is Peter Sgromo. I am an escaped victim of Bruce McArthur."

• • •

I leapt from my chair, dashed into a nearby boardroom, and slid the door shut. The voice at the other end of the line was professional, articulate, direct. The caller didn't ramble. There was no uneasiness. I get a lot of calls from conspiracy theorists and people experiencing delusions. My phone number isn't hard to find. Peter Sgromo didn't sound like a kook.

Peter and Bruce McArthur were friendly acquaintances. Peter said they met through a support group for gay dads—Peter didn't go to the meetings, he wasn't a dad, but he would join the others for brunch afterwards. In the late 1990s, McArthur had just arrived in Toronto from Oshawa, and was living as an openly gay man for the first time. McArthur joined a small social group of other men, mostly fathers, who had come out of the closet later in life. That's how he met Peter. For years, they'd find themselves around the table, with an assortment of other middle-aged gay men, most of whom had kids, having coffee or cocktails. They were hardly best friends.

Sgromo left Toronto in 2001, moving to the United States for a good job in corporate America. He came back to Toronto in early 2017 and soon saw McArthur's face in his inbox on Bear411, a dating app preferred by burly men of a certain age.

"I just remember him really being persistent and tenacious about getting together, which has never been our history, so I got a little bit nervous," Peter told me. "Chalk it up to being a bit paranoid."

The fact is, Peter is *a lot* paranoid. That became clearer later in the conversation. At this point, Peter was plain-spoken, self-effacing, entirely credible.

"I didn't really think we were hooking up for sex," he told me. "We flirted, but I flirt with telephone poles." You don't have sex with your friends, he added. And he and McArthur were friends. Not best friends, but old friends. Or at least somewhere in that grey zone of friendly acquaintances and friends. Sgromo felt uneasy, so he invited a friend to tag along for the rendez-vous with McArthur. And around a table, over some beers on Church Street in the spring of 2017, the conversation was as fun and engaging as he remembered. They gabbed about travel. "He was talking about the men in Italy."

The only thing that took Sgromo aback was McArthur's talk of one guy he'd met in Italy. The Italian liked it rough, McArthur reported. "I never would have thought of Bruce as a person who would've liked rough sex," Peter told me. It took all kinds, he figured.

Apart from that, it was a pleasant evening catching up with an old friend he hadn't seen in twenty years. But Peter's friend was set to go home, and he himself was ready to pack it in. "[Bruce] had his van parked on Church Street, by the school, just across from City Apartments." Those are the apartments where McArthur, more than fifteen years before, had attacked a sex worker with a lead pipe. Peter didn't know that.

"So we're chatting, talking, ready to say goodnight, it was a nice hug, and a little peck, and he started kissing me. Hey, I liked it. I was like, okay, this is kind of fun. It was consensual. So he said, c'mon, I'll give you a ride to your hotel. So he opened the door."

There was nothing in the back of McArthur's van—the seats had been removed entirely. "I thought, oh, that's kind of weird," he remembered.

But Peter knew that McArthur was a landscaper. This was his work van. Maybe that was normal. It took him a minute to realize the back served a dual purpose. The two crawled into the back and shut the door.

"It was like this was a little travelling playroom."

McArthur took out poppers—amyl nitrate, the party drug he had temporarily been banned from using back in 2001. Peter said no. He was never fond of poppers. Then they got down to business.

"He kind of pushed my head to perform some oral sex on him, and I did a bit, but he wasn't really erect. We started kissing again." Peter wasn't describing this interaction to me with any kind of relish. His tone was matter of fact. "Then he grabbed me by the back of the neck. And I was like—" He paused. "Woah." The grip, he said, was intense. "Then he twisted my head down to his crotch." This wasn't playing anymore. "I thought, any second he would've broken my neck."

I don't know whether McArthur had planned on killing Peter Sgromo that night. Maybe he had. "I have a big neck, for one hand. He nearly snapped it," Peter remembered. But maybe he was simply looking to—as his online dating profile put it—"push buttons." Either way, he didn't have Peter's consent. And he picked a bad target.

Peter Sgromo is, to borrow a phrase, built like a brick shithouse. I had to look him up after our chat, but his photos immediately confirmed his description of himself. He's short, that much is clear. But he's got thick biceps. His shoulders are broad and strapping. He looks like he could lift a bus. And, he tells me, he has self-defence training. He's been robbed before and seems intent on making sure that never happens again.

There was a struggle. "I was able to free his hand by squeezing his elbow," he told me. He didn't get into the full play-by-play, but, he told me, he broke free of McArthur's grip. "I was like, 'Bruce, what the fuck are you doing? After all I've been through to do something like that?'"

It was odd. At first, Peter thought it was a kink. Maybe McArthur liked going too far—but only a bit too far. Peter discarded that theory quickly. "He was flaccid," Peter said. "It was not a sexual thing."

Peter, in the moment, made a judgement: "This guy knows how to kill somebody."

The whole episode was disturbing. Peter broke off the hookup, but let McArthur drive him home. He was unsettled enough to put some distance between him and McArthur in the van but not enough to refuse the lift.

And that was it. That was Peter's interaction with McArthur.

I asked, "Did you report it to police?"

That's where it got complicated. The exact details aren't necessary, but Peter Sgromo went on to explain that there are some people out to kill him. Maybe it's a reasonable reaction to some of the hairy situations he's found himself in. Maybe he needed a broader explanation for his bad luck. Whatever the reason, Peter saw a plot behind McArthur's attack on him. A broader conspiracy at play, one that does not appear to exist—or, if it does, McArthur has nothing to do with it.

I paced the boardroom anxiously as he told me, in perfectly lucid detail, how he had reported these plots to police and how they hadn't believed him. He went on to say that he'd explained McArthur's assault on him, months after the fact, to an officer. It's not clear if that officer filed a report.

I finally covered everything, thanked Peter, and hung up. I walked out to the office and grabbed Ha and our managing editor, Nicole MacIntyre.

"I've got good news and bad news," I told them. I recounted Peter's encounter with McArthur. They were transfixed.

I finished. "But there's something else."

I filled them in on the supposed price on Peter's head. The assassination plot. Their faces fell. "But here's the thing," I told them. "I think he's telling the truth. I think the assault happened."

Beyond the fact that I just trusted his voice, Peter's story was consistent and detailed. He mentioned sitting with McArthur on a patio on Church Street. When I asked what time of year it was—he consulted a mental calendar. It was spring, he concluded. I grimaced a bit. *He probably wasn't on the patio if it was spring.* Unprompted, he added that it must have been May, and he recalls it being warm. The conversation continued like that. Me, offering innocuous questions that are continuity tests, to see if he's remembering or inventing. *So you said you walked across the street* . . . I would ask. Or: *So you were in the front seat?*

Every one of his answers was consistent. So, yes, I thought he was telling the truth.

"Can you prove it?" Nicole asked.

"I dunno."

I left the conversation with Peter armed with a handful of names. The friend who sat on that patio with Peter and McArthur, and a friend who had been in the same circle as Peter and McArthur in the nineties. It took some doing, but I got both on the phone, and their stories matched with Peter's, almost identically. Peter Sgromo knew Bruce McArthur, they shared drinks in the spring of 2017, and they left the bar together.

I broached the question of Peter's mental state with his longtime friend, who sighed heavy. Yes, Peter was paranoid. Yes, he was fixated on this supposed plot on his life. Then came the all-important *but*—he wouldn't make something like this up. He's not malicious, not a crackpot, he doesn't hallucinate, he's just been through a lot.

All that was enough to go to print. Just a week after McArthur's arrest, our story appeared in the paper:

Suspect in killings of gay men had history of violence.

10

DEAN AND SOROUSH

IT'S January 29, a week and a half after McArthur's arrest. Detective-Sergeant Hank Idsinga walks up the ramp in the Toronto Police Service's media theatre, past the throng of reporters and cameras, and stands in front of the microphones.

> As you know, on January 18 Bruce McArthur was arrested
> and charged with two counts of first-degree murder in
> relation to the deaths of Selim Esen and Andrew Kinsman.
> Since then, we have continued our investigation, including
> searches of numerous properties associated [with] Mr.
> McArthur, a review of material evidence, and interviews
> with dozens of people, many of whom have come forward
> to us. I do want to offer some clarity on the intersection
> between Projects Houston, Prism, and the homicide cases.
> We know the community has been, and continues to be,
> deeply concerned about these past investigations,

specifically the seriousness with which we looked at these
cases. . . . On Wednesday January 17, investigators uncovered
evidence which provided them with grounds to believe that
Mr. McArthur was not only responsible for the death of
Andrew Kinsman but was also responsible for the death of
Mr. Esen. Further evidence was uncovered which led
investigators to believe that Mr. McArthur was responsible
for the deaths of other unidentified victims. On Thursday,
January 18, Mr. McArthur was arrested by members of Project
Prism. He was charged with two counts of first-degree
murder in relation to Mr. Kinsman and Mr. Esen. Today Mr.
McArthur was brought back before the courts. Mr. McArthur
has now been charged with three additional counts of
first-degree murder. These new charges are in relation to the
murders of Majeed Kayhan, Soroush Mahmudi, and Dean
Lisowick. . . . Majeed Kayhan was one of the males whose
disappearance was investigated by Project Houston.
Soroush Mahmudi was fifty years old when he was reported
missing in Scarborough by his family, in 2015. Dean
Lisowick was never reported as missing, but we believe that
he was murdered between May of 2016 and July of 2017.

I'm standing in the back of the room. My stomach sinks. Those
last two names I'd never heard before. It isn't five victims. It is
seven. And if it is seven, it could be more. I thought I had pored
over every outstanding missing persons report in Toronto—maybe
the country—that fit McArthur's profile. How did I miss two?

After the shock wears off, I sprinted out of the police station to
catch a cab, my mind racing, kicking myself. It's irrational, I know,
but guilt set in. How could I have failed these guys so badly? I had
spent countless hours trying to see if other cases fit the pattern—
Mahmudi, at least physically, fit that pattern to a T. If I had found

him back then, in 2015 when he went missing, might this case have been reopened sooner? Might McArthur have been arrested sooner? I circle around the comment about Dean Lisowick: he was never reported missing. How was that possible?

As I mentally will the cab to go faster through the traffic, I'm hunching over my phone screen, plugging in permutations of the names into a search browser and firing off emails to the newsroom and trying to figure out what to do next.

This story was far from over.

• • •

Back at the *Globe and Mail*, the research library was already in full swing. By the time I got to my desk, there was already a zip file in my email, full of reports on Soroush's debts, all the property registered to his name, any records for bankruptcy he may have filed. It's an eerily intimate look into someone's life, but it's often a helpful one—not to explain why they died or to expose their money troubles, but to help put together the scaffolding of where they lived, where they were employed, who their family was. Ha and I got to work.

At the time of his disappearance, Soroush was working as a painter. He was married to a woman named Fareena and was stepfather to her son. He was listed as the owner of a half-dozen different properties, mostly in Barrie, north of Toronto. At first we figure he was working as a landlord. Then we realize that he was buying and selling properties, slowly downsizing as he moved from one property to another. He and his wife filed for bankruptcy in the spring of 2014, shortly before his disappearance. Soroush's financial situation wasn't entirely dire—he reported just over $140,000 in assets and just over $150,000 in liabilities, mostly unpaid loans and condo fees. Even so, the bankruptcy report states that he failed his repayment plan.

Soroush seemed like a regular guy, living a suburban life. The mundane details made the story all the more tragic. Fareena later spoke to the *Toronto Star* about her husband. She was from Sri Lanka; he hailed from Iran. They had met later in life in Canada. "He loved me too much," she said. He worked late, she said, and Soroush became a loving stepfather to her son. On the Saturday he disappeared, in mid-August 2015, Soroush woke up and made breakfast for his stepkid. He walked out of their house in Scarborough, and he wasn't seen again.

Next, we took a look at his criminal record, which is never a comfortable process. As a reporter digging into a murder victim, you're caught in an uncomfortable tension between hoping they lived clean, honest lives and hoping a lengthy criminal record reveals some part of their history. For Soroush, it was the latter.

There were more than a dozen charges on the list, but these charge sheets aren't terribly informative. They detail the offence committed, the date, a file number, and the courthouse where the case was heard. In other jurisdictions, those criminal files can be accessed online. Not in Canada. I needed go to the courthouse to see the documents. I had to empty my pockets to walk through a metal detector. I would wait in a hallway as raccoon-eyed public defenders and beat cops bustle past. I shuffled up to a Plexiglas window and shouted through a speaker, spelling the name and birthdate of the offender I was looking for files on. I'd grab a pen on a chain and fill out page after page of paper. Sometimes the clerk behind those counters will tap the names into their terminal and lean close to the Plexiglas to whisper details from the court files, and put a rush on pulling the boxes from storage. Other times they'll shrug and say, in monotone, "That will be four to six weeks."

Four to six weeks is an eternity. Sometimes, you just never hear back.

So on a cold day that winter, I drove from courthouse to courthouse in and around Toronto to try to help build our profile on these victims, Soroush in particular. Not to slur them as criminals, but to try to understand the lives they lived a little better. A piece of those lives, anyway.

I was on the highway north to Barrie, to another courthouse, when I realized the sun was setting. It hit me that I might not make it in time. I pulled over at a gas station and prayed I'd reach someone sympathetic. I did. A soft-spoken woman in the records department was eager to help. I asked for one file number. Then another. Then another. And the wonderful clerk, her cheery disposition waning only slightly as the requests went on, pulled up each file and gave me as much information as she could. We filed the request for the full court files. The ball was rolling. The files came back in days, not weeks.

The list of convictions was long. Digging in to each one individually, however, painted a more complex picture. Soroush had run-ins with the law, but he also seemed to get caught by the unforgiving machinery of the justice system. There's a 2000 conviction for driving under the influence. A 2008 conviction for failing to appear in court. A 2009 conviction for driving while disqualified. Another conviction from that year for failing to appear, again—though it's withdrawn, later, after Mahmudi pleaded guilty, again, to driving while disqualified. Then he pleaded guilty to the same charge in 2010.

It's a mess of a rap sheet, and it must have been full of red flags for his car insurance company—never mind a prospective employer. It betrays the story of a man struggling with alcohol abuse, and who seemed to insist on driving anyway. At the same time, each criminal charge seemed to lead to a litany of procedural ones.

Sometimes, one infraction leads to another, and they can snowball. Each time the system offers a little less lenience. Paradoxically, each charge makes your life a little harder, makes it a little less easy to live a normal life. The constant court appointments you need to make it to—except you can't drive. The checking-in with your parole officer, who expects you to get a job—except getting a job is impossible when you need to regularly appear in court or report to your parole officer to conduct a urine test. It's a series of catch-22s. It's quicksand.

One charge sticks out, though. Everything on his sheet is related, one way or another, to driving under the influence, except one. This conviction, from 2001, is very different. It's an assault charge. On the document, which reports that Soroush pled guilty, there's little detail. It lists the accused's name, Soroush Mahmudi; the alleged offences; the plea; and the victim's name.

The victim's name is a male name. Ha jumps on it. I'm very good at finding people—he's much better. Ha reports back a few days later. He's found the victim. Her name is Sarah Cohen.

• • •

I'm waiting in a booth in a bright chain restaurant north of the city. I order a coffee while I wait for Ha, who volunteered to pick Sarah up on the way. They walk in, and I stand up to shake Sarah's hand and thank her profusely. I know this is an intimidating experience.

She's nervous, but doesn't need the encouragement. Sarah is a warm, soft-spoken person. She admits to being anxious, but she relaxes quickly. She's eager to help.

We make some small talk as we get to know each other and decide on some breakfast. I don't even know how it comes up, but she's a huge *Golden Girls* fan. She can recite entire chunks of the show from memory. I love the *Golden Girls*. She's never spoken to the press before and wants to know how it's all going to work. We do our best to lay out what we're going to ask about, how we're going to portray her.

After we order, I suggest, "Why don't we start at the beginning?"

For the better part of an hour, we let Sarah talk. A waitress drops off my bagel and lox. I'm starving but hold off as I try to take in every word Sarah is saying. As she opens up about meeting a man she loved, and the day that would be the worst of her life, we nod and sip our coffee.

Her story starts as a sunny, romantic montage, scored by the cheesy adult contemporary hits playing over the restaurant sound system.

. . .

Sarah met Soroush at Woody's, on an evening in 1997. It's right on Church Street, it's got cheap drinks, it's huge, and it has a mix of drag shows and displays of attractive men—there's a best abs competition, best ass, best arms, and so on. Men get onstage and show off their best attributes for a chance to win a prize. Even if you've never been inside, there's a chance you've seen the place before. It served as a prime location for *Queer as Folk,* the show that opened up a generation of queer youth to gay culture. That includes me. For all those reasons, it's been one of the most popular bars in the Village for decades.

The night Sarah met Soroush, she had been across the street, at Crews & Tangos. She and a girlfriend had been talking about romance, and she was waxing in a self-pitying style about being single. *Go on, then,* her friend challenged her: *Go pull up a spot at Woody's, and see what happens.* That's what she did. She sat there, at the bar, nursing a drink. Before long, she made eyes with a dark-skinned man leaning against the wall. Soroush charmed her immediately.

The two began dating. Soroush was about the most tender, warm, affectionate man you could hope for. Straight, Sarah still thinks, but he had no issues hanging around a gay bar. And he was attracted to trans women, Sarah notes, which isn't the case for many men. They moved in together before long. Soroush was hurting for work, so Sarah pulled some strings through her dad and got him a job at a factory. Some harmless nepotism. But Soroush was a hard worker, and he was incredibly strong, Sarah remembers. Sarah made him lunch every day and packed it up. She gushes, recalling how Soroush would come home with stories of how the other guys on the job site were envious of the lunches she had made.

Soroush had dark corners, though. He would drink. He confessed to her that he had done terrible things, hiding in the mountains north of Turkey, across from the Iranian border. He had fled, fearing persecution from the government. He relayed only bits and pieces of his past, often by being ominously vague—he had done what he needed to do to survive, he told her. He had killed. He drank to cope with that.

When Soroush was pulled over while driving drunk, his licence was suspended, so Sarah stepped up again and drove him to work. His English was rough, and she worked with him to improve it. He would get frustrated, but it was coming along. As far as Sarah was concerned, it was a perfect domestic life.

Over time, things got darker. Soroush had demons, Sarah knew that. But he was never physical towards her. They had been together for three years before it got violent. The first time, they were chatting as he drove, and she corrected some error in his English. He got angry, extending his hand behind her head, grabbing a clump of her hair, and twisting it in a painful way. That was strike one. Days later, they had an argument in their apartment, and he pushed her into the dishwasher. There was no use waiting for strike three: Sarah knew it was time to go. She just had to pack.

A couple of days later, after getting her affairs in order, Sarah confronted Soroush in the kitchen. She recounted grimly what happened next. It was obvious these memories were still fresh and vivid, still incredibly painful.

She told him it was over. At first, he seemed resigned. He didn't say anything. She turned around to go and get her bags. A second later, a flash of pain. There's broken glass. She's on the floor. Soroush had grabbed the glass jar from their blender, picked it up off its base, and swung it around, bringing it down on her skull. He climbed on top of her and began punching. Sarah's mind was reeling. She was stunned. Then the adrenaline kicked in. This wasn't just an outburst. This was an attack. She fought back, but he was too strong. He was on top of her. She couldn't escape. He could kill her. A neighbour heard the assault and when they came by to investigate, Soroush backed off. Sarah thinks he might have stopped before they were interrupted, knowing he had gone too far—she doesn't quite know when the beating stopped. What came next is a blur. She was admitted to the hospital, but she has trouble putting timelines to subsequent events. She spent months in rehab and physiotherapy. She talked to the cops and opted to press charges. Soroush was arrested, but the cops told her it was unlikely Soroush would see jail time—what was more likely was just a fine, anger management classes, and probation. She sat in the courtroom once, but it was too hard. She thought about suing Soroush, but she was told the fine he'd paid was substantial, so she settled for that.

Sarah is still wearing the scars from the attack, literally and figuratively. She admits that her cognitive functions are a bit slow at times. She gets migraines. She came to love the *Golden Girls*, to memorize entire episodes, as she lay in bed recovering from the attack, watching and rewatching the entire series. It was a familiar safety blanket.

As Sarah tells me all of this, it takes all my effort not to stand up from the vinyl booth, walk over, and wrap Sarah in a hug as her eyes well with tears. I'm happy Ha is there; otherwise, I might just do it. That's just not something a journalist is supposed to do—and it's probably why I am, by my own own admission, a terrible interviewer. I don't enjoy probing the worst moments of people's lives, and I often find myself holding back to avoid causing pain.

But over breakfast, I do my job. I prod Sarah to go on. And she recounts how hard it was to escape that attack, how she felt incapable of holding down a job; how hard it was to show up in court to watch Soroush plead guilty; how hard it was knowing that he wouldn't see jail time for what he'd done to her. She nearly spits out her coffee when we tell her how much his fine worked out to. She was told it had been more.

It's a heartbreaking interview. Sarah is the victim of a horrible assault at the hands of Soroush. Soroush was the victim of a horrible murder at the hands of Bruce McArthur.

These men left real lives behind. Messy, human lives. Soroush's disappearance meant Sarah never fully got a chance to close that chapter on her own terms. He did something awful to her, and she never forgave him. But his murder isn't solace, Sarah says. It's salt in the wound.

Although Soroush robbed Sarah of so much, he went on, by all accounts, to get his life on the right track, even if she couldn't do the same. While the punishment he received for his assault on Sarah was insufficient, at least in her eyes, he nevertheless seemed rehabilitated. His wife, Fareena, seemed smitten.

Driving back to the city after our breakfast, I realize something key about Sarah's story. Soroush Mahmudi was reported missing to 41 Division in August 2015. Police investigated the disappearance and found no answers. But Sarah never got any calls from the cops. Nobody, it seems, had enquired about Soroush's past. If they had consulted the various police databases which he should have been in, they certainly hadn't followed up on the name of his victim. Nobody had figured out that he had been a Church Street regular. That Soroush liked Woody's. That he hung around gay bars. That he wasn't an isolated case—that he was, instead, the fourth brown queer man to disappear from Church Street in five years.

They didn't connect the dots.

• • •

Dean Lisowick was one of thousands who lived on the streets of Toronto or in one of the underfunded and overcrowded shelters around the city, particularly in the neighbourhoods around the Village. Dean, who had no fixed address, was never reported missing. It took only a few phone calls to learn these details about him— that he was homeless, panhandling on Church Street, a familiar figure in Barbara Hall Park, just next to the 519 Community Centre. Like so many others who end up street-involved, Dean's story is not a simple one.

Dean grew up poor. His family moved from their native Winnipeg to Toronto in search of economic opportunity—but things didn't improve. His parents split. Dean was eight when he was taken by the Catholic Children's Aid Society and placed with a couple in Udora, Ontario, a small town once described in an official town document as "neighbourly but not intrusive."

In the farming town, Dean grew up in a nice home facing a cornfield and was soon joined by two other foster brothers. Such an arrangement wasn't terribly uncommon in the communities scattered around the fertile lands of Lake Simcoe—communities that had welcomed droves of children throughout the early twentieth century, sent away by their families or placed there by aid societies. Bruce McArthur's family, in nearby Eldon, had done exactly that two decades before.

Even after Dean arrived in Udora, his biological family stayed in contact, with Dean's father visiting on the weekends. In his new home, he forged a close bond with his adoptive brothers. "He wouldn't let anyone hurt me," Jerimiah Holmes recalled. They played outside, accompanied by the family dog. A photograph of the two of them shows them leaning against their bikes, Dean's arm slung around Jerimiah's shoulder. Jerimiah has kept the photograph in near-perfect condition, the edges of the print frayed only slightly.

The warm facade of rural life in Udora was hiding a dark secret, however. Evidence surfaced that Dean had been sexually abused during his time in foster care. Jerimiah learned of the claims years later, after he left the idyllic fields of Udora, when an officer investigating the claims rang him up. After that call, Jerimiah couldn't shake the feeling that the abuse, if it occurred, stayed with Dean. "We're somehow broken. We don't know how to get ourselves fixed. We don't have the tools," he said.

When Dean grew up, he left the foster home and returned to Toronto, where he reconnected with his extended family. But that life proved tumultuous. Dean began spending time in the Village, and he found himself, especially in the mid-1990s, thrust into a scene where drug use was hard to avoid. Run-ins with the law followed, mostly for drug possession. There's an assault charge that appears to stem from an altercation at home, where he was staying with his great-aunt. In 1994, Dean became a father. He was in no place, it seems, to raise a family. He disappeared not long after his daughter's birth and headed to the Village.

Dean and I have a mutual friend: Monica Forrester, the activist who had agitated for answers in Alloura Wells's disappearance. I bumped into her at bar across the street from the *Globe* offices one afternoon and, over a beer, she told me about her history with Dean. She had seen him often, over many years, standing on Church Street. She swore she had seen him just a few months prior.

Dean and Monica were both fixtures at Sneakers, a hustler bar on Yonge Street. It had opened during the gritty mid-nineties amid a sea of smutty movie theatres and sex stores and had earned a well-deserved reputation as a place where older men could find a young, attractive escort. The short strip of the street just north of the bar—colloquially known as Boystown—was a stroll for many of those sex workers.

Dean, a charming and outgoing guy with a boyish face, had no trouble finding work at the bar. He fell into a community of sex workers—Monica was one of them. "He always identified as bisexual," she remembered. He had a street name: Laser. Monica and the others in Boystown, at Sneakers, in the Village: they were his chosen family.

Sex work is a complicated business for many queer people. Trans people, in particular, face barriers to traditional and legal employment. In an economy that often treats people's queerness as an economic liability, using your sexuality or gender for profit can be liberating. A way to game the system, almost.

But with economic necessity comes risk. Drug use, particularly crack and meth, can push some sex workers to taking dates they might not otherwise. Violent johns are a constant threat. While sex work can be a very safe business, police repression pushes dates into the shadows. Even having an establishment like Sneaker's, while not perfect, offered a protection.

As the 1990s gave way to the booming 2000s, Sneakers shut down. Boystown was slowly snuffed out by the Toronto Police vice squad and encroaching gentrification cheered on by the city. A few of the porn theatres and sex stores have held out, but the street slowly got "cleaned up." That push had been going on for decades, having already claimed victims like the St. Charles Tavern and the Manatee.

"When Sneakers closed down, a lot of hustlers . . . were sort of lost," Monica remembered. That left Dean high and dry. He was a sex worker with a criminal record for drug use. Finding another job, even as he worked to get sober and find a place to live, wasn't really an option. So Dean was forced to panhandle on Church Street. He'd visit soup kitchens in the area for a warm meal. He'd sleep in a shelter. But everyone I've spoken to who knew Dean said this wasn't supposed to be the end of his story. They all had a pang of remembered optimism in their voice, a belief that he would struggle against the current and get back on his feet.

Through all those years, Dean always made sure to write a birthday card to his mother. One read:

Someone who's as nice as you
deserves life's best each day.

Below, he wrote:

Hi Mom this card took the words right out of my mouth, hope you like it, Love you Lots and Lots. He promised to visit. *CANT WAIT!!!!* He wrote below a string of Xs and Os.

His own daughter, Emily, would still ask about him. When she was growing up, students at her school would ask: *Where's your biological dad?* "I don't know, on the street somewhere," she'd say.

"I even thought maybe he turned everything around and found work and a nice lady, and maybe lived in a nice big house with kids of his own," she would say, years later. But she admitted a dark reality was more likely. "Maybe he was gone, passed away somewhere, and no one knew."

Dean's cousin, Julie Pearo, was one of the few family members to stay in touch. She would even go visit him. They had been close—they were born a day apart. "The last few times I saw Dean he was making plans, setting goals, and doing the things needed to accomplish them," she recalled. "His face lit up when he talked about his daughter—almost dragging me around downtown to show me the electric bike he wanted to buy her and how he was going to get his life together so he could do that."

Dean never got to do that, but he tried. He took odd jobs. He would find an affordable apartment and stay for a few months, but he would ultimately take off. He never got to repair that relationship with his daughter—or meet her two kids.

"Now I have to go every day knowing that my father is gone and the way he left us," Emily said.

The day I learned Dean's name, I drove up to the Village after work. I awkwardly stalked up and down Church Street. I wandered

into a convenience store, Dean's photo loaded up on my phone—
Recognize him? They didn't, but the shopkeeper had a rant prepared
about the rampant violence in the neighbourhood. I caught the
owner of the Village hardware store. He remembered Dean perfectly well. Dean had hung around out front of the store sometimes.
Friendly, lovely, a fixture of the community. Until he stopped
coming around.

Monica swears she had seen Dean around the Village as recently
as the summer before, in 2017, but cops believe Dean disappeared
in the spring of 2016. "I could've sworn . . . ," she starts. Later, she
becomes more confident. "It's been recently," she said. "He's been
around. I've seen him." Monica had been living with the memory
of her friend, smiling, hopeful, standing on Church Street.

At the same time, Monica admits, the Village is a meeting place
of many identities that seem to disappear. Sex workers, queer
people, refugees, Indigenous people, street-involved people, drug
users. The city seems to accept that's normal. For Monica, that makes
it so hard to keep track. "It's really hard to say who's missing."

DEAN LISOWICK

11

INSIDE THE TORONTO
POLICE SERVICE

THE floor-to-ceiling windows that wrap around the *Globe and Mail*'s fifteenth-floor office let you gaze out all across Toronto's east end—the bustling Gardiner Expressway, the dilapidated portlands and Lake Ontario, the historic Distillery District. You can look past an array of mid-range buildings and see the neighbourhoods where so much of this story takes place.

You can pick out Cabbagetown, where Skanda and Andrew lived; the coffee shops Basir frequented; the Eagle, where Hamid would drink; Woody's, where Soroush met Sarah; the corner where Dean hung out; the park where Selim sat and read. If you squint, you can maybe even see the towering apartment building where McArthur lived.

I've got a whiteboard on wheels parked next to my desk. It's been written on and erased a few times already, but, one day, later in the afternoon, I wheel it into a boardroom. Ha and some other co-workers shoot me furtive glances, wondering just what I'm up to.

I print off photos of the faces of the missing men, most taken from their missing persons posters, taping them to the board. I print off calendars, from 2010 to 2018, and start marking them up. There are names. Places. Open questions. Major events. I'm scribbling in the margins of the margins.

Obsessive as it may look, there is reason to it. Police have laid five murder charges against McArthur, though I expect charges for the murders of Skanda and Basir are to come—that McArthur isn't responsible for those murders feels unlikely. I can spot a few trends immediately.

At this point, in late January, police have not nailed down the dates some of these men disappeared. For others, they have a pretty good guess but can't be entirely sure. It does seem all the victims were killed over long weekends—Christmas, Thanksgiving, Easter—or in the doldrums of summer. So what does that say? I reasoned: those were the days when nobody was home at Mallory Crescent. Karen would later tell me there was some truth to that idea—that they spent a lot of time at their cottage, especially on long weekends. McArthur would have had free run of their property.

Zooming out, there's a conspicuous gap. Skanda, Basir, and Hamid all disappeared in a relatively short period between September 2010 and October 2012. Then, based on the rough timelines provided by police, McArthur killed Soroush in August 2015. Dean, investigators believed, disappeared between the spring of 2016 and the summer of 2017. Then, in 2017, there was Selim, who vanished in March; and Andrew, who went missing in June. The largest gap was between late 2012 and the summer of 2015. Why stop? Was the media attention around Project Houston too much?

Or were there more victims?

• • •

It's been two weeks since McArthur's arrest. I walk into a Second Cup coffee shop on Church Street—I've been told this particular café was a favourite haunt for McArthur. I order a coffee and make some small talk with the barista. In a moment when we're out of earshot from others, I lean in: Did Bruce McArthur come here? I'd been told by several people that it was a favourite haunt of his. The barista nods. In a hushed tone, he tells me they chatted on one of the dating apps. He even knows the address of one of McArthur's landscaping clients. The barista and I exchange numbers. Within a half hour, he sends me screenshots of his conversation with McArthur, and tells me what bus stop he had been waiting at when McArthur messaged him, from just metres away.

I order an espresso, even though the sun has already set, and head to my car. I drive south, get on the Gardiner Expressway, headed towards the address the barista texted me. I park on a side street and count down the numbers on the houses until I find the one that, the barista says, McArthur had worked at in the previous summer. In the cold glow of the street light, the front yard looks manicured and alive despite the cold. I knock on the door, but there is no answer. I peer in the windows—all dark. No car in the driveway. I try the neighbours. One man greets me suspiciously through a door held a crack open. Yes, the cops were here this past weekend, he says.

Back on the sidewalk, I stare at the property. Some small planters sit out front, but there's no big backyard, from what I can see. A grim thought pops into my head: Not a prime spot to hide bodies. Not like the secluded Mallory Crescent.

I get back in the car and drive home, still buzzing. Walking from my parking lot to my apartment, I get to thinking—just how many clients did McArthur have? Police said they had a list of dozens of names.

Around the corner from my place, I spot a police car. The cops had been parked outside when I left that morning, too. I noted it was a K9 unit. Across from my building is a municipal parking lot. Flower beds, dead plants in the desolate soil, surround it. I stop and stare at these beds. Having spent all day, every day, contemplating where McArthur might have hidden more bodies, I couldn't shake the thought. Standing next to these drab midwinter soil beds, I pull out my phone. I message a city councillor I know: *If McArthur had gotten a city contract, could you find out?*

It is nearly midnight by now. I've been chasing leads the entire day. I am seeing Bruce McArthur around every corner.

I unlock my door, say hi to my boyfriend, fall into bed and am immediately asleep.

• • •

While we tried to identify other properties McArthur had worked on, police were stepping up the investigation on Mallory Crescent. An impromptu war room had been set up in front of Karen and Ron's home. Toronto Police had a mobile command unit—a long trailer—parked on the street.

On an earlier visit, police cadaver dogs had pointed officers to the large planters that sat in the backyard of 53 Mallory Crescent. Police had loaded those into a truck, delivering them to a forensic lab to be painstakingly excavated. They continued to comb through the house and backyard. A large white tent sat near the edge of the property.

On February 8, just a few weeks after McArthur's arrest, Hank Idsinga decided to deliver his weekly update standing on Mallory Green. TV stations sent satellite trucks, and journalists milled about Mallory Green, shifting from foot to foot in the snow, waiting for his update. I hadn't been expecting an outdoor press conference and had worn a light coat and dress shoes. I had started losing feeling in my feet when Idsinga finally walked to the array of microphones.

I can now confirm we have recovered the remains of at least six individuals over the last week and a half, and we've identified some of the body parts as belonging to one of the victims who we charged Mr. McArthur with the murder of. And that's Andrew Kinsman. That's where we stand right now; the identification of the other remains is still ongoing.

Do you anticipate more charges being laid?

I do anticipate more charges being laid. I don't have a timetable for that, I don't have a number for that, but I would expect more charges will eventually be laid.

What about the planters?

We have approximately fifteen planters in total. So exactly where we are in the examination of those planters, I'm not going to say.

What's under the tent?

All that is under that tent is a grassy area that we've scanned with the [Ontario Provincial Police] ground-penetrating radar. We've identified some spots in there that we're interested in. And we've been heating that ground, now, for over a week, and I'm led to believe that it's probably still not completely thawed. So we hope to dig down until we can't dig anymore— which may be a matter of inches—and then we may have to leave it for another day or two let it thaw some more, and then continue again. So it's going to be a long process.

Through February, progress was slow going. The forensic patholo- gists painstakingly excavated the contents of the planters, while the crews at Mallory Crescent burrowed into the frozen ground, inch by inch. Another team of detectives were going over every inch of McArthur's apartment. The digital forensics team was analyzing McArthur's phone, computer, and various email and social media accounts for more clues. The vans, both the one McArthur had tried to scrap and the one he was driving the day he was arrested, were being analyzed for DNA. The property in Madoc, owned by his business partner and which McArthur spent time at, was being searched for evidence that he may have hidden some of the victims there. The cops were even searching Reza's condo, the man McArthur had been seeing when he was arrested. Reza, still bewildered and horrified by the news, was forced to couch surf. The scope of the investigation was staggering. Police were already calling it the largest forensic investigation in their history.

Police wrapped up their search of Karen and Ron's home and released it back to the couple in early February. Even so, their work outside continued. On February 13, police called in a backhoe. They had decided to remove a section of the sewage line leading to the home, suspecting that it contained vital DNA evidence.

With the forensic work ongoing, I reluctantly boarded a plane for Eastern Europe. Before all this began, I had booked flights for another project—Russian disinformation and cyber warfare. But even halfway around the world, in another time zone, I kept on top of the updates.

On February 23, police laid a sixth charge against McArthur, for the murder of Skanda Navaratnam. I watched from Kyiv, Ukraine, holding my breath, hoping there would be no more victims.

As you know, on January 18, Bruce McArthur was arrested.
He had been charged with five counts of first degree murder
in relation to the deaths of Selim Esen, Andrew Kinsman,
Soroush Mahmudi, Dean Lisowick, and Majeed Kayhan.
Since then, we have continued our investigation including

searches of numerous properties associated to Mr. McArthur, the review of material evidence, and interviews with dozens of people many of whom have come forward to us. One of the focuses of the investigation has been on human remains found in the planters from 53 Mallory Crescent. The remains of at least six individuals have been recovered from these planters. I've already released the fact that the remains of Andrew Kinsman were located within the planters. There are several ways of identifying remains in a case such as this, including fingerprints, dental records, and DNA analysis. Some of these processes are obviously more time-consuming than others. We have now identified the remains of three individuals from these planters. Number one being Andrew Kinsman, number two being Soroush Mahmudi, and number three being Skandaraj Navaratnam.

It was the news that so many in the Village had been aching to hear. I fired messages back and forth with friends of Andrew and Skanda as they finally got the news that their friend had been identified. In the end, I had picked a bad week to be gone. While I was out of the country, the *Globe* received an unlikely visitor: Mark Saunders, Chief of the Toronto Police Service.

Saunders had ascended to the helm of the Toronto Police in 2015, at a time when the force was under immense existential pressure. On an operational level, the force was facing a budget crunch. On a political level, it was facing intense scrutiny over practices and programs that can only be described as racial profiling. One such policy, commonly referred to as "carding," allowed police to perform random and arbitrary checks, collecting demographic data on those they stop. That practice was, unsurprisingly, disproportionately impacting racialized Torontonians. Nearly one-quarter of those entered into Versadex were Black, despite Black people making up just over 8 per cent of the city's population.

The hunt was on for a chief who could confront those criticisms. The race ultimately came down to two candidates, both of whom were well-qualified deputy chiefs, and both of whom were Black. The rumour was that Saunders, who defended carding, was the preferred candidate of the police association. His opponent, Peter Sloly, was preferred by community groups most vocally against discrimination and carding. The *Toronto Star*, which extensively covered the behind-the-scenes race to be chief, set up a tension between two sides of the service. On one side were the rank-and-file officers who may well have recognized the need to address racism in the force but who remained skeptical of change that was too drastic. On the other side were reform-minded officers and leaders who wanted to build better bridges to marginalized communities.

In the end, incrementalism won out. Mark Saunders was appointed police chief in April 2015.

Three years later, he walked into the *Globe and Mail* offices to discuss, among other things, the investigation into Bruce McArthur. About forty-five minutes into the conversation with an array of *Globe* editors, reporters, and writers, columnist Marcus Gee launched a pointed question. "Wasn't this a pretty serious failure for Toronto Police?" he began. "I mean, we had a serial killer for several years now. Everybody in the gay community suspected that might be the case. And you didn't see it. Isn't that failure?"

The first word out of the chief's mouth said a lot. "No."

What he said next helped set off a firestorm in the community and the city. It would threaten to knock him out of the job entirely.

"Listen, we knew something was up, which is why we went in to begin with. It was—we did not have the evidence and, working it back again in hindsight, it's very clear that he was able to navigate in the community."

That answer has always struck me as absurd. Police had repeated throughout 2013 that there was no evidence of a serial killer, even though what evidence there was pointed to the idea that the disappearances of Skanda, Basir, and Hamid were suspicious. Police downplayed the idea of a serial killer again and again through the summer of 2017, even though Selim fit the profile of the earlier three cases. Hindsight shouldn't have been necessary. There were enough unexplained disappearances, enough concern in the community, that the prospect of a serial killer should have been on the table.

McArthur wasn't some undercover agent, working diligently to evade detection. He was no mastermind. He *navigated the community* because he was of the community. And he must have known, better than anyone, who could go missing from his own community without appropriate follow-up from police. He knew who could go missing and be written off as a drug user. Who could be brushed off by the media as some closeted, conservative, Muslim man who probably ran off.

There's a maxim that might be more owing to police procedurals than real detective work, but it holds that 80 per cent of victims know their killers. Skanda dated McArthur. They had been together the week Skanda disappeared. Skanda's friends called McArthur controlling, manipulative, jealous. McArthur had been hanging around Hamid's apartment before his disappearance. Basir had talked to McArthur online. Hamid had a long-running relationship with McArthur. Why weren't those connections enough to paint McArthur as a suspect?

The community may be a village, but there were so many obvious vectors between three missing persons and a man with an assault conviction for a violent, unprovoked attack against another gay man, just blocks away from where these guys were last seen. Red flags should have been shooting up everywhere.

But not for the chief. He kept going. He did more than that: he doubled down.

"[McArthur] had friends, family. Loved ones. He would be in

bars. He was Santa Claus and all of these things. And, all the while, nobody knew—if anyone would know before us, it's people that knew him very, very well. And so that did not come out. And I'm not going to point fingers because we're past that. With the loss of life, it is catastrophic, here." He continued by asking: "What can we do better?"

"Our role is to follow the evidence," the chief went on. "And if you don't have any evidence, then you dig harder to see, to make sure. You do the checks, double-checks, with all of these investigations. You don't just sit back on your hands and go 'Nothing's coming and see you later,' we go out, we aggressively try to pursue and look for that.

"We knew that people were missing and we knew that we didn't have the right answers, but nobody was coming to us with anything. Nobody."

It was this comment that floored everybody in the room. But that was nothing to the reception it received in the community when the interview was reported. There was incredulity. There was pointed anger. There was grief. Maybe the most common shared reaction was a despondent validation—*We knew you never took us seriously, and here's proof.* The community had screamed from the rooftops. Friends had yelled it through bullhorns. Queer people had sat, uncomfortably, in police stations, spilling out the details of their sex lives and their intimate relationships to an institution that had spent so much time and money over the years abusing them, all in service of trying to find answers, to catch the serial killer that many had believed was stalking Church Street. And what recognition did they get for that work? Dismissal, from the police chief who should have been seeking penance.

Months later, well after this meeting with Saunders, I asked Mita Hans, the community activist who knew some of the victims, about the interview. Sitting on her back porch in the August heat, she replied icily to the chief, through me.

"How much more do you expect from us? Do you expect this from other communities, to do your work for you?" Her voice tightened even more. As though she wasn't even breathing.

"And how dare you—*how dare you*—further victimize the people that are already not getting the good end of this deal, the societal deal we have, where we pay your salaries to do your job, and you don't do it. And when you *do* do it, you do it completely wrong, and your focus is completely wrong. There's so much to be angry at." She laughed joylessly.

I also brought up the comments with Nicki Ward, the transgender activist. She said, "Even by the poor communications standards we've come to expect, I was still kind of stunned at the barefacedness of it. It was quite brassy, to use an old-fashioned word."

There was never any anger in Nicki's voice. She opted for mirthless humour over outright anger, underscored by her dampened English accent. I knew, beneath, there was frustration that has been left out in the sun too long. It was indignation that had never been resolved. It was disappointment that had fermented into dark comedy. She called it a "shame and blame philosophy." Her description seemed pretty apt to me. Saunders had managed to snidely suggest that it was McArthur's wife, his kids, his roommate, and his friends who ought to have solved this murder. Then, in the same breath, insisted that he wouldn't be pointing fingers.

After the interview went online, protesters gathered outside police headquarters. Reporters muttered to each other: *How long until he resigns?* In the following weeks, op-eds went farther, actually calling for him to resign. The *Globe* editorial board endorsed an external review of the investigation, writing: "Chief Saunders seemed to implicate a vulnerable community in its own suffering, which alone would be bad enough. But now it appears that his statement wasn't even accurate: that people did indeed come forward with information during Project Houston about Bruce McArthur."

Only the *Toronto Sun* seemed totally deferential to the chief, with marquee columnist Joe Warmington writing that, in fact, "the chief deserves an apology."

The force tried immediately to stem the bleeding. A spokesperson for the service suggested the chief's comments had been taken out of context. The *Globe* called their bluff and released the full audio recording of the conversation, which had happened exactly as reported. To hear the chief actually say it was even more damning.

Did some potential witnesses stay mum? Perhaps. But turn the question on its head—did police do enough to stress the importance of what was at stake? Did police do enough to find those witnesses? And what did police do with the information that they *did* have?

That was the million-dollar question.

• • •

By the time I slept off my jet lag upon returning at the end of February, my social media feeds were crammed with earnest outrage over the blame Chief Saunders had heaped onto the shoulders of the queer community. When I pulled up to my desk, my whiteboard of calendars and photos was still there, untouched. I was immediately overwhelmed all over again. The release of information had been tightly controlled, but some police sources had passed details of McArthur's arrest to the *Toronto Sun*. One source close to the Ontario Provincial Police had been feeding me updates on the search of the property McArthur worked on in Madoc. But, beyond that, the main source of information came from Idsinga's semi-frequent press conferences.

Sometimes in journalism, serendipity takes hold. Saunders's comments had dislodged something. Someone approached Ha and me. I'll call them Chris.

Chris wanted to meet. They had information from inside the Toronto Police Service. We agreed to meet in an out-of-the-box English pub in Toronto's east end. On a sunny Saturday, when spring felt just around the corner, Chris walked in a few minutes after we arrived. It took only a couple of minutes of pleasantries before we got to the information they were bringing us: police had Bruce McArthur's name in 2013, under Project Houston. The Prism investigators knew this detail, of course, but this was news to us and the general public.

That revelation was extraordinary, and Chris knew it. This was the type of thing that could, if true, cost the chief of police his job. As soon as they said it, the ramifications ran through my head: police had picked up on the connections between McArthur and the three missing men and pulled him in for questioning. They should have known about his 2001 conviction, we figured. If they had interrogated him, they might have discovered his penchant, and reputation, for taking consensual sex too far, verging into straight-up assault. They might have discovered his ties to the victims. They might have discovered his access to an array of properties where hiding bodies would be chillingly easy.

But there was danger. If we reported this revelation and it wasn't true, the *Globe*'s reputation on this story would be taken out at the knees. Despite support for Saunders during his run for the top job, the police association had now largely turned on the chief. Just weeks before we met our contact, the association had run an informal plebiscite, the results of which showed that 86 per cent of the officers who voted said they had lost confidence in the chief. Might the association be using us to oust the chief?

Chris was credible, but there was a problem: they didn't know this information first-hand. They had one source, inside Toronto Police, who represented others, none of whom wanted to talk—for good reason. Leaking from inside the force was not just frowned upon, it could be a punishable offence. Police forces countrywide have been notorious for running aggressive internal investigations to root out leakers. The officers who were coming forward with this information were terrified—none were willing to access the internal files on McArthur, which could establish a record of that 2013 interview; and none were willing to communicate with us directly. Opening those files created digital trails. They knew that any conversation with journalists could lead to their emails being surveilled by fellow officers or their phone records being pulled. Getting caught could mean they would lose everything.

Chris's story, however, made a lot of sense. We knew from friends of McArthur and the victims that McArthur had dated Skanda and was friendly with Hamid. The connections with Basir were a little bit less solid, but we suspected that the two would have met, given McArthur's taste in men and the bars that both frequented.

But Chris was alleging that there were firm connections that brought investigators to McArthur's doorstep. That was hugely significant, but we couldn't report it based on second-hand, or even third-hand, knowledge.

I made a pitch to Chris: What if we delivered you a burner phone that you passed off to your contact? After hearing "no" repeatedly, finally we heard a "maybe." We left the bar and crossed our fingers.

By Monday, word came back: it's on. Get the phone, and the officer will call you.

I grabbed my coat and bounded out of the office. I was on the hunt for a phone that couldn't be traced back to the *Globe*. Obviously, owning a burner phone is suspicious in and of itself, but I was striving for plausible deniability. Having investigated firsthand how thorough Canadian cops can be in tracking down leakers and informants, I left nothing to chance. I walked west from the office and grabbed cash from an ATM. I jumped on a streetcar and headed to the Eaton Centre, the sprawling downtown shopping mall. I walked around for a while until I came across a small independent cell phone store. I pointed to a flip phone, one that dated firmly back to 2005.

A friendly woman came to help me ring up the purchase. I had two questions: How much, and can I pay up front? It was a high level of paranoia, but paranoia is the art of knowing what you're up against.

She grinned, nodded, and led me to a chair. Her co-worker eyed us suspiciously from the other end of the shop as I started to inquire about the cheapest plan. When I asked, directly, whether I could pay in cash, he cleared his throat loudly, staring at her. She shot back a look and asked him, with some acidity: "Do you have a cold? Do you need a cough drop?" He sheepishly shook his head and went back to what he was doing, looking up only occasionally to eavesdrop. He was distracted later by a teenager who walked in, trying to hawk a cell phone he had obviously stolen. The stickler employee turned him away.

The employee who was selling me the burner was eager to help. For $100, I bought a brand new, old cell phone and an unlimited calling and texting package within Ontario. We went through the required paperwork.

"Name?"

I shook my head.

"We'll call you Mr. X."

"What's your address?" she asked, before quickly correcting herself. "I'll put in mine."

I grinned. "Thanks."

I assumed at the time that she had pegged me for a drug dealer. Which is probably why I confused her when, after handing her a wad of $20 bills, I asked for a receipt.

• • •

We passed the phone on to Chris. Who passed it to someone else. Who passed it to the source.

On that Friday evening, I received a text from the burner phone number—the message read simply "J." We had expected a call—Chris had said as much. I puzzled over the letter for a minute, before realizing it was probably an officer fumbling with the clunky keyboard. I took it as a sign they were ready to talk.

Sitting in my living room, I texted back and told them to go ahead. The phone rang, I picked up. Out my window, beyond the buzzing neon sign of the restaurant below, twilight was coming. I joined Ha to the call. I hadn't turned on any lights, so as the conversation went on over the next hour, and as the late winter sun slowly sank, my apartment grew darker. The only lights in the room were my cell phone, pressed to my ear; my laptop screen, at which I was typing furiously; and the neon light, emanating through the window.

We exchanged some pleasantries. We tried to establish how we could report the information we were about to receive. Then we got down to business.

A minute into the call: "Okay, so, basically, Project Houston was not started because of three missing gay men. It was started because of a tip that was received. That Skanda was part of..." They paused, searching for the right word. "... was, basically, consumed. It was a cannibalism case. That's how it started. There was a tip that he was a victim of cannibalism."

Even as they said it, the detail was still impossible to believe. Days earlier, Idsinga had spoken to CTV News about this cannibalism tip. Idsinga himself seemed to downplay the importance of the tip, saying that "during Houston, part of the investigation was into an online cannibalism ring." Ha and I hadn't properly dug into the detail, as it seemed like an outlandish sideshow. We knew the police had ruled out the cannibalism tip. Although they had arrested a child pornographer—a hockey coach, in Peterborough, not far from where McArthur grew up—they had got no closer to explaining the three disappearances.

Through my years of working on this story, I had an incredibly hard time getting a straight answer from the police as to when, exactly, the investigation into these missing men had begun, and when it ended. Police insisted Project Houston had been launched in 2012, but we knew that they did not publicly link the three disappearances until the summer of 2013. The police said roughly a dozen investigators had been assigned, but the investigation had been suspended sometime in early 2014.

The cop on the other end of the line was providing a very different timeline. They told us that Project Houston had been launched, not to investigate three missing persons cases, but to investigate a tip about one man and an online cannibalism ring. Skanda's disappearance had been linked to that tip, but Basir and Hamid's cases had not been tied in until the spring of 2013. Once the cannibalism theory had been discounted, Project Houston was wound down. "They left two inexperienced officers on Project Houston," our source said, through the crackling line of the old flip phone.

What was incredible is, even with a small team, just how close they got. The investigators had tied together Skanda, Basir, and Hamid. They followed the clues, and it led them right to McArthur. "They knew they had a serial killer. They were just—just didn't have the evidence," the cop told us.

I push: They were *sure* they had a serial killer?

"Okay, maybe it was more of a suspicion."

How did they get to McArthur?

"So McArthur was associated [with] Skanda and he was also associated with Faizi. After they had put out the fliers in the community they got information that Bruce was associated [with] Kayhan as well. So they had McArthur on all three of them."

It was the next three words that really mattered.

"They interviewed him."

"And do you know how that interview went?" I ask.

"No, I don't."

• • •

There is a chain of command in journalism. Journalists get a significant amount of leeway to work, but everything always goes up the food chain—to editors, managing editors, editors-in-chief, publishers, and so on. It's a hierarchy that serves the profession very well but is rarely praised in the maddening anxiety of a situation of this magnitude.

After we finished the call, we knew the story we had. The story of how police interviewed a serial killer but released him. We furiously typed the article laying out the bombshell.

While we were confident in what we had, our editors decided it wasn't enough. The paper could not, it was decided, run a story based on a single, anonymous source. After some arguing, the position softened: we could run the story based on one source, but only if the source were willing to disclose their identity, at least to us. I called our source back and pleaded: *Your name, all we need is your name.* The answer was no. Discussions went back and forth over the weekend, as we put pressure on the Toronto Police Service for confirmation of the details we had learned. They didn't get back to us.

We slept on it and the next day came up with a decision: we would ask the force, yes or no, whether McArthur had been interviewed in 2013. If they denied it, we would hold the story and continue investigating. If they confirmed it, we knew we had it. The answer came on Sunday night from Meaghan Gray, the service's spokesperson.

"We will not be commenting on who we may or may not have spoken to."

The answer sent blood pressure levels skyrocketing. It was worse than a denial. There were more frantic late-night phone calls. Finally, a decision: we were holding the story. We might never run it.

We trusted Chris. Even if we couldn't identify our cop, everything they told us had checked out. Even so, no matter how hard we lobbied to get their name, it was a no go. These cops' jobs were on the line.

Over the next few days, Ha and I worked double time to find corroboration for aspects of our source's story. I tried Debbie Harris, the retired supervisor who had overseen Project Houston. I reached her at home, and she politely told me she wasn't interested in commenting—as I pressed, her politeness turned into curtness and she made it clear she wouldn't be helping shed light on anything about the original investigation. I reached out to other detectives who had worked the case, but to no avail. Others in the *Globe* newsroom worked their sources, but we didn't get anything definitive.

It so happened that, early that week, police would be providing an update on the case at the force's headquarters. We couldn't risk asking about the original investigation in front of other reporters, but we informed Meaghan Gray that we wanted a minute on our own with Idsinga. She acknowledged the request.

At the end of the update, Idsinga stepped away from the podium, walked through a throng of reporters and TV cameras, and sped down the ramp that led away from the auditorium used by the service to hold media availability. Ha and I followed. We made it to the antechamber, where Gray was standing. Idsinga was behind her. The detective, she said, wouldn't be commenting. He nodded at us, turned, and left.

I looked at Gray, realizing full well that our leverage was shot.

"Listen, we want to get this right," I told her.

"I appreciate that," she said.

Press flaks, especially those who work for law enforcement, need to be unreadable, but Gray's poker face is especially incredible. She reiterated that her comment, the one that torpedoed our story on Sunday night, stood.

I kept trying. "I understand that you can't comment on who you did or did not interview. But I am assuming that, if our information is incorrect, you would tell us." It was a Hail Mary. Sometimes confirmation comes via a wink and a nudge. While government press officers are not always the most forthcoming, at least they rarely lie outright.

"I wouldn't assume that," Gray said, deadpan. It's the worst possible answer. It created the journalistic equivalent of Schrödinger's Cat: the story was both wrong and right.

More days of agonizing over the story followed. Lots of phone calls. We rewrote and rewrote the story to try to win sign-off, but it never worked. The story wouldn't run.

It wasn't just demoralizing; it was devastating. We had this clue that broke apart the narrative that McArthur was somehow invisible as he stalked his victims, under the radar, but we couldn't run it. It had been a tough week.

Then came another moment of serendipity, by way of an email that landed in my inbox with a succinct subject line: "Fuck." There was a link to a news story:

"Bruce McArthur was previously questioned, released by police in separate incident," read the headline from the *Toronto Star*. Gray had, it seemed, spoken to the *Star* at length.

"We know this information will be disappointing to some members of the community," she told the *Star*, seemingly confirming details of the interview.

We suspected a con job. We suspected that, alerted to the fact that we had information regarding the 2013 interview, the police force leaked the story to the *Star* in the hopes of more sympathetic coverage. Sometimes, when journalistic adrenaline runs through you, certain words and sentences disappear or turn translucent.

Here's a sentence that I read intently that night.

"Years before he was named as an alleged serial killer, Bruce McArthur was brought in by police for questioning . . . and was let go, according to sources familiar with the incident."

But there were a few words in the middle of that sentence that I glossed over: "—in a separate incident unrelated to men missing from Toronto's Gay Village—" Everyone else at the *Globe* had the same myopia as I had. Convinced that the Toronto Police Service had pulled a fast one on us, we hit publish on our story that night.

"Toronto police interviewed Bruce McArthur years before his arrest for six murders," our headline blared. The story filled in details: "A source with knowledge of the investigation told *The Globe and Mail* that police had linked Mr. McArthur to two of those three missing men through his dating apps. An anonymous tip from 2013 then led police to interview him."

The next morning, after we published, something stood out about the *Star* story that I had a difficult time squaring: the interview, as they reported it, had occurred *after* Project Houston wrapped up, in 2014. Our source was convinced it had been in 2013 and confirmed it when we followed up. Could our source be wrong? Or was it the force who had tried to muddy the waters?

We realized in the days after our cowboy move, perplexed over the discrepancy in dates, something mind-boggling: it wasn't the same interview.

McArthur had been interviewed twice.

SOROUSH MAHMUDI

12

A SWISS TIP

ON a Friday, in the late fall of 2012, Detective Debbie Harris had a phone call from police in Berne, Switzerland. On the other end of the line was Detective Roland Keller. He was calling to talk about something police there had learned from an informant. It was information, Keller told Harris, that could explain what had happened to a missing Canadian man, Skanda Navaratnam. That's about as far as they got beyond the language barrier.

Harris put out a call to the division for an officer who spoke high German. Detective Constable Patrick Platte raised his hand. By Monday, they had Keller back on the phone, with Platte interpreting. The Swiss detective laid out the information: in 2011, Keller's informant had been spending his time on Zambianmeat.com, a web forum that advertised itself as "the #1 site for exotic meat." It was a community for those interested in and attracted to cannibalism. It would be easy to write off the site, and the informant, as a bizarre wild goose chase. But, as Detective Keller explained to the Toronto detectives, this informant had been right before.

Just a couple of years before, while on the site, the informant had communicated with someone who went by the screen name Kanibm. Online, he and Kanibm had discussed their kinks. It became clear to the informant that, unlike many of the conversations he had had on the site, this obsession with cannibalism was more than role playing. Kanibm made an offer: come to Slovakia. The agreement was one that, Kanibm said, he had made with others: "If you can come to Slovakia, I'm seriously interested in eating you. This is not a joke or a game."

At first the informant agreed, but it suddenly all got a bit too real. He changed his mind, then he went to the police. The Swiss cops passed the information on to their Slovakian colleagues, who set up an online sting. They made plans to meet up with Kanibm. When the undercover officer arrived, Kanibm tried to kill him—a gunfight ensued, and a sniper shot the would-be cannibal five times. Police found human body parts in his fridge.

Kanibm's real name was Matej Čurko, and he was believed to be responsible for the deaths of at least two women and, potentially, many more. So the information that Keller was bringing to Harris came from a pretty reliable place. He passed on to her a transcript of a conversation with the informant.

"I am for several months in contact with a suspicious person who claims to have eaten a human being," it began. This self-purported cannibal went by the screen name Chefmate but introduced himself to the informant as John Jacobs. The informant insisted that the context of the conversations he'd had with Jacobs made the prospect "believable." He "lives alone on a farm near Toronto. He hunts and kills animals regularly so he is armed and trained in the killing with firearms." He went on, with the informant reporting that Chefmate "knows the taste of human flesh from experience." The informant reported that Chefmate joined Zambianmeat in December 2008 and so, he deduced, Chefmate's first victim may have been killed sometime between 2009 and 2011.

The informant, who knew that Chefmate was primarily interested in men and that he was based in Ontario, began searching
for a possible victim. That's when he discovered the missing persons listing for Skanda Navaratnam online.

The forum on which these conversations took place is macabre. Visually, the screen had a black background, dark red accents,
white font. A cartoon pig grinned from the top left-hand corner
of the website. The site was riddled with gruesome images and
stomach-churning conversation. It's offline, now, but it was still
up when I tried to retrace the Swiss investigators' steps. The forum
was members-only, with most of the site hidden behind a log-in
screen. Users had to be approved before joining. My first attempt
was denied—moderators, it seemed, sniffed me out from a mile
away. I read up on the codewords and slang used by those in this
incredibly niche community and tried a username and fake email
that played into the fantasy and tried again: I was approved.

The forum was reminiscent of a time when the internet was a
more localized place, organized more on specific interests than
social groups. On this particular corner of the web, there's a board
for welcomes and introductions. Another for role-playing and
erotica. Another for meet-ups. Another to discuss current events.
It's odd, obviously, to stumble on to some secluded corner of the
internet to discover cannibal aficionados discussing the housing
market. But that's what it's like. By design, the members of the
forum work to blur the line between what is real and what is fantasy. Upon registering, you are asked whether you are showing
up just to role-play, whether you would be open to going further,
or whether you are looking to seriously go ahead *IRL*. That is, in
real life.

There is no evidence that I'm aware of that Skanda was ever
into cannibalism—as a fantasy, as a possibility, as a plan, or as anything more than what it is for most of us. That is, a gruesome and
unsettling nightmare.

However bizarre and dark, this was the best tip police had got so far to explain Skanda's disappearance. So Detective Harris did her due diligence. On the same Monday she got the rundown from Detective Keller, Harris filed a production order in an Ontario court to obtain the IP address attached to the email chefmate50@yahoo.com. That IP address, in turn, came back with a name and address, but it didn't connect to a secluded farm. Neither did it trace back to a man named John Jacobs. Chefmate was Alex Brunton, a sixty-four-year-old minor league hockey coach. He lived in Peterborough on a quiet, suburban street with his wife.

Harris worked out of 51 Division, the unit that covers the Village and its environs. Given she now had evidence of murder, even if it was circumstantial, the case got bounced up to headquarters, where the Homicide squad took responsibility. Harris stayed on the investigation, but homicide detective Hank Idsinga would head up the case. Police gave the team a name: Project Houston.

A week before Christmas 2012, police placed a tracking device on Brunton's SUV. They flagged his name and passport with U.S. Homeland Security. They surreptitiously entered his home while he was away, in the United States, and cloned his computers. In his inbox were hundreds of messages to and from men around the world, of various ages and ethnicities. In the pictures he received, some were older, some were clearly in their teens. Brunton told these men, in graphic detail, his plans to kill and eat them. In Brunton's inbox was evidence that he had actually met men from the forum in person. In some cases, he paid to fly them to Toronto. In his chat logs, dating back years, Brunton had communicated with teenagers as young as fifteen. In one case, he had smuggled one of his partners across the U.S. border in the trunk of his car. On his phone, police found photos taken inside the locker room of the youth hockey team he coached.

Police meticulously went through Brunton's emails and instant messages for evidence that could connect Brunton to Skanda. They collected the pseudonyms of the men with whom Brunton fantasized, working to unmask them and ensure they had not become victims of a gruesome fantasy, crossed over into reality.

This work was joyless. These grotesque fantasies were often accented with gruesome images Brunton and others had found in the dark recesses of the internet—photos of car crashes and murder. Police pored over this information for months. As the winter of 2012 turned to spring 2013, police made a series of connections that proved prescient. As they worked to connect Skanda and Brunton, Detective Constable Josh McKenzie was assigned to reverse-engineer the problem—to see if it was possible that Brunton was responsible for other murders or disappearances. McKenzie began searching through open missing persons cases. That March, the investigator came across two more missing persons files that bore a striking resemblance to Skanda's: Abdulbasir Faizi and Majeed Kayhan.

Police began finding lots of indirect connections. Platte, whose fluency in German made him an asset on the investigation, began interviewing friends of the missing men, alongside McKenzie and others. Detective Constable Charles Coffey, meanwhile began combing through their online lives. Skanda and Basir, they discovered, were members of silverdaddies.com, a dating site for those seeking older gay men. So was Brunton. Skanda would visit Remington's strip club, on Yonge Street, near the Village. So did Brunton. And two days after Skanda went missing, Brunton searched "non-consensual torture" on zambianmeat.com.

That appeared to be the sum total of the connections. It was not a slam dunk, but it was enough to bring to a judge. Brunton was looking good not only for the murder, but maybe for other unsolved homicides as well. And the more they looked into

Brunton, the more they began asking whether he could be con-nected to another case that had just shocked the country.

• • •

In May 2012—just a few months before Chefmate came to the attention of detectives—I was sitting in my apartment in Montreal when my phone rang. On the other end was my editor at *Xtra*: "Did you see this video that's going around?" It took me only a second to figure out what video he was talking about. I had, I told him. There was some speculation that it had been filmed in Montreal, he said. I told him that this story was not for me.

I hung up. I sat in my home office, forgetting entirely what I had been doing before my phone rang. I stared at my laptop and pulled up one of the numerous websites hosting the video. Even the title made my skin crawl. *1 Lunatic, 1 Icepick*. I watched a minute of the video before I hit pause.

I sighed and called my editor back. *Fine,* I said. *I'll do it.* I needed the work. I would end up working side-by-side with Tu Thanh Ha, who was then working for the *Globe* in Montreal.

The video showed the scene immediately before and immedi-ately after a gruesome murder. It wasn't hard to figure out that this wasn't some special effects wizard or some elaborate prank. The perpetrator in the video appeared to take sick joy in desecrating the body. The very real nature of the video was confirmed when packages began arriving in Ottawa, one addressed to the Liberal Party and another to the governing Conservatives. Body parts, wrapped in tissue, had been sent to each. The next day, a suitcase was discovered outside an apartment building in Montreal. Inside was a human torso. Cops investigated the building and discovered a blood-splattered unit, the name on the lease: Luka Magnotta.

By that point, Magnotta had already fled the country. He wasn't arrested until June 4, in an internet café in Berlin.

I spent months covering the investigation and the fallout. I was sitting in a courtroom in Montreal as Crown prosecutors laid out their evidence against Magnotta, just as police in Toronto were poring over Alex Brunton's voluminous digital footprint.

The links that led investigators to believe that Brunton and Magnotta had some kind of relationship weren't rock solid. In his chat logs, Brunton made repeated mentions of a "Nathan"— another cannibal, supposedly, who had also worked as a dancer at Remington's, the same strip club Skanda liked. Brunton and Nathan met at the club sometime before 2003.

Magnotta had used the pseudonym Nathan on and off and had been stripping at Remington's from 2001 to 2003. For a time, Magnotta lived in Peterborough, just a few minutes from Brunton's home. In medical records, he confessed to a doctor that he was trapped in an abusive relationship with an older man. And, of course, in the video uploaded online, Magnotta styled himself a cannibal.

Toronto Police drew up a general warrant, looking to review Magnotta's phone logs for evidence of his ties to Brunton. Meanwhile, they continued scheduling interviews in their search for mutual acquaintances of the missing men, hoping that someone would be able to provide the crucial link that could explain how and why—and if—these men had crossed paths with Brunton and Magnotta.

• • •

On May 13, 2013, police arrested Alex Brunton on sixty-six criminal charges. They included producing child pornography, sexual assault, extortion, and kidnapping. Not on the list, however, was murder. When police brought Brunton into an interrogation room, they hoped to connect the dots between him, the three missing men, and maybe even Luka Magnotta. It didn't go that way.

He explained to the officers the culture of Zambianmeat, telling them it was all fantasy. They pressed him on what it meant to "butcher" someone. He insisted it was all role-play.

"I didn't really think someone would do such a thing until Luka Magnotta . . . came along," Brunton told the cops. Brunton confessed to putting a teenager in his trunk and driving across the border but tried to deny intentionally filming the players on his hockey team. The interview turned towards the missing men. Brunton denied knowing Hamid and Basir but acknowledged that Skanda was familiar, from Remington's.

Detectives reached out to Montreal police and began investigating the possibility that Magnotta was the one responsible for the three disappearances, as he had been living in Toronto around the time of Skanda's disappearance. Right until September 2013, police continued investigating the possibility that Brunton or Magnotta had something to do with the three disappearances. It got them nowhere.

By August, the police still had nothing tying Brunton to the murders. Police requested new warrants to search Brunton's computers and hard drives seized from his home. It was then, in mid-September 2013, that they went back and double-checked all the evidence they could find on the missing men. That's when Detective McKenzie opened up Skanda's computer and noticed something in his contact book—a deleted file, containing just an email and a phone number. McKenzie recognized the address. Detective Constable Charles Coffey had seen the same address written on a notepad found in Faizi's home: silverfoxx51@hotmail.com.

The cop did a record check on that Toronto-area phone number. There's a hit for a traffic stop from 2005—the driver didn't have a valid insurance card. The name on the file was Bruce McArthur. The last warrant in Project Houston, filed on September 23, 2013, reads: "An interview is currently being scheduled with Bruce McArthur in regards to the disappearances of Skanda Navaratnam and Abdulbasir Faizi." When called, one detective said, "he had no problem coming in." McArthur sat in the police station and answered the detectives' questions directly and plainly.

He told investigators he knew Skanda, but that they were "only friends." They would hang out at the Black Eagle, but he insisted that "they did not have a sexual relationship." McKenzie showed McArthur pictures of the missing men. McArthur recognized Hamid, he admitted, and had known him for about a decade. "They had been sexual," the investigator wrote. "Kayhan was employed by McArthur for one month doing landscaping," they found. He denied knowing Basir. As one investigator put it, "he was very comfortable telling his side of the story."

In April 2014, Project Houston was suspended. Investigators were "unable to account for the disappearances of Kayhan, Navaratnam and Faizi after exploring all available leads."

13

RED FLAGS

CHIEF Mark Saunders's trainwreck editorial board meeting with the *Globe and Mail* had set off two different chain reactions.

The first: A group of officers inside the service began talking among themselves about the flagrant contradiction between the chief's public messaging about Project Houston and what they, themselves, knew about the investigation. That's how Ha and I came to hear of the 2013 interview, when Chris had approached us.

The second: The police leadership recognized that they had a problem. That they had interviewed him in 2013 looked bad, although McArthur was then just another community member with ties to the missing men, not a person of interest in the trio of disappearances. The brass knew there was that second interview, from 2016, when McArthur was actually under arrest for his attack on Matt. So the service decided to get ahead of it.

On March 6, two weeks after the editorial board meeting at the *Globe*, the *Star* broke the story of the 2016 arrest. The story quoted police spokesperson Meaghan Gray: "Information was brought forward by our investigators that was concerning. That information was referred to professional standards and, as early as yesterday, an investigation was started. . . . The chief has always said, if we come across issues that need addressing, we would not wait. We would act as soon as practical."

Detective Sergeant Hank Idsinga told the Canadian Press that week that he, himself, had referred the matter to the professional standards division, which handles internal affairs. "I saw something I felt needed to be investigated further," he said.

From the day that story broke, though, something struck me as odd. It was connected to something our anonymous cop told us. Ha asked the cop: "Do you know if there's a paper trail? Like, some kind of a record that they did talk to McArthur in 2013?"

"That they spoke to him?" the cop replied. "I would like to think so." If McArthur had been brought into a police station for anything, much less in connection with three suspicious disappearances, they added, "he should have been flagged."

I kept running it through my head: When McArthur was arrested in 2016, why didn't the officers notice the red flags that would have popped up in Versadex? The 2013 interview under Project Houston should have been in there. Even the 2001 assault should have popped up. Neither the 2001 arrest nor the 2013 interview would have been proof of criminality, and it would not have been enough for any kind of search warrant from a judge, but it should have, at the very least, spurred the officers to call up the detectives from Project Houston. All it would require is running McArthur's name through Versadex.

I ran through the options: maybe they never ran his name through the system—but that made little sense. Toronto Police are supposed to enter every interaction with the community into Versadex. Every person stopped and carded, under the Toronto Police's racist stop-and-check policy, had a Versadex record just for walking while Black. Why not McArthur, a man who had been interviewed due to his connections to three suspicious disappearances? The officers had evidently used Versadex to record the incident, as that's how the detectives on Project Prism had discovered it in the first place. How could they enter his name into the database without seeing he was already in there?

What if, when they ran his name in June 2016, there had been nothing in the system on McArthur? That, when the officers plugged the name into Versadex, the only thing that showed up was a 2005 traffic stop.

With the investigation underway, police remained tight-lipped about the 2016 interview. One of the officers who had interviewed McArthur had since gone on to another police force, which left Sergeant Paul Gauthier, the officer who first processed McArthur, to face possible charges under the *Ontario Police Services Act*.

While we waited for the results of the investigation, I turned my focus back to the search for more of McArthur's victims.

• • •

Early that March, Sean Cribbin went public with his story. Sean had—like Peter Sgromo, Matt, and John—known McArthur for some time. They had chatted on various dating apps. One day in the summer of 2017, they finally decided to meet.

"It was a beautiful sunny day, clear, clear, clear sky," he recalled to Global News in March 2018, his voice already shaking. The two met up, and Sean climbed into McArthur's van. Quickly, the conversation turned to what was on everyone's mind in the Village that summer. "I had a conversation with Mr. McArthur about a serial killer being at large," he told the reporters. McArthur, he recalled, didn't say anything.

When they got back to McArthur's apartment, they had agreed on the ground rules of what was going to happen. McArthur was going to mix Sean a cocktail of GHB—giving him explicit instructions on how much of the drug to use. Too much, he knew, would incapacitate him. McArthur had boasted of his experience in BDSM, and Sean had agreed to let him lead the way.

Early on, Sean recalled thinking something was wrong. "I couldn't breathe. I have memories of not being able to catch my breath." In BDSM, rules and boundaries are incredibly important. Sean recalled that "the first red flag went flying up" and he knew that he wanted to go home. "He wasn't, I felt, respecting my limits."

Another red flag went up. "At this point I started to sweat quite a bit, which, for me, would be an indicator that I had a larger dose [of GHB]." At that point, it was too late. Sean went unconscious. The next thing he remembered was hearing noises from the other room. McArthur's roommate had come home. By now, he was regaining his wits—either because the effects of the drug were wearing off, or because adrenaline had kicked in—and Sean used the return of the roommate as his excuse to leave. He collected his things and left but has no recollection of how he got home.

Six months later, police arrested Bruce McArthur. Sean was sitting in bed when he saw the news. "Oh, they caught the serial killer," he remarked to his partner. There was no photo with the article, and the name in the story meant nothing in particular to Sean. A few minutes later, when McArthur's photo hit the news, he realized who it was.

Sean started imagining what would have happened if McArthur's roommate hadn't come home that day. Sean's partner would have had no idea where he was or what had happened to him. Just like so many other families. "To put him through that would have been hell."

Later that day, January 18, Sean heard from the police. In his interview, the detective started asking for his memory of his encounter with McArthur. One investigator kept asking one particular question: Do you recall seeing cameras in McArthur's bedroom?

He couldn't remember any, but investigators eventually let slip what they were getting at, and how they came to know he had been in McArthur's bedroom that summer. "They had photographs of me," he said. That's when he realized just how vulnerable he had been. "I was unconscious and, in that [photographic] evidence, there [were] definite signs that I was in a position, bound, and ready to be killed."

. . .

In the years I've worked on this story, tips have continually filtered in. On just about every platform, I heard from people who worried that whatever had happened to the five missing men had happened to their friend or loved one as well. They reached out online, in person, some reached out totally anonymously. Some people waited to run into me before tugging my sleeve and pulling me aside to whisper some bit of information they thought would be helpful. I heard from old acquaintances I hadn't spoken to in nearly a decade and from people I'd never met.

Some of the tips were about McArthur himself. One old friend recalled walking home through the east end of the city when a van pulled up, offering him a ride. The white-haired man in the driver's seat, who he recalled seemed to leer, had set off some red flags. My friend is brown-skinned and had spent the months since McArthur's arrest glad he had refused the ride home.

I heard from a friend of Reza, the man I saw all over McArthur's Facebook page. He told me the relationship between the two was often "tumultuous." Reza is a passive guy, which his friend says let McArthur take advantage of him. "Bruce was a very controlling man," he recalled. Their relationship had been off-and-on for years, and yet even separation couldn't control McArthur's manipulative nature. "They're not dating, and yet Bruce is dictating to [Reza] how to redecorate his place." The pair would argue and fight endlessly, he recalled. It seemed that the relationship had ended, for good, in mid-2017, and Reza had tried to put distance between him and McArthur. "They were working on a friendship," he said. After not talking for months, McArthur invited Reza to his annual Christmas party, which he held at his Thorncliffe Park apartment. That was likely the last time he saw McArthur before his arrest, three weeks later. Testament to how seriously officers treated the idea that McArthur may have had an accomplice, investigators seized Reza's phone, car, and condo.

Through the investigation, however, the evidence confirmed that McArthur acted alone. His partner, friends, roommate, business partner, and family were all as in the dark about McArthur's crimes as the community at large.

Many spoke to me instead of going to the police—old distrust of the cops runs deep, while others feared being outed by an investigation. More than one sent links to cases that I had researched years before—coming to the same conclusions I initially had, that their physical appearance and abrupt disappearance looked so similar to the other cases. Many pointed to Cassandra Do and Lien Pham. Cassandra was found strangled in August 2003. In October, Lien was killed in a similar fashion. Both were Asian, and both worked as out-call escorts, advertising their services in the back pages of local newspapers. Cassandra and Lien, friends said, were very good at screening clients. They weren't interested in taking risks. Lien was working to put her kid through college and take care of a sick father back in Vietnam. Cassandra was a former nurse who was looking to fund her gender confirmation procedure. In their attempts to solve these crimes, police appeared before a group of sex workers, asking for information about their killings. Detectives suggested that the slayings of Cassandra and Lien had connections to other murders of sex workers around the province. Today, more than fifteen years later, those killings remain unsolved.

Mita Hans reached out to ask me to look into a mutual friend of hers and Skanda, a man who had worked at the St. Lawrence Market selling scarves. Mita hadn't seen him in some years and started to wonder. He was, as it turned out, still very much alive and still selling gorgeous imported scarves. That was a relief.

Mita had another missing friend: Jon Riley. Jon lived most of the year in Meaford, Ontario, a small retirement community on the shore of Georgian Bay, about two hours north of Toronto. He would spend the summer sailing through the bay, island-hopping on the various islands and spits of land scattered throughout the bay. "Jon lived for his sailboat," his sister Judi said. The rest of the year he spent in Toronto, taking odd jobs, living in the small condo his mother owned in High Park, in the city's west end.

In 2012, his mother gave up that condo, moving in full time with Jon in Meaford. After that, always one to live frugally, Jon took to staying in shelters when he went to Toronto. Sometimes he would head to the Second Cup coffee shop on Church Street, the local haunt for Hamid Kayhan and Bruce McArthur.

Jon generally took contracts and gigs for IT work, but he wasn't picky. "Painting, landscaping, heavy lifting"—Judi says he would do whatever. A lot of businesses that needed day labourers would reach out to the shelters, looking for workers. That's how Jon found a lot of his gigs. Judi and Jon were incredibly close. In the months leading up to his disappearance, they talked all the time, even though Judi lives in Hawaii.

Jon had left Meaford in April 2013. He left a note for his mother, saying he would be in Toronto for only a few days. Thanks to some crossed wires in the family, it took a few weeks for Judi to realize that nobody had heard from Jon in weeks.

"I knew right away something was wrong," Judi said. Jon had left both his cell phone and computer in Meaford. He had cashed a government sales tax rebate but left everything else back home. Judi pushed down the anxious thoughts, instead telling herself that Jon had just found a long-term job and had been too busy to contact his family. "There was some level of panic in me, but I wasn't freaking out."

Towards the end of the summer, Judi did start to panic. She opened up Google and began to research how one goes about filing a missing persons report. Even as she called a toll-free line set up by the provincial government to help people report those cases, she started second-guessing herself. "I felt the sense that I am over-reacting, my brother is fine," Judi said. In the end, she didn't file a report.

This is a routine many families of missing persons go through. They feel that bringing in the police is a kind of nuclear option. That, maybe, that person just needed some time alone or hasn't been able to be in touch for logistical reasons. It's a really understandable, maybe even rational, form of denial.

By September, it was impossible to deny that something was wrong. Judi asked a friend and former neighbour in Toronto, Joan, to file the report with the Toronto Police Service, as that is where Jon was last known to be.

"She tried to file the report and immediately wasn't taken seriously," Judi said. The cops at 22 Division wanted to know why Jon's mother, in Meaford, wasn't the one reporting him missing. "A couple more weeks went by and she went in and said, 'I just want to make sure that Jon is in the system. Is he recorded as a missing person?'" The front desk clerk at the detachment looked up his name. "No, there's no record of Jon Riley," the cop told Joan. So she reported him missing again. Joan ultimately had to make four trips to the police station before the cops took it seriously.

As Joan and Judi tried desperately to get police to take Jon's disappearance seriously, Project Houston was in full swing, investigating the suspicious disappearances of Skanda, Basir, and Hamid. But the police precinct that Joan walked into, in Toronto's west end, didn't appear to be talking to headquarters or 51 Division.

In November, three officers arrived at Joan's doorstep. "They were suspicious of why Joan, a former neighbour, was reporting him missing and why my mom wasn't. So that sort of became their investigation: Did Joan do something to Jon?" Jodi said.

In the end, Toronto Police pushed the case off to the Ontario Provincial Police. An officer got in touch with Judi to give her some bad news: "Unless foul play is suspected, we cannot investigate," the officer told her.

"The police's immediate reaction was that he went on one of these long trips. They kept saying that he 'vacated his life,'" Judi says. It struck her then as absurd. "Where would he go? He had $280 on him." His debit card was at home. He hadn't packed anything. "I couldn't get the police to take me seriously."

The Ontario police did search his house but refused to go through his laptop. Judi sat on the other end of the phone, in tears, begging an officer to take this seriously. "There's something wrong. Something happened to my brother." The officer tried to offer Judi some solace, telling her that Jon's name would be added to the Royal Canadian Mounted Police's missing persons database. His name would be posted online, which could help garner clues.

"I found out a year and a half after my brother's disappearance that he was never put in the RCMP database," Judi says. While he may have been added to the internal database of missing persons, his case was never uploaded publicly. She was told the issue was that Jon's file hadn't been translated into French and therefore couldn't be uploaded to the website. So Judi did that, too. "I had a friend translate the report into French, I submitted it, and within twenty-four hours he was in their database and he was on the website of missing persons.

"Over the five years, it was always me calling, me calling, me calling," she said. One day, a shoe with a human foot washed up on the shore of Georgian Bay. Judi called immediately—it wasn't Jon.

Judi has spent years continuing to press on this. His case looks so damn similar to the other missing men. Echoing many of their families, she wonders: "How does someone totally disappear? How does that happen?"

Jon looked like the other men, too. Broad-shouldered, with salt-and-pepper hair, he often sported a stubble. Jon wasn't, like some of the victims, South Asian or Arab. The other big difference between Jon and the others is that Jon, as far as anyone knows, was straight. Judi wrestles with this. "He didn't have a girlfriend for many, many years," she says. It is possible, she adds, that he was queer—she would have readily accepted Jon, and he knew that, but confessing to their mother would have been difficult. She would have been less accepting. Mita told me he would go to gay bars on occasion.

Judi makes a point of always speaking of Jon in the present tense. "He is the best big brother," she said to me.

14

KIRUSHNAKUMAR

ON July 24, 2010, a rusted ship crawled through the waters off Canada's West coast. Weeks earlier, it had tried to dock in Australia but was turned away. Then it had been spotted off the coast of Guatemala. The coast guard were keeping an eye on the ship but, as one Canadian Forces official confessed to the *Globe and Mail*, "as long as it is on the high seas and proceeding with peaceful intent, there is no legal framework for inhibiting its journey."

TV news blared images of the woebegotten ship as it approached port in Vancouver, its grubby blue-and-red hull spewing water from various cracks. The whole ship listed to one side, as though it were set to lie down and never get up. The deck was blanketed in silhouettes, peering out towards the shore. On board the MV *Sun Sea* were 492 Tamil refugees, escaping the still-smoldering civil war in Sri Lanka. They had been at sea for months, hoping desperately that some country would take them in, even though they were flouting international standards of refugee law. They hoped the risky voyage would bring them a better life. One man had died during the journey—his illness treatable, but not in the middle of the Pacific Ocean. "The day that we reached the shores of Canada, as refugees, was the day we found courage and hope in our hearts," recalled Piranavan Thangavel.

That optimism landed roughly, as the asylum seekers learned the harsh realities of Canada's immigration policies. It was two weeks after they reached Canadian waters before the ship docked in Vancouver. That didn't end the harrowing journey for those aboard. Vic Toews, then Canada's public safety minister, announced that the migrants would be detained to "ensure that our refugee system is not hijacked by criminals or terrorists."

The government made an example of the MV *Sun Sea*, in part to deter future asylum seekers from landing in Canada. A year before, another ship, the MV *Ocean Lady*, had similarly docked in Vancouver. Ottawa was not looking to play host to a third ship, no matter how treacherous the journey or how desperate the migrants' cause. Ottawa insisted that some, maybe all, of those aboard the ship were members of the Tamil Tigers, which Canada considers a terrorist organization. They were all detained while the Canadian Border Services Agency fought to have them deported. A pregnant passenger was the first to be released, a month later. Others sat in detention for six months. But Canada's immigration system, while often arbitrary and unfair, was still one of laws. In the end, fully 228 of those who came to Canada on the MV *Sun Sea* were, according to the Immigration and Refugee Protection Act, refugees. Another 116 had their claims denied. The board rejected most of those claims because, as the civil war had officially ended, the government concluded they no longer faced risks back home. The government established that just 11 of those who arrived on the MV *Sun Sea* were members of the Tamil Tigers.

Evidently mortified by the higher number of refugees accepted into Canada from aboard the ship, the government introduced the

Preventing Human Smugglers from Abusing Canada's Immigration System Act in 2011, which codified the mass-detention process and fast-tracked the applications of refugees who arrived as part of a group, with an eye to kneecapping their ability to make full claims.

One of those 116 who had their claims denied was Kirushnakumar Kanagaratnam. He was ordered removed from the country. But, unlike many of the others, Kanagaratnam was never deported.

• • •

Detective-Sergeant Hank Idsinga's next update came on March 5. The detective put on his glasses and forged ahead on updating the media about where the investigation was. This time, however, Idsinga seemed a bit tense. Maybe uncomfortable.

> The release of evidence by the Toronto Police Service has to strike a balance between the public interest and the fair court process due to Mr. McArthur. We solve many crimes through the release of evidence to the media. Today, we are going to be releasing a photograph of an individual who we believe is an unidentified victim of Mr. McArthur. We have utilized numerous investigative techniques to identify this individual and so far have been unsuccessful. We have also shown the picture to numerous contacts within the community and have been unsuccessful. I do not want to release this picture and I'm doing so as a last resort.

A photo appeared on a screen to his right. On it was a startling apparition. A man's face. His neck is tilted back in an unnatural way. His dark beard, greying at the tips, is unkempt. His hair is frizzy and tangled. He's wearing a grey T-shirt. He appears to be lying on his back, but the background is a blinding white. The photo gives the impression he was photographed floating in a void.

I was standing a few feet from the television, and what struck me most were his eyes. They are nearly closed, but a tiny sliver of his irises are visible. They are reflecting the flash of the camera. It looks like he was fluttering between awake and asleep, looking wearily at the photographer who had woken him up.

> I would also ask the media to be mindful that, by broadcasting this picture, a family member or friend, not realizing that their loved one is deceased, may come to that realization from the moment they view the picture.
>
> I will not be commenting on how this picture came into our possession. I would ask anyone who recognizes the individual in this picture to contact us as soon as possible. We need to put a name to this face and bring closure to this man's loved ones.

• • •

The unsettling photo and the revelation that there was an eighth known victim hit the community hard. More than that, it was disturbing news for dozens, if not hundreds, of families still missing a loved one. Judi Riley had gotten a call from police in the days before the press conference, asking if she had a photo of her brother in a beard. She recalls thinking: "Why are they asking me these cryptic questions?" The release of the photo explained it. But it also left everyone wondering whether there were more photos.

I stared at that photo for hours that week. An unsettling thought emerged. *What if he is never identified?* Given that six of McArthur's seven known victims were immigrants or refugees, it would have fit well within his victimology to target a man new to Canada, with little family or social connections in the country. It was quite possible that this unnamed man couldn't be identified by anyone in Canada.

That was unacceptable. But Nicki Ward had a hunch. "It was very disturbing to look at it. And, as a result, most people's reaction, when they saw it, was to turn away in horror," she told me. Asking a community steeped in trauma to stare at a post-mortem trophy photo of one of their dead was a massive, unfathomable ask. She has "seen some shit," she told me. She could stand to stare at the horrible image for a few hours, even while many couldn't stand to look at it for a few seconds. She said, "I went back to my house and spent the next eight hours photoshopping it, just to get rid of the distortion and get rid of some of the bruising and discoloration so that you could actually look at it."

Nicki's strong stomach was an asset. She sat at her computer, some six hours in, with a fresh cup of coffee, and looking at the photo she had worked away on. "I was like, oh my god, that's a face. That's a person."

Police technicians had worked to strip the photo of its metadata and some of the identifying background. But they hadn't worked to make the photo look like a human being. They hadn't worked to make it look like a *living* human being. But when Nicki sent the photo to investigators, they, to their credit, recognized they had something valuable. The updated photo was still haunting, but the man looked alive. His eyes were open. His hair and beard trimmed. He looked put-together. It was clearly the same man as in the original picture, released a month earlier, but it was less jarring—it could have been a passport photo.

More than a month after releasing the original photo, police held a press conference and unveiled the photo Nicki had touched up.

. . .

Immigration is a difficult business. When noncitizens, already in your country, apply to stay, processing their claims can take an extraordinary amount of time. Whether it's for a work visa, residency status, or an application for asylum, the nature of bureaucracy and the courts can drag the process on for months and, more likely, years.

There are trade-offs with different approaches, especially when it comes to refugees. Some countries, in recent years, have preferred to detain refugees making in-land claims until their applications can be processed and heard—America has, recently, joined this club. Canada employs this method in some circumstances, such as in the cases of the MV *Sun Sea* and MV *Ocean Lady*. To lock up every would-be refugee who arrives in your country is rife with problems—it is, often, inhumane; unpopular, mostly; and incredibly expensive. So most countries release refugee claimants on their own recognizance, instructing them to report for various check-ins and court appointments. Even those whose claims are rejected and who are eventually ordered deported are often left to their own devices—as they should be. A failed refugee claimant is not a criminal and shouldn't be locked up. But those who are facing deportation, especially those who do have a genuine fear of being forced to return home, can be desperate. Even if hiding from local authorities means being undocumented, impoverished, and alone, it can often be better than the alternative.

That is exactly the calculation that Kirushnakumar faced when his claim was denied and his appeals were exhausted. Although the Canadian government considered the civil war in Sri Lanka over and done with, Kirushnakumar knew the dangers he faced at home. He and his family, like many in Sri Lanka's Tamil-majority north, had their lives thrown into peril by a bloody civil war and were forced to move because of the fighting. His studies were abruptly ended when the schools were shuttered. Any hopes he had of playing soccer or cricket professionally dissipated. Survival was the primary concern. His family was poor, not only forcing the kids to worry about avoiding being pressed into military service but also forcing them to put food on the table. One brother owned a dress shop, and Kirushnakumar helped out. But life was a struggle. His elder brother was shot to death in 2007, in the latter years of the protracted fighting. To this day, his family won't say who was responsible for the assassination out of fear for their own safety. That traumatic event pushed Kirushnakumar to flee to Canada just a few years later.

Kirushnakumar survived the long and perilous journey across the Pacific Ocean. He kept himself sane by playing poker with his fellow passengers. He started a makeshift band with some of the musically inclined onboard. The threat of death, however, hung over the passengers. Upon reaching Vancouver, they were left to bob in the ebbing and flowing tides as politicians decided what to do with them. When they were finally taken ashore, the passengers were detained. Kirushnakumar was ordered deported.

Being sent home wasn't an option. So he made a rational decision: he hid. He made it to Toronto, where he had extended family. It's hard to say exactly how he got by—he never told his family back home—but it seems clear that he sought odd jobs and under-the-table work. He washed dishes at a restaurant, he shovelled snow. He likely took landscaping work. He managed to send home $300 to his family every couple of weeks. But "I don't know what he did to survive," Kirushnakumar's cousin told me.

When his family stopped hearing from Kirushnakumar, they suspected he had gone deeper into hiding to avoid being sent back home. They worried, they waited to hear from him, but filing a missing persons report was out of the question—alerting the police to his presence in the country would only be a licence to find and deport him. Without his support, they suffered. As they do even today.

• • •

More than a month later, on April 11, Toronto Police still had not identified the man in the photo. But their forensic investigation had been making steady progress. Detective Sergeant Idsinga reported,

> One of the focuses of the investigation has been on human remains found within planters from Mallory Crescent. As I have stated before these remains are of individuals who have been dismembered. They are in various stages of decomposition, and doctors from Ontario forensic pathology services have been doing some very difficult and time-consuming work in attempting to reconstruct these remains and identify them. I have previously stated that the remains of at least seven individuals have been located within these planters. The remains of Andrew Kinsman, Soroush Mahmudi, and Skandaraj Navaratnam had previously been identified. I can now add that the pathologists have identified the remains of Selim Esen, Dean Lisowick and Abdulbasir Faizi. At least one set of remains has yet to be identified, and the remains of Majeed Kayhan have not been identified.

The news was both encouraging and confounding. This other body that was found in the planters—did it belong to the mystery man from the photograph? Or was it someone else? And if Hamid's body wasn't in the planters, where was it? Idsinga said investigators were still hoping to search seventy-five properties when the snow melted later that spring.

Idsinga added that they had received five hundred tips relating to the identity of the man in the photo. Most had already been ruled out. He also released the photo that Nicki Ward had helped enhance, hoping it would garner more tips.

Investigators weren't just looking to dig through the thawing ground. They were also going back in history: "Our investigative team are currently reviewing fifteen homicide cold cases from 1975 to 1997. This number is fluid and may increase or decrease." Police were cagey about the details, but investigators were considering the possibility that Bruce McArthur had been responsible for that rash of murders that hit the Village decades before— including, possibly, the slaying of Sandy LeBlanc.

While work on those cold cases was slow going, police had a breakthrough on the unidentified man in the photo very quickly. Nicki's Photoshop skills had worked wonders.

Five days later, on April 16, Idsinga held another briefing: "I can now report that the remains have been identified as Kirushnakumar Kanagaratnam. Mr. Kanagaratnam arrived in Canada in 2010 from Sri Lanka and lived in the Scarborough area of Toronto. He was not on file as missing, and we have no prior evidence which would link him to the Gay Village. We believe that Mr. Kanagaratnam was murdered between the time period of September 3 to December 14 2015."

Police believe he was killed just two years after his refugee claim was denied.

• • •

The news was a gut-wrenching realization for Kirushnakumar's family. Those who spoke English, who received the news, chose to tell a fiction to Kirushnakumar's ailing parents: Kirushnakumar had died in a car accident, they said.

Suthakaran Thanigasalam, Kirushnakumar's cousin who spent years in hiding with him during the civil war, served as a point of contact for me after the police identified the photo of the unidentified man. He confessed that the discovery of what had happened to his cousin threw his whole life into tumult. He found himself irrationally afraid of the gay dating sites mentioned in the international coverage of the murders. The photos of McArthur in a red suit and white fake beard meant that Santa suddenly seemed dark, morose. Eventually they had to tell Kirushnakumar's parents the truth about his murder, and they fainted in despair. While Suthakaran had viewed Canada as a safe haven, he was suddenly struck by the enormity of its failure in his cousin's case. "They abandoned us," he told me.

In late April 2018, Suthakaran sent me a poem he had written.

Hey Canadian government!
Where is my brother?
He came to you
But you say he is not alive
What happened to my brother?
He reached you, safe, by ship
But you say he was not safe after he reached land
Why you did not understand his fate?
He trusted you to keep him safe and happy
But you kicked him away
Who killed my brother?
He never thought about harming anyone
He ran to you to protect him
But you threw him to danger
Krushnakumar, who lost his brother to a gun
That is why he thought you would keep him alive
But you ignored him
He did not come from rich family
He begged you to keep him safe
But you kicked away his refugee alms plate
He expected humanitarian aid from you
But you showed him, and us, inhuman conditions
What are you going to say to us?

I could not stop his mom's tears from falling
He is our homeland's refugee
Hereafter please be thoughtful
You have given our lives endless sadness

KIRUSHNAKUMAR
KANAGARATNAM

15

DUMPING GROUND

WITH Kirushnakumar identified, police had put names to all seven bodies hidden in the planters from Mallory Crescent. But just days after the city learned the news of the eighth victim, Toronto was shocked into confronting another gruesome mass killing.

On April 23, 2018, twenty-five-year-old Alek Minassian drove his rented van along Yonge Street, aiming it at pedestrians crossing the street, even jumping the curb and targeting those on the sidewalk. He made it nearly two and a half kilometres, and left ten dead in his wake.

Investigating that act of domestic terrorism stretched police resources to their limits, but work continued just the same on the McArthur investigation. Police identified more and more properties linked to McArthur, but as the weather warmed, the snow melted, and the K9 units were able to visit those properties, they were struck off the list of properties to search. That left just Mallory Crescent, where police hoped they would discover what had happened to Hamid's body. An uneasy optimism grew that the total number of victims would stop at eight. However, that left Judi Riley, and others like her, bereft of answers all over again. Jon's disappearance matched the circumstances of McArthur's victims closely, but nothing in the investigation seemed to point to a connection.

The frequency of updates slowed. With less news trickling out from the investigation, Ha and I set to work putting together a comprehensive profile of each victim, trying to set the stage of their lives and lay out the scene of how they ended up involved with Bruce McArthur. When that task was finished, my contract at the *Globe and Mail* was up. That was when I set out to try to learn more about McArthur himself and piece together his life before the killings began in 2010.

I was standing in a dirt field in rural Ontario in June, when I took a call from the Canadian Broadcast Corporation. I was en route to Eldon, where McArthur grew up, to get a sense of the rural setting of his early life. I had pulled over and was pacing around the patch of dirt, trying in vain to get better reception. The CBC was pitching me on the idea of a podcast, and I was doing everything I could to say no. Bruce McArthur had now been in the news for six months, and we had spent so much time prying into the lives of his victims. Personally, I was exhausted. Tired of looking at this perfectly mundane picture of evil. I can only imagine how those closer to the investigation felt. This trip to McArthur's hometown was supposed to be the last piece of the story, at least for a while. But the conversation turned to something that did pique my interest: the cold cases.

Police were reviewing more than a dozen cold cases but were tight-lipped on details. I was still struck by how these cases had been left to sit in a vault, unsolved, for decades. I kept thinking how close we had been to having more files sitting in that archive: Skanda,

Basir, Hamid, Soroush, Kirushnakumar, Dean, Selim—without the investigation into Andrew, they might have never been solved.

I gave in. I spent that summer in the Canadian Lesbian and Gay Archives, now called the ArQuives, trying to piece together why so many grisly homicides had gone unresolved in the queer community. But more news from Mallory Crescent was just around the corner.

• • •

Police returned to the Leaside property on July 4. The news vans were back, the sight of reporters milling about on Mallory Green returned. Some neighbours wandered onto the green to chat with us, but the stately brick buildings next to Karen's home had put back up their hand-scrawled signs on pieces of wood: PRIVATE PROPERTY. NO PRESS.

In the midafternoon, just as the day hit its hottest, Detective Dave Dickinson, clad in a black suit, walked to an SUV. He opened the door, grabbed the handle of a leash, and led a police dog out of the car, into the tangle of leaves and branches that sloped down into the ravine. The pair emerged ten minutes later, a toy bone in the German shepherd's mouth—a prize for a job well done.

Dickinson and McKenzie conferred behind a command vehicle, a massive truck resembling a tactical RV painted in Toronto Police colours. The pair, Dickinson in his suit and McKenzie in jeans and a black shirt, made their way over to me. We made some small talk and then Dickinson said, "You'll want to stick around for a few hours."

Not a big ask. Despite a profession-wide problem with impatience, half of journalism is waiting. At least there was no snow.

As investigators trudged through the woods behind the house, photojournalists, camera operators, on-air reporters, and print

reporters milled about, sitting on park benches and wiping the
sweat from their brows.

Late in the afternoon, a black van arrived. It pulled onto the
grass and backed up beside the house, just in front of a white tent
erected in the side yard. Three-quarters of an hour later, three
officers emerged from the ravine, barely visible through the gap
between the van and the tent, carrying between them a sagging
black bag. They loaded the bag into the back of the van, and ten
minutes later they were gone. On the side of the ravine, a deep
hole was left unfilled. With little ceremony, amid silence only
punctuated by birds chirping, Toronto Police had found Hamid.

• • •

The next morning, Detective-Sergeant Hank Idsinga was standing in front of the house on Mallory Crescent, looking off-balance.
The detective was fighting off a summer flu, and the temperature
had already hit 25 degrees. The sun was oppressive.

"Yesterday afternoon, human remains were located at one of
the first digging sites," he told a small gaggle of reporters huddled
around him, his raspy voice barely managing to rise above the
sound of a news helicopter hovering overhead and a chorus of
cicadas in the trees nearby.

Idsinga's update was vague. He wouldn't give details of what
had been discovered—the police had not yet identified the body
parts, and the search was bound to continue for days, if not weeks.
But we suspected it was Hamid.

Before he'd come out to give the press conference, Idsinga
had pitched an idea to Meaghan Gray, the main Toronto Police
communications officer on the file: Why not bring the journalists
down the ravine, where the excavation work was going on, and
show them what goes into a forensic investigation like this?

"Do you think they would like that?" Idsinga asked.

Gray laughed. "Uh, yeah."

So after wrapping up a brief question-and-answer, Idsinga walked over to the yellow police tape that stretched around the property, separating the police vehicles from the quiet neighbourhood. As he did this, a young woman made it through the pack of journalists, sticking out her hand towards the detective. She caught him off guard, and he looked confused. "Can I have a photo?" she asked. With a crooked grin, he obliged. She scuttled off. It was a weird moment, but no stranger than where we were about to go.

The detective lifted up the yellow tape to shoulder level—high enough for most people to walk under without ducking—and ushered the reporters underneath. The hillside was steep, so police tied a rope around a tree, offering anchoring for everyone trying to make it down the precipitous decline.

We scrambled down, one by one, stepping over tree roots and rocks. The camera operators were trying to keep one hand on the ropeline and another on their bulky gear.

At the bottom, there was a small clearing. To the left, twenty police officers and investigators diligently contributed to a makeshift assembly line. One would collect a bucket of dirt and pass it on to another. The last person dumped it onto a wooden table, sifting through it, scanning the remnants. It was sombre, methodical work, accompanied by the faint buzz of the cicadas and only the faintest hum of traffic off in the distance.

They were searching for human remains—two words that, together, still strike me as dissociative. Clinical. The investigators were searching for bones. Skin. Teeth. They believed that, over the course of seven years, McArthur had made the decision to pack bodies, dismembered, into large planters, cover them in soil, and top it off with an assortment of seasonal plants. When it came time to discard the dead flowers or cycle out the perennials, he dumped the flowers, the soil, and the bodies onto a compost pile, down the face of the ravine. It was meticulous, organized, purposeful. But it was also obscene, risky, indifferent. He was hiding his crimes in plain sight. And he was scattering pieces of his victims all over the yard.

I stood there, staring at the investigators sifting through buckets of dead flowers and soil, looking for the tiniest bit of evidence.

I felt sick.

• • •

A tremendous amount has been written about what serial killers do. How they act. The rituals they practise. Their mental illnesses, their modus operandi, the drivers that make them do what they do.

What has become clear to me, over time, is the extent to which the cottage industry of serial killer profiling is a lot of quackery. When McArthur was arrested, out of the woodwork came supposed serial killer experts, offering a full range of conclusions about McArthur. Many saw his techniques as refined, advanced. They offered pronouncements on how many victims he likely had, what sort of rituals he observed, how he selected his victims, or why he committed the murders he did. Some had even come out to say that their computer models had predicted someone like McArthur.

I couldn't agree with them. That summer, staring at the reckless way in which McArthur had hidden the bodies, it struck me just how impetuous his crimes had been. He had attacked men in his van and in his own bedroom. He had saved pictures, of both the men he murdered and the ones he had failed to kill. I'm not sure any of that told me why he did what he did. If anything, that all felt personal. The way he disposed of the bodies felt detached.

A piece of wisdom had once been imparted to me, and I kept coming back to it: Anyone who says anything conclusive about what serial killers do, who they are, or how they act, is full of shit. There's lots of experts, academics, retired cops, and former profilers who provide useful context—who are careful to explain that *generally* serial killers begin at a certain age, that *most we've seen* have certain rituals, that *more often than not* they share certain characteristics. Many others are less careful with those caveats and are quick to make sweeping conclusions.

The reality is that serial killers, despite the massive media industry that trades on profiling them, are an exceedingly rare phenomenon. And with a sample size so small, making meaningful conclusions is difficult and unreliable. Concluding that serial murderers begin at a certain age or that they tend to act a certain way is often little more than guesswork. Of the small cohort of confirmed serial killers, most are unremarkable criminals. They target the vulnerable, usually women, and murder them in a sloppy fashion. It's certainly true that, of those who have been caught, serial killers tend to have started younger than other killers. That finding comes with the crucial caveat *of those who have been caught*. It can take years to catch serial killers—many of those who target marginalized populations can operate for some time without being detected, if they are ever detected at all, or they can begin later in life and die before the authorities identify a pattern. When those patterns are identified, it tends to come from good police work—like it did in this case—not from profiling or predictive modelling.

Our understanding of the criminal mastermind serial killer generally comes from the glorification of a handful of prominent cases. The documentation of those criminals also tends to play up the masterful skill of the killer, not the failures of police to catch them. Even self-professed serial killer buffs likely wouldn't be familiar with the rash of freeway killings that plagued California in the 1960s, '70s, and '80s. Dozens of young men, often gay or transient, were found along the highways that run throughout the state. The victims were often dismembered and put in trashbags, which were discovered sporadically over the years.

The cases garnered shamefully little attention, but over time, many of the cases were solved, though far too late. Patrick Kearney was arrested in 1977, after killing a young man—the victim had, luckily, told a neighbour where he was heading before leaving home, giving police a clear lead. Kearney admitted to a total of thirty-five murders to police. He had dumped some of his victims along the California highways, some in the state's deserts.

Another suspect, Randy Kraft, was interrogated by police over one murder in particular but was ultimately released. That paused, but didn't stop, his reign of terror. He was ultimately convicted of sixteen counts of first-degree murder, ranging from the early '70s to the mid-'80s, although a record he kept of his killings suggests he was responsible for as many as sixty-one killings. His victims, too, were left along the highways in California, as well as Oregon and Michigan.

William Bonin had been arrested and convicted of raping a young hitchhiker he picked up in 1975. His killing spree began after his release: he was ultimately convicted of twenty-one killings, along with several accomplices. It's likely he committed other murders, though his 1996 execution makes solving those cases more difficult.

These three men may have killed, together, more than one hundred men—many of them vulnerable, many of them queer. These criminals were not geniuses, and their crimes were solvable. And yet, for so many years, police failed to catch them.

As I looked back through those freeway killings, the rash of murders in Toronto, and other strings of homicides targeting gay men and trans women around the world, it struck me that this was a commonality with many: murders targeting queer victims were more violent. Normally, cops told me, that signifies a more personal bond between killer and victim. And yet, often, the bodies were dumped. Disregarded. More than what it tells us about these serial killers, I think it tells us something about how society viewed queer people, and in many cases views them still. It's a view that many of these killers, I think, internalized.

It is a belief that queer people are disposable.

• • •

A final update from police headquarters, on July 26, 2018.

> I can now report that we have recovered and identified the remains of Majeed Kayhan from the ravine. Bruce McArthur is already charged with the murder of Majeed Kayhan, who we alleged was killed in 2012, although the examination and identification of remains continues. We do not have any evidence to suggest that Mr. McArthur is responsible for any more than the eight murders, for which he currently stands charged. At this time we have no evidence to suggest that there are any further remains to be located at any further locations. The review of numerous cold cases and outstanding missing persons cases continues.

With the forensic investigation winding down, many families had to begin planning funerals. That was a logistical nightmare for many. Selim's, Skanda's, and Kirushnakumar's families weren't even in Canada.

In Toronto, Haran Vijayanathan, executive director for the Alliance for South Asian AIDS Prevention, stepped up. As a native Tamil speaker, he was able to help the families in Sri Lanka understand what was happening. He remembers speaking to Kirushnakumar's mother. "You know, this elderly woman who doesn't speak a lick of English, and you're looking at her face and trying to explain that there is not a lot of answers that she is going to get."

As he helped coordinate with the families, trying to ensure the appropriate burial rituals would be respected, it became incredibly personal. "I can hear my mother asking this question—she's wondering, 'Did I do everything that I could do to ensure that he has a good afterlife?'"

There was an enormous amount of trauma and pain involved in planning those memorials. For Dean's family, it was too much. Haran volunteered to claim the body himself and organize the service. For other families, he organized a crowdfunding effort to pay for the services and offset travel costs.

Soroush's widow held the service in their home, cooking piles of food for the dozens of mourners. Selim's service was held in a church but was distinctly secular—representatives of the queer community were asked to speak. Sammy, his partner, wasn't invited, a product of how Selim's family viewed their complicated relationship. "This was in tune with him," his brother told the *Globe and Mail*. Andrew's family, chosen and biological, celebrated his life by swapping stories of their irreverent friend, as punk rock blared from a stereo.

Each family had their own way of remembering the man they lost.

. . .

It is August 5, weeks since police packed up their equipment and left, weeks after police recovered Hamid's body, and I'm back on Mallory Crescent. This time, I'm in Karen's backyard. Karen points down into the ravine. Where there used to be trees, now there's nothing. Mesh is all that's stopping large chunks of her backyard from sliding down the hill onto the rail tracks that sit below.

"We have a little blind raccoon we've been feeding for three years," Karen says, to no one in particular. "No one has seen her since the police were here the last time."

Karen loves animals. Every squirrel, raccoon, deer is a ward for her to look after. The police presence has disrupted the whole ecosystem of her backyard. She never complains about it, but she does constantly fret about the fate of the species who share her space.

Karen and Ron have invited a small group over for lemonade in their backyard. Amongst us are some of the leadership of the Metropolitan Community Church, a queer-affirming congregation that were quick to offer Karen and Ron a place to stay when they were abruptly asked to leave their home. Karen invited me, I think, to help document how she was trying to take back her home from Bruce McArthur—and, in so doing, how she was trying to welcome the queer community. Also there is a woman who, they hoped, would become their new landscaper—McArthur's successor. She's short but with an intense energy, and she flutters around the property with two thick picture books of flowers tucked under her right arm, pointing to spots where she could revive their barren backyard. On Karen's front lawn, we sip homemade lemonade and snack on carrot cake.

Karen, whose soft, airy voice is the perfect mask for a bone-dry sense of humour, doesn't undersell how gruesome and unnerving the recent months have been—and anything she has endured, she underscores, is dwarfed by the suffering of these men and their families.

Karen, back in 2012, had, unwittingly, recognized the vulnerability of the missing men. After McArthur had brought Hamid to her property, Karen noted that he seemed a bit downtrodden. She remembers McArthur being hard on him. Karen sent an email to McArthur a week later, writing: "I hope the guy worked out." He looked like he needed the work, she told McArthur. Little did she know.

When you bring up Mallory Crescent, you get a range of opinions. Most people, however, come around to one question: How can they stay in that house? There's a sense of judgement, an underlying question: Are they enjoying this attention?

I wondered that too, until I got to know them. Even though they lived just kilometres away from several of McArthur's victims, they lived in a very different world than those men. And yet McArthur's victims wound up very close by. McArthur's arrest brought those worlds together violently. Rather than fleeing or hiding, Karen and Ron embraced a community in mourning. They used their endless empathy to try to lessen the hurt.

Karen and Ron's decades in community service prepared them for exactly that moment. Some time later, on a grey Sunday afternoon, I drove to the East York Community Centre to watch Karen Fraser receive the Agnes Macphail Award, a recognition for contribution to the community. The award was named for the first woman elected to the House of Commons—a woman who served as an advocate for social justice and for prison reform.

Standing in the back of the room, leaning against the door frame, I watched one speaker after another step to the podium. There were stories about Karen fundraising to buy prom dresses for disadvantaged high school students. She helped get a literacy school in Jamaica off the ground. She took to the lectern and recounted marshalling all her connections to help families get by during the 1998 ice storm in Quebec.

When tragedy hits, it can be easy to imagine the players as one-dimensional figures, as actors who walk onstage to read their lines, then disappear from sight and mind. I think many people cast Karen Fraser and Ron Smith, the homeowners who chose to stay in their house, in those roles. The two are more complicated than that. They tried to use their unexpected central role in this story to help everyone get through it.

Walking through her backyard another day, Karen put her hand on my arm and turned to me. "If any of the families . . ." she started. There was some fumbling with the right terminology. How does one extend an open invitation to visit the scene where your loved one was buried, hidden for so many years?

And yet, Karen said, if it would bring them closure, she would be happy to open her home.

MALLORY CRESCENT

16

KILLING WITH EASE

BY the time city supervisor Harvey Milk stood to address the 1978 San Francisco Gay Freedom Day Parade, his stump speech had taken shape. Like all good politicians, he road-tested messages. He added ideas, turns of phrase, and calls to action—some worked, and he kept them. Others didn't, and he jettisoned them. So when he stood to address the crowd, his words had been honed and, to the extent they could be, perfected. It's commonly referred to, now, as the "Hope Speech." It starts with his rallying cry: *My name is Harvey Milk, and I'm here to recruit you.*

For a speech about hope, it spends a considerable amount of time focusing on the dark. Anita Bryant, a country singer and orange juice pitchwoman who found popularity in professing support for so-called family values, was named twice in the speech.

"About six months ago, Anita Bryant in her speaking to God said that the drought in California was because of the gay people," Milk told the queer crowd. The mere sound of Bryant's name was often met with boos in any queer crowd. But Milk turned her into a stand-in for a homophobic society. A caricature.

"The day after I got elected, it started to rain. On the day I got sworn in, we walked to City Hall and it was kinda nice, and as soon as I said the words 'I do,' it started to rain again. It's been raining since then and the people of San Francisco figure the only way to stop it is to do a recall petition. That's the local joke."

Bryant, in an era of sexual liberation, became spokeswoman for a suffocating heternormativity. She hopped throughout North America, lobbying to have governments repeal the limited pro-gay ordinances and laws that queer activists had fought tirelessly to bring in over the years. Toronto was one of her targets. Even as police arrested men in bathrooms, parks, and bathhouses around the city; even as gangs of men drove around the village looking for fags to beat down; even as the murders of gay men went conspicuously unsolved—Bryant's concern, in a city where she had no ties or business, was that it might be a tad too gay-friendly. In many cities she visited, she succeeded in encouraging councils to roll back the small instances of legislation and bylaws designed to prevent discrimination and harassment of queer people.

This woman was a central figure in Milk's crusade for queer acceptance. But rather than hold her up as a domineering spectre or a symbol of the threat that loomed, he did exactly what made Harvey Milk such an effective organizer—he made her a cause to rally around. To rally *against*.

"The young gay people in the Altoona, Pennsylvanias and the Richmond, Minnesotas who are coming out and hear Anita Bryant on television and her story, the only thing they have to look forward to is hope. And you have to give them hope. Hope for a better world, hope for a better tomorrow, hope for a better place to come to if the pressures at home are too great. Hope that all will be all right."

He issued a rallying cry for the *us'es*—throwing grammatical rules to the wind, Milk turned a plural into a plural—and called on not just gays but African-Americans, seniors, those living with disabilities. If you give the green light to a gay person, he told the crowd, it gives a green light to everyone. "It means hope," he said. Especially to those who had given up.

Giving up would have been understandable. Just a few years before, San Francisco's gay community had been petrified. A serial killer hunted among them. Police suspected the murders of fourteen gay men in the city were the responsibility of one assailant. Other men attacked by the killer survived but refused to cooperate with police.

"My feeling is they don't want to be exposed," Milk told the Associated Press in 1977. "I can understand their position. I respect the pressure society has put on them."

But that was the core of Harvey Milk's radically inclusive message. *I understand, but there's hope.*

Maybe that's why Milk's own killing became an inflection point for optimism, not despair. Why, when Milk was gunned down by a former colleague, it was not a sign of defeat but a call to action. Milk himself issued that call in a prophetic poem he penned before his murder.

I can be killed with ease.
I can be cut right down.
But I cannot fall back into my closet.
I have grown.
I am not myself.
I am too many.
I am all of us.

• • •

Harvey Milk's optimism was contagious, but there was a dark irony to his words. He *was* killed with ease. Dan White, the city councillor who walked into city hall and gunned down Milk and Mayor George Moscone, got away with murder. White was convicted of manslaughter—in part using the ludicrous "Twinkie defence," wherein he claimed his junk-food habits were evidence of his clinical depression. That depression, his lawyers successfully argued, made him not culpable for the assassinations.

That case is infamous. But there is a slew of cases that well established that killing a queer person, for one reason or another, did not constitute murder. In Toronto, in 1977, Joseph Patrick Donoghue, found guilty of the lesser charge of manslaughter, got a seven-year prison term for killing Cameron Noel Allgrove and dismembering his body. When Paris Colin Rogers beat Gerald Douglas White to death in 1978, he was charged with second-degree murder, but the court convicted him of manslaughter, and he served just six years. William Richard Andes was sentenced to eight years for manslaughter after viciously stabbing Shirley Hauser, a trans woman, to death in 1979. Eric Swanson beat Edwin Kasdan to death in 1986, but a jury acquitted him of murder after hearing that Swanson feared being raped by the gay man.

A common defence in all these cases was that of "provocation." It was argued, and accepted by the judge or jury, that the victim had made a pass at their killer. And that the sexual advance was so threatening that it provoked the killing—a killing done in self-defence is manslaughter, not murder.

The defence is patently absurd. And yet it has survived for an awfully long time and was used as recently as 2005 in another murder case involving two men. Bumping along in a car on a dirt road in rural Ontario, Robert Nicholson confessed his love to Sebastien Bouchard. He leaned over and planted a kiss on his friend's neck. Bouchard reacted violently. On the side of the road, Bouchard beat Nicholson until he stopped moving. Bouchard walked the rest of the way home and cleaned the blood off his boots. At trial, Bouchard's lawyers argued that the kiss had amounted to "provocation," that the murder was wrong, yes, but that it was spurred by the gay man's confession of love and that kiss. The judge disregarded that argument, and the jury sentenced Bouchard to life in prison. But Bouchard appealed. The Ontario Court of Appeal found that the judge should have underscored this idea of "provocation" to the jury. Not doing so was enough to taint the verdict—they ordered a retrial. The Crown attorneys appealed to the Supreme Court, which denied their request. So a new jury was impanelled, and the case was heard all over again. In the second trial, in 2016, Bouchard was convicted of murder just the same and again sentenced to life in prison. His second conviction was a victory, but the idea that a kiss can warrant a fatal beating, if the victim was gay, lingers in the justice system.

In New York, in 2016, James Dixon copped a plea deal for manslaughter and twelve years in prison, after beating a trans woman to death in public—his manhood was threatened, he told investigators. A former Austin cop, James Miller, got off with ten years of probation—no jail time—for killing his gay neighbour in 2018.

There has been an unspoken conspiracy for too long. It's one that has told the world that a murder isn't a murder because the victims' sexuality meant they were asking for it. Only nine states have banned the defence, and some courts have forbidden it. While jurisprudence has largely eliminated the defence, it is not formally forbidden in Canada.

Even today, you can still literally get away with murder. If your victim is queer.

• • •

On the crowded dance floor of the Village's busiest gay bar in 2017, Kalen Schlatter stalked through the throng of dancing women. A roster of Crews & Tangos's best drag queens took to the stage, one at a time, playing to the adoring crowd. Schlatter was more interested in the spectators than the performers. Schlatter was bisexual but liked gay bars, he later admitted, primarily because women were easier to pick up in queer bars.

Many of the things Schlatter did he did to pick up women. Nude modelling, staffing parties at art galleries, frequenting gay bars. Schlatter liked the sport of picking up women—apps like Tinder, he said, were too easy. He liked the thrill of the hunt.

"Sometimes you have to push the boundaries with women," Schlatter said to an undercover cop.

He had a routine. He would flit through the bar, introducing himself to women. Later, he would lie in wait outside the bar until he recognized a woman he had met inside. There on the street, he would walk up to them and say hi again, hoping to split women off from their group.

That's what Schlatter did to Tess Richey when he found her with a friend outside the club in the wee hours of the morning. He walked her to get a hot dog from a food cart, then waited until her friend left. He suggested they go somewhere private and led her down the stairwell of an under-construction building. The two made out, but Tess declined his advance to have sex. Schlatter, as he put it, was "pissed off." In his mind, he deserved sex. When she continued resisting, Schlatter sexually assaulted her and wrapped his hands around her neck. He left her body there.

As the media circus swirled around McArthur's arrest, Tess's story fell off the front pages. Even as her killer stood trial, Toronto media salivated instead over the charges against a woman accused of throwing a chair from a high-rise balcony to the street below.

Tess's killing says a lot about the miserable chasm the queer community has found itself in. Public acceptance has turned the "gay ghetto" into a cultural hub and a party destination, especially for young women looking to escape the leering and pick-up tactics ubiqitious at straight establishments. Part of the logic had long been that straight men wouldn't be caught dead in a gay joint. The Villages of the world have generally been accepting to straight, cisgender women. As frequent victims of the insecure sexual rage of straight men, queer people would be hypocrites to turn away women looking for a safe space to let loose. But as cultural mores changed, straight men no longer found it as threatening to their own masculinity to dance in rainbow-flag–draped bars—or, at least, they believed, such a hit was worth it for the access to women. With that, queer spaces suddenly became much less queer. Just other spaces for men to harass women.

Many in the dominant straight culture have also grown fond of smugly insisting to the queer community that, no matter how bad things used to be, they are fine now. While I was writing this book, I've lost count of the number of times I was told, pointedly, to stop talking about homophobia. Adherents to this simplistic worldview argued that this story is about gays killing gays—that's the end of it. That marginalization is just a myth, that straight white men have held the reins of power for a reason, and that any attempt to forge a unique culture or space beyond them is just a culture of victimhood and self-pity. This thinking tells straight men that they are the real victims, that they are entitled to certain things in life—access to any space, attention above all others, sex, to name a few. And if they don't get it, they should take it. That is the mind-set that told Kalen Schlatter he had a right to walk into Crews & Tangos that night, to elbow his way up to every woman he found attractive, to wait around outside hoping to pick her up. It's that entitled mentality that told him, even as Tess refused, that she owed him sex. When Tess kept resisting, he got so mad he took it anyway, then killed her.

It's a similar mentality that motivated Alek Minassian, the twenty-five-year-old self-styled incel—involuntarily celibate—who, prosecutors allege, rented a van and used it to mow down pedestrians along Yonge Street in April 2018. He had spent his time in online communities that railed against women for withholding sex from them. If Schlatter's entitlement came from confidence, Minassian's came from insecurity.

"A lot of incels think they're owed shit from the world," former incel Jack Peterson told me once. "The mindset is kind of like this: 'I've been bullied and rejected my whole life so because of all the suffering I've experienced, now the world owes me sex, it owes me friends, it owes me success, because of all the failures I've had.'"

The city of Toronto experienced so much violence in such a small span of time: the misogynistic murder of Tess Richey, the act of terrorism that targeted women on a busy street in broad daylight, the systematic killing of marginalized queer men, the ever-present targeting of trans women and sex workers. It's easy to think of murder in abstract terms—in terms of a podcast, or a Netflix documentary, maybe even through the lens of a true crime book—but there is something profoundly unsettling about coming to *expect* murder, to reckon with the idea that your mere presence in a space can make you a target. Acting a certain way, or failing to, or perhaps even just how you look or carry yourself, can be a bullseye, an invitation to kill. It's a feeling that marginalized people know all too well. This internal monologue is one queer people have been going through for decades. Probably centuries. Women go through a version of it, too. As do racialized people. Maybe you opt not to wear a particular piece of clothing, not because you don't want to wear it but because you worry it is a little too loud. Or maybe you put on some make-up but wipe it off out of fear of the message it sends. Maybe there are certain mannerisms you teach yourself to avoid because they are a little too flamboyant. Or you lower your voice to make it more masculine. Perhaps you opt for that pared-down look, then shoot your friend a furtive, frustrated glance when they choose not to—you worry they'll call attention to you, endanger you. Feeling yourself in the middle of the scope forces you to do constant self-analysis to make sure you're not stepping out of line.

What is so hard, but so necessary, is to push past that. There are plenty of platitudes out there, often slapped next to corporate branding, instructing legions of consumers to be yourself. But there is scant investigation of one of the main reasons why that is so hard—fear. Literal, physical, fear. The struggle has always been to turn that fear into resilience and solidarity. For years, that feeling of being targeted did mean going back into the closet. It has been a long arc, but queer willingness to step over those lines has been emerging. That too, though, has always come with risk. To walk out on that glass cliff is to invite attention, disgust, hate. That's what history teacher Kenneth Zeller discovered when he was beaten to death in High Park, in Toronto, in 1985, by a group of youth the same age as his students. Joe Rose, an HIV/AIDS activist with bright pink hair, was the target when he was beaten and stabbed on a Montreal bus in 1989. Matthew Shepard found out the penalties for stepping out of line when he was beaten and tortured to death in Colorado in 1998. Dandara dos Santos was the target, in Brazil in 2017, when she was beaten to death by a gang who uploaded her murder online for the world to see.

These stories are repeated thousands of times over. But that message of solidarity preached by Harvey Milk on the stump forty years ago has become foggy with time. Even if many queer people have benefited from the boldness of their ancestors, the togetherness has, for some, been lost. The horrific murders and queer bashings that shocked North America into action to stop violence against queer people haven't stopped—they have only found new targets. The victims of these attacks are queer people of colour, Indigenous people, trans people, sex workers, those with mental health issues. But violence against any member of the queer community constitutes an attack on the entire community. Just like the abduction and murder of an Afghan refugee, or a Turkish ex-pat, or a street-involved sex worker should have motivated us into concern and action about the targeting of our entire community. But it didn't. The targeting of trans women of colour, a scourge that has plagued the United States in recent years, hasn't activated a collective defensive mechanism.

Enacting change isn't easy. In June 2020, a gay bar in North Carolina set up a first aid station to treat protesters who had been shot with rubber bullets and teargassed. This was in the midst of the Black Lives Matter protests that had swept across North America. In Raleigh, police arrived, armed with an anonymous tip that the group had been helping the protesters. The officers fired concussive rounds at the bar owners and tried to clear them out.

Online and in-person, neo-Nazis, homophobes, transphobes, and white supremacists have targeted queer movements to try and scare them off this crucial work. To make them afraid again. Even as figures like President Donald Trump profess to care about the queer community, they have emboldened these groups. They have let the rhetoric and the attacks go by without comment or condemnation. Here in Canada, erstwhile Conservative Party leader Andrew Scheer spent an entire election campaign, in 2019, refusing to engage with the queer community, even after a traumatic year.

This book lays blame at many doorsteps: on the front porch of city hall, parliaments, police stations, media offices. But some blame has to stay with us, with queer people. Complacency with violence has become complicity to it. Losing sight of Harvey Milk's instruction to not be oneself, instead to be *too many*, has left communities alone. It has left vulnerable peoples isolated, even inside a community.

Andrew Kinsman heeded Harvey Milk's call. After Omar Mateen killed forty-nine patrons of the Pulse Nightclub, Andrew published his essay, asking: "Are you willing to succumb to apathy?"

I know it's a dirty, problematic (and many will say an ill-timed) question. That's one reason to bring it up now. You should be uncomfortable, both because of recent murders and due to the fact that you're more likely to actually do something if you can't sit in your rut and be a passive fucking piece of shit.

A whole lot of shit happens to us because we don't resist. And by shit, I mean the odd slur yelled out of a speeding car—and mass murder. It's not even fair to call it apathy because the sickness is believing we are of less worth than a heterosexual version of ourselves that might have been if we hadn't been born queer. We'd sure as hell like it if everyone happily waved rainbow flags and knew how to properly use pronouns but we resign ourselves to the sad realisation that one day we might get deliberately run over by a truck.

Is this passivity so entrenched that we can't address it for ourselves now or for future generations?

We submit, and we choose to submit.

We're even allowed to help elect the victims: Trans folk, people of colour, effeminate men, dykes who just need a good lesson, the bad queers who are too open, too sexually active, too willing to speak out for themselves and the rest of us. Kill them off, and maybe we'll be allowed to live, and hey; our cage will be roomier, with more food in the trough.

This submissiveness is killing all of us.

The Greek Fates were known as the Moirai. There were three of them. The root word, moira, means proof or certainty, otherwise known as justice. Rather than embracing our fates, we may be attesting that we deserve this, that this is our due.

Can we stop allowing them to murder us?

Some of us see the homophobia that is all too apparent. Some of us see the role of religion, particularly extremism. Some see access to guns, mental illness, toxic masculinity, the media, the failure of society to raise children not to want to commit atrocities.

Murder is the symptom, not the disease.

Our society is homophobic.

I was tasked today with writing a few lines to address the mass murder that just took place. I dislike buzzwords, platitudes and treacle, and crafted a measured and professional notice. The result was fine, and largely used after editing by committee.

It was full of emptiness, and the inability to directly address many disturbing issues weighed heavily on me.

I want to see change. I need to help effect that change. I work at helping gradual, systemic improvements take hold, sometimes planting seeds and often nurturing the seeds others have planted.

We need community centres and AIDS Service Organisations to teach and promote self-defense for queers and allies. We need to build in the idea that not only can we stand up for ourselves but that we damn well should be doing so. We need to stop allowing ourselves to be murdered.

We have to do this for ourselves. They're not going to help us; they're going to pit us against one another, jail us and murder us with impunity. We'll get purposefully distracted with treats and baubles, threatened with despair and reminded of how much worse things can be if we become too demanding.

And they're going to get away with it, because we let them and they are us.

The blame isn't absolute. There are those who work hard every day to ensure, in Andrew's words, that they don't get away with it. All the activists and agitators who have never lost sight of the plight of missing and murdered queer people whose cases haven't been solved are the flagbearers. The ones who have worked to ensure that sex workers aren't isolated and at-risk are doing that hard work every day. Those who have pushed for justice for missing and murdered Indigenous women and girls. The fighters who have kept up the pressure for real police reform are doing the difficult policy work that needs doing.

But the community, as a whole, is letting down its own. Every unsolved queer death is a failure on that front. Every queer bashing that is left to be quickly forgotten and off the front page is an abrogation of duty. Every politician pushing an anti-queer platform, unchallenged, is a catastrophe.

Today, we shouldn't need Harvey Milk to recruit us. We should recruit ourselves.

17

"THEY'VE ALL PURPORTED
TO LISTEN"

WHEN someone disappears, we imagine, forces are marshalled. It's a scene right out of a movie: someone doesn't show up for work one day, or they are supposed to pick up their kid but she's left standing in the rain, and maybe their phone goes straight to voicemail. There are sirens. A team springs into action. Some policing axiom tells us that if you don't find them within forty-eight hours, the chances are slim you'll ever find them. So time is of the essence. Someone's living room becomes a de facto war room. Police retrieve toothbrushes, or maybe a comb, to get DNA. They bring in a K9 unit to sniff an old sweater. Officers canvass the neighbourhood. News anchors shuffle papers. *Good evening. Local police are seeking help in finding* . . . The missing person's picture is there, over the anchor's shoulder. The internet has made it all easier. Social media blasts go out. There's a tip line, maybe even a reward. People are reaching out with anything they know. Cops are already poring over CCTV footage. They've called the missing person's cell phone provider, bank, Google, and Facebook to get their most recent GPS coordinates.

Hours go by. They don't come home. A cop folds out a map across the dining room table and points to a park. Hands go up. Volunteers are dispatched. They link arms, shuffling through the tall grass, looking for clues. Or a body. If they aren't found, we imagine that they will never really be forgotten. Maybe the missing posters won't be stapled to telephone poles forever, maybe the evening news won't remind the city of their disappearance on each anniversary of their disappearance, maybe the cops won't issue new calls for information every year, but we expect that there will be some follow-up, some effort to keep those cases front and centre, especially in the internet age. These are myths.

The fact is, thousands of people disappear every year. People walk out of assisted-living homes and wander off—maybe with purpose, maybe not. Teens make good on their promises to run away and plunder their savings account for a bus ticket. Unassuming men with secret lives get caught up in the underworld and are grabbed out of their cars on rural roads. The Royal Canadian Mounted Police report that, in a year, some thirty thousand adults go missing across Canada. In many of those cases, there is no great mystery. The police force, which compiles statistics from all local police forces, says nearly two-thirds of those missing adults are found within 24 hours. Nearly 90 per cent are found within a week. So there is rarely a command centre. No city-wide response. Often not even a local news bulletin—if there is, it's brief and easily missed. The file may land on a beat cop's desk, but if there's nothing to suggest foul play, it hardly takes priority. Usually they send out social media posts asking for information. If there is enough evidence to suggest the missing person is in danger, investigators can make a request to the missing person's cell phone company for help locating them, but details on their cell tower pings might not come in for weeks. Often, that data is vague and unhelpful. Nobody is dragging the lake. And why would they? Odds are, the individual will be home before the weekend. Even as police budgets have ballooned in recent years, the funds have largely gone to specialized policing. Frontline officers have felt the squeeze—they don't have the time, the resources, the capacity to dedicate teams for every missing person. So that 10 percent who don't come back in the days after they're reported missing, go missing again: they go missing online. If you open up Google or Facebook, hunting for details of someone who had gone missing years prior—someone like one of McArthur's victims—you aren't likely to find much. They disappeared once in the physical world, and again in a digital one. A human 404 error.

Often, when the friend isn't back that weekend, it's up to their friends and family to step up. Their friends know something is wrong. The missing person just adopted a puppy. They have kids. They always return phone calls. So the friends and family put up their own posters. They go to the media. They keep up with police, asking for updates. Maybe a few weeks go by. Police begin to realize the disappearance is in the 10 per cent, not the 90. So now there's a police spokesperson standing in front of a news camera, telling the city: *It's unusual for them to be gone this long.* Their car is found, miles from the office, keys in the ignition, and police tear it apart. More requests go out to more companies—looking for social media history, GPS tracking, calls made, purchases logged.

This story exposes the absurdity of this situation. From Dean and Kirushnakumar, who were never reported missing; to Soroush and Selim, who weren't connected to the pattern until it was too late; to Skanda, Basir, and Hamid, who were left to lie in a case file for years—the mobilization we expect from a city just isn't there. Even with Andrew Kinsman, it took a village to stand up and say: no more missing men. Justice was, eventually, found for the other seven men. But there are so many names and faces who, even amid the massive investigation and media circus, continue to be forgotten, like Jon Riley. Even though his case closely resembled the others, it remains unsolved.

Many tried to explain this phenomenon with a very simple theory: *It took a white guy to go missing for police to care.* It's a sentiment I appreciate, but it's wrong. The problems are much more endemic and structural than that. Andrew Kinsman's case was treated with seriousness and urgency because he had an army of pissed-off queers and allies behind him, a group that would not allow his disappearance to go by without police taking it seriously. The thing is, Skandaraj Navaratnam benefited from a similar support system. His friends were dogged, determined, and organized. Skanda and Andrew had community networks that the other missing men, to varying degrees, did not. Basir, Hamid, Selim, Soroush were all reported missing, but they simply didn't have the organized support needed to pressure the cops into taking those cases seriously. Dean and Kirushnakumar were marginalized onto the frayed edges of society. To conclude that police forces are racist, and conclude that is an answer in and of itself, misses the more pernicious problem: that to be prioritized as a missing person, you need social capital. And social capital is not an infinite resource. It is not equally available to everyone. This is a fundamental, structural failure of the way every single police department in the world handles violence against marginalized people.

Blame shouldn't be exclusively reserved for the police. The queer community was built on the premise that, if the structures of power that exist can't or won't do anything to protect them, the community would do it itself. To do that, all the letters in the acronym—all the colours in the flag—were supposed to stand for each other. That dream has never been realized. Queer people of privilege have, generally, not stood up for others in the community who have faced oppression or violence. The community should not have been a place where men disappeared with little notice or panic, especially from the bars that were supposed to be safe havens.

• • •

"They've all purported to listen," Wally Oppal scoffed to me over the phone. He stressed *purported* with scorn. He was talking about police departments, governments, entire systems. Oppal had tried to be the canary in the coal mine.

I had spent that day reading through a report published in 2012 by the Missing Women Commission of Inquiry. The commission had been chaired by Wally Oppal, a former B.C. attorney general, and had been given a mandate to investigate police failure in the disappearances of sex workers from Vancouver's Downtown Eastside. When I finished reading the report, I was shaking in rage and disbelief. So I'd called him.

One of the issues the commission was to focus on was why attempted murder charges against farmer Robert Pickton had been stayed in 1998. From at least 1997 to 2001, Robert Pickton preyed on women who worked in the Downtown Eastside area, infamous in Canada for its liberal drug use, homelessness, and prolific sex trade. Pickton abducted and killed women in that neighbourhood with virtual impunity. His victims, mostly sex workers and many of them Indigenous, were reported missing by their friends and family, and sometimes police earnestly investigated their disappearances. Other times, their files were thrown in a pile on someone's desk, as good as ignored. There were officers who cared. "Every day, I was asked, 'Are they really missing?'"—meaning, 'Maybe they just don't want to be found,' wrote Lormier Shenher, a former Vancouver Police detective, in the *Globe and Mail*. "The police rarely ask that question when they receive reports of non-marginalized missing people."

Even if some officers tried their best, the police were slow to connect the cases.

In 2002, Pickton was charged with six murders. It is believed he could have killed as many as forty-nine women, dating back to 1983. He took aim at a community that was, at best, ignored and failed by the power structures and, at worst, actively marginalized and oppressed by police. He hunted sex workers, Indigenous women, and drug users knowing full well that police would be more likely to brush off their disappearances and mistrust their friends when they came forward with information. Even if Pickton appeared on bad john lists—social databases of dangerous men compiled by sex workers and shared with each other—that would mean little for investigators.

Robert Pickton was right. Maddeningly, infuriatingly, he was right. He predicted the police response perfectly. One woman survived an encounter with him, and when she tried to relay her concerns to police that Pickton was dangerous, she was ignored. Shenher wrote that it was a mistake to keep quiet about their suspicion that Vancouver had a serial killer. "The reluctance to warn the public of the possibility of a serial killer is not only disrespectful to the people you serve, it's also dangerous."

The fallout from the lack of investigation led to Oppal's commission of inquiry into the police handling of the investigation. The report is wide-ranging and damning of the interlocking system of failures that contributed to so many women being killed.

There's one recommendation in particular that infuriates me: "I recommend the development of a provincial missing person website aimed at educating the public about the missing persons process and engaging them in proactive approaches to prevention and investigation."

It's a fantastic idea—a structure that would make sure we would never really forget about those missing persons. However, it was a structure that was never really built. What was built in no way fulfils the report's recommendation. In response to that recommendation, the Royal Canadian Mounted Police set up a missing persons database and linked it to a public-facing website. To this day, that website is virtually useless, hosting just a tiny fraction of active missing persons cases in the country. The RCMP leaves it to local police to elect which cases to upload to the database—and most police departments lazily leave cases off, especially those of the most vulnerable, and the most likely to be targeted. It is a platform that serves to marginalize them all over again.

Oppal also recommended police forces in the country create dedicated missing persons units, to ensure that missing persons in different jurisdictions—or even within different divisions of local police forces—can be linked up if there are, in fact, tangible connections. That recommendation stopped somewhere on the journey from the west coast to Toronto. The Toronto Police Service did not actively use the RCMP database. They did not have a dedicated missing persons unit, and they ignored the recommendation to create one. Fully aware that failing to do those things would enable future serial killers, the Toronto Police seemed indifferent.

Oppal's inquiry drew a red line under the severity of the deficiencies of police in Vancouver. They didn't take these missing persons cases seriously. They didn't value the vulnerable people who vanished. They didn't do enough to search for similarities between the missing. They didn't alert the public or seek outside help.

It's worth focusing on that word for a second: *vulnerable*. Pickton's victims were vulnerable for a lot of interlocking reasons. They were criminalized for their work. As Indigenous women, many experienced racism first-hand by the police. They were arrested for their drug use. Those vulnerabilities came from choices the city and the police force made. Indigenous women are not, by virtue of their biology, vulnerable. Sex workers and drug users do not set out every morning with the determination to commit crime. Generations of over-policing but under-protection, of racial profiling, of cold indifference—those are the catalysts for marginalization. Those are the factors that make someone vulnerable. After McArthur's arrest, Shenher wrote of the sad predictability of the outcome, of how often he is asked about whether things have really changed. "Time and again I answer, no, nothing has changed, and yes, this will happen again," he wrote. A trans man, Shenher seemed to take the killings to heart. "No one feels sicker than me that a new community is grieving, this time in Toronto."

Bruce McArthur's victims were vulnerable in similar ways. They were marginalized because the police spent so many decades marginalizing the entire community. Individual detectives may have treated this case with all the seriousness and empathy it required, but that can't undo every other homophobic remark from someone in uniform, every morality raid on a gay bar, every queer person who died in police custody, every trans homicide that was allowed to go unsolved. More than that, his victims faced trauma that helped create narratives to explain away their disappearance. War, torture, violence, illness, assault—those experiences shaped these men's lives, and may have contributed to their mental health struggles and substance abuse. But it should not have meant that their disappearances deserved less public scrutiny, or concern from the police.

Oppal's final report was published in November 2012, around the time Hamid Kayhan went missing. When I sat at my computer, three years later, using that RCMP portal to sift through missing persons reports, there were only a dozen cases in it from Toronto, spanning decades. The Toronto Police had uploaded Skanda Navaratnam's case, but not Hamid Kayhan's. Neither Toronto nor Peel police included the details of Basir Faizi's disappearance. The reports there were just a tiny fraction of the thousands of unresolved missing persons cases from Toronto. Even years later, in 2018, Toronto Police listed just eighteen missing persons cases in the federal database, spanning forty years. By 2020, there were just sixty-four, still a fraction of the unsolved missing persons cases in the city.

Infuriating doesn't cover it. It's blood-boiling.

What needs to happen to underscore the value in keeping these names in the light? What *more* needs to happen? It brings back the comments from Chief Mark Saunders that still rattle in my head: *He was able to navigate in the community.* I still get angry at it. The leadership of the Toronto Police failed to create a dedicated, trained unit to investigate missing persons cases. They failed to make information on missing persons cases available to the public. When they found three linked missing persons cases, they ran the investigation for less than a year. Other cases, with clear similiarities, were never connected—and were further not publicized. Through it all, and even after an arrest was made, the Chief of Police tried to gaslight the community into thinking it was their fault.

Their failure.

• • •

Toronto Police seemed to recognize some of their failures. Chief Saunders ordered an external review to be conducted of the way police handled these cases, as announced in the *Star*'s report on March 6. Even before the results came in, he announced that the city would, finally, be getting a dedicated missing persons unit.

At the same time, the leadership looked to make Sergeant Paul Gauthier a fall guy. Even though the investigation began in March 2018, it took a whole year for Gauthier to be charged under the *Ontario Police Services Act*. His case is still ongoing. Officially, the charges against him are insubordination and neglect of duty. Part of the allegation seems to hang on his failure to videotape the interview with McArthur. It's not hard to read into those charges that Gauthier was being held responsible for McArthur getting away, for killing again.

"My employer has effectively set me up to be their fall guy for all this," reads a letter from Gauthier, published not long after the charges against him were filed. "Simply because they need a scapegoat."

In early 2020, I got a call from an officer who had been working in 41 Division that night, who knew what transpired on the night Bruce McArthur was arrested and released for the 2016 assault.

The two officers who interviewed Matt and McArthur that June evening in 2016 were faced with an uncomfortable situation, I was told. Matt alleged an assault, but McArthur's interview made it a he-said, he-said situation. There were no physical marks, no evidence to support either side. You can argue that McArthur should have been charged on the spot, in 2016, for assault, but he would never have been convicted. You can argue that a search warrant should have been ordered for his van, but it never would have been granted. You can argue that Matt should have been interviewed again, but he wouldn't have changed his story. "He was so fucking believable," the officer told me.

The one thing that would have fundamentally changed the outcome of that night would have been if Bruce McArthur's name had popped up in Versadex. The system should have indicated that McArthur was interviewed as part of a murder probe in 2013, and that he was arrested and charged for an unprovoked assault fifteen years before, in 2001. Those two pieces of information would not have given police enough to charge him, but it would have likely been enough for them to keep looking at him.

McArthur's name, the officer told me, wasn't in the system at all.

Where, exactly, the system failed is hard to say. "Bruce McArthur was in a database," Detective Dave Dickinson told me. The detectives of Project Houston, he underscored, did their job. They filled out the paperwork and put McArthur in the system. Why his name didn't pop up in 2016, though, is still unclear. Dueling databases may be part of the problem. Versadex was supposed to centralize various other record management programs used by the service, although fusing them together was not seamless.

Whatever the cause, there appeared to have been no reason for Gauthier or the other officers to connect the dots. If they had had that piece of information, history might have been very different.

My conversation with that cop in 2020 raised something really troubling. If that officer knew there was no record for McArthur in Versadex, so did Idsinga and Saunders. That meant the Toronto Police Service were forging ahead on charges against Gauthier, knowing full well that there was no way he could have known of McArthur's past interactions with the police.

The timing of the charges against Gauthier, too, was incredibly odd. The chief had said in 2018 that "if we come across issues [of concern] that need addressing, we would not wait. We would act as soon as practical." Idsinga forwarded the charges against Gauthier in March 2018. However, investigative documents show that the officers of Project Prism were well aware of McArthur's 2016 arrest as far back as late August 2017, when they first ran the licence plate for his Dodge Caravan.

Detective Charles Coffey asked Gauthier his opinion of McArthur. Dickinson called Gauthier to ask if he had any other notes that could be helpful.

So why wait more than six months to launch the investigation into Gauthier's supposed incompetent handling of the incident?

The answer doesn't require much theorizing. Chief Saunders's job was on the line. Not only was his force facing accusations that they had bungled this investigation, he had just tried to blame the queer community for his own inability to get the job done.

Gauthier made a convenient villain.

• • •

In 2020, the conversation around defunding the police hit the mainstream. This story is both a ringing endorsement of the idea, and a note of caution.

It's undeniable that Bruce McArthur escaped justice for so long not because of the police who worked this case, but in spite of them. The dizzying amount of physical and digital evidence, coupled with the voluminous hours of interviews conducted, required dedicated and well-trained investigators. It was a seasoned investigator who identified McArthur's van as the one that picked up Andrew Kinsman on that hot summer day. It was an eagle-eyed detective who spotted the minuscule blood droplets on the floor of McArthur's van. It was a meticulous forensic computer expert who found the fragments of pictures that offered irrefutable proof of McArthur's victims. We can't make do without those officers.

At the same time, we can't accept the status quo. The external review of this case is bound to find systemic deficiencies that should have been addressed decades ago. The newly formed missing persons unit is welcome, but it is lightly staffed, and the competition for resources within the service is increasingly fierce. As police perform ever-more specialized operations, from counter-terrorism to the problematic "guns and gangs" operations, missing persons are vulnerable for neglect. Governments, too, have been keen to craft new laws to curtail civil liberties in the name of national security, but have been less enthusiastic about requiring social media and internet companies to join the search for our missing. There has been little apparent interest in prioritizing critical work like missing persons investigations. Yet, looking back, if only Project Houston had been given a few more detectives, some more resources, a little more time, maybe things would have been different. That failure goes beyond Chief Mark Saunders, to his predecessor, Bill Blair—now the federal minister of public safety. Despite a budget that has surpassed $1 billion, the Toronto Police continue to warehouse missing persons cases on the fleeting list of press releases on their website.

Missing man, Bloor Street West . . .
Public Safety Alert . . .
Missing woman, Queen Street West . . .
Missing man, located . . .
Raptors Playoff Tailgate Party . . .
Missing girl, located . . .

Missing woman, Brimley Road . . .
Missing man, Church Street . . .
Missing man, Carlton Street . . .
Missing man, no fixed address . . .

Police officers are not Swiss Army Knives. They cannot fix every problem. The core jobs of police are to keep the peace, collect evidence, and lay charges. Missing persons cases sit uneasily outside of that triangle. Tasking officers to investigate those cases, even as there is no evidence of criminality, is not always the right approach. It puts the onus on friends and family of the missing to lobby police that the disappearance is strange and unusual enough that it necessitates police intervention—had Andrew's friends not been as effective as they were on that front, the critical security footage may have been written-over and this case may still be unsolved today. That structure asks people who have been underserved and criminalized by the right arm of the police to work enthusiastically with the left.

These eight missing persons investigations, Project Houston, and Project Prism each make abundantly clear that there can't be justice amidst the ongoing criminalization of sex work and drug use; as police harassment of queer people continues; with the scourge of police brutality against racialized people; and next to the pernicious failure of police departments to address violence against Indigenous people, particularly women and girls. While we must demand more sensitivity to culture, identity, and trauma, asking the police to also untangle the Gordian knot of centuries of injustice is absurd.

It is time to open this work to non-officers, bringing in social workers and outreach officers to engage with communities, especially marginalized ones, in a way that recognizes the trauma inherent—both in being marginalized and in being in the gravitational pull of a missing persons investigation. There is no particular reason why missing persons investigations must be done exclusively by police officers. Indeed, how many times must we learn that it is a faulty premise? That should be just a first step.

Change needs to come, not only to the Toronto Police but to every police service throughout North America. Fealty to the status quo is doing a disservice to those who have been failed by it. A dogmatic insistence by the Toronto Police Service to wear their uniform, including sidearm, in the annual Pride parade is emblematic of that intractability. At the same time, we can't expect police to volunteer these solutions. We must push for them. Despite some early outrage and clamouring for change, the public anger dissipated. Chief Saunders ignored calls to resign. No action was taken to fundamentally fix the relationship between the police and the community. Just as it wasn't done in 1981, just as it wasn't done in Montreal, or New York, or San Francisco: just as it still isn't being done in cities around the world.

Chief Saunders did step down, announcing his resignation just as I finished writing this book. He made the decision, on his own terms, to cut his contract short. Speaking to TVO before his departure, Saunders continued to insist the community's distrust of police was a one-sided problem. "Some people, when I go into the community, fine, love me," he told host Steve Paikin. "Others, not so great. I understand, and if we're going to get this right in law enforcement, then the inclusion of all communities is necessary for us to get it right. I've made a lot of effort to try to make things work." The outgoing chief lauded the gender-neutral bathrooms installed at police headquarters. He pointed to the community officers who work the streets of the Village. "A lot of the members of the communities are really onside with the police but we still have a lot of work to do to get to certain corners that are hard for us to get to," he concluded.

The police have been dead set on convincing the community to abandon its grievances. To celebrate the successes, and breeze past the failures. To accept this would be another tragedy. The police need to be defunded, yes, so we can remake those structures in such a way that serves the community.

• • •

In the summer of 1981, a balding man in a white priest's collar sat in the visitors' gallery in Toronto City Council chambers. Thin, sickly, he had trudged to city hall from his office near a smattering of gay bars dotted around Yonge Street. Next to his desk was a cot, where he had been sleeping most nights. His colleagues had been worried that, had he tried to take the subway, he might have fainted.

"That city council meeting was the last one before they were taken to a four-week break," he remembered.

That was day twenty-five of Reverend Brent Hawkes's hunger strike. As it happened, a concurrent hunger strike was going on in an Irish jail. Members of the Irish Republican Army, imprisoned by the British government, started their strike to protest prison conditions. Those hunger strikers began dying at day forty-six. So Brent knew the risks inherent in this plan. If he had to wait for city council to return, his hunger strike would have to stretch to more than fifty days.

It was that city council meeting. "That, or nothing," Brent remembered.

His demands were simple. The reverend, who served the LGBTQ-friendly Metropolitan Community Church, wanted an investigation into police practices during the bathhouse raids, which had taken place earlier that year. He wanted a study of how and why police broke down those doors, rounded those men up, rung them up on charges. He wanted accountability for the vividly remembered comment made by one officer that the bathhouse showers ought to have been hooked up to gas. He wanted answers for why a police commissioner called up school boards to out teachers who had been rounded up in the police action.

Many felt Brent's tactics were over the top, even those who supported his goals. He remembered a column in the *Toronto Star* that dismissed his hunger strike as "trying to kill a mosquito with a hammer." They weren't wrong, Brent confessed. "Unless you have an exit strategy that's not death, it's a difficult tool." He confessed, "I didn't have an exit strategy."

The provincial government would normally conduct such a study, but the Conservative administration with little love for the queer community had already rejected calls for any inquiry into the raids. That left Toronto City Council as the avenue of last resort.

Last-minute negotiations took place on the margins of the council floor. *There's a motion,* Brent was told. *It's not perfect, but it's something. It's a study.* Good enough, Brent decided.

The motion adopted proposed that a study should be conducted by a sociologist "to look into the disagreement and difficulties surrounding relations between the Police and the Gay Community and that he submit a report to His Worship the Mayor and City Council recommending ways to bring about improved relations." They cobbled together a small budget and put forward the name of a sociologist to do the study.

Brent and his supporters headed to a nearby diner to celebrate victory and the end of his hunger strike. Brent looked at the menu: he settled on mushroom soup, something light. He still remembers how it tasted.

The sociologist tapped by the council to do the study, in the end, declined the invitation. Council, instead, turned to a former newspaper journalist-turned-law student named Arnold Bruner. Given he was inexperienced, both in his legal career and in his knowledge of the queer community, his name was hardly met with excitement, but the study was, at last, underway. Bruner delivered the report two months later. A committee of one, Bruner had his wife and son help him type out the report, which clocked in at nearly two hundred pages. It is sharply and plainly written and not only lays bare the systemic and endemic problems with how Toronto Police handled relations with the community but also offers a clear view as to the broader societal issues at play. Some of the problems identified and solutions suggested are very much of the time. Others still feel painfully relevant, forty years later. Like the suggestion to create a liaison committee between the community and policy. Today, there is just one dedicated LGBTQ liaison officer. There was a recommendation to stop the surveillance and arrest of people engaged in sexual activity in public washrooms and parks—replacing that with dialogue and alternative solutions. That was readily ignored when police authorized a sting operation in Marie Curtis Park in 2016.

"The issue of relations between the police and the gay community of Toronto is a human problem," he wrote.

The Bruner Report marked a noted shift in community–police relations, and many of the recommendations in the report were adopted to some degree, but the relationship remained strained. As evidenced by the number of recommendations that, decades later, still remain aspirational, it's clear that Toronto Police seemed intent on keeping them strained. The force has repeatedly made choices irrespective of the concerns of the community. These issues are not Toronto-specific. The abuses aren't either. Neither are the reports, the recommendations, the apologies or the failures. Pick a city—Montreal, New York, London, San Francisco, Vancouver, Sydney, Paris—it's tough to find one among the world's richest nations where there hasn't been some kind of wide-reaching failure to address violence against queer people. Harder still to find one where some part of that violence wasn't perpetrated by the state itself.

Toronto is a perfect storm of those issues, a parable for what happens when lessons aren't learned again, and again, when failures follow well-worn paths.

THE BATHHOUSE RAIDS

18

GUILTY

WITH the McArthur investigation essentially over, the slow work-ings of the judicial process began in earnest. We knew investiga-tors had been meeting through the summer and fall of 2018, although progress seemed slow-going. The Crown prosecutors and defence normally get together to negotiate inside an anti-septic white room, probably figuring out dates and disclosure. I once tried to saunter into the conference room where they were meeting, ahead of one of McArthur's scheduled appearances. I noticed Detective Dave Dickinson walk in and tried to follow him. A bailiff gave me a hearty laugh. "Even I'm not allowed in there," he said. I shrugged and smiled. "Worth a shot," I told him.

As 2018 rolled over into 2019, it looked like we wouldn't see a trial until 2020 at the earliest. I was getting asked with some fre-quency whether McArthur was going to confess and plead guilty. Without fail, I told them no. Why plead? Bruce McArthur was facing eight charges of first-degree murder. Even with just one charge, under Canadian law he would be eligible for parole only after serving twenty-five years. He would have to live into his nineties to ever set foot outside prison walls again, and parole for his case was a long shot. Even then, it seemed unlikely he would live to ninety-one. Karen Fraser told me that McArthur had developed diabetes when he was working for her—she had nagged him about seeing a doctor, but he seemed nonchalant about it. His health didn't seem of great concern to him anyway.

On January 28, 2019, nearly a year to the day since McArthur had been arrested, I get a message, from Jayme Poisson, the former *Toronto Star* reporter. At that point, we were both working for the CBC.

"We hear cops are making a McArthur announcement tomorrow?" she writes. I tell her I haven't heard anything. "Guilty plea?" she writes back.

Within a few minutes, Meaghan Gray, the Toronto Police spokesperson, sends me the media advisory. "A significant development in this case is expected," the news release reads. I try for more info, but it's a no-go. "I can only reiterate that a significant development is expected when he appears in court tomorrow," she writes.

So I try Dickinson.

"Sorry Justin . . . mum's the word," he writes.

Jayme thinks it's going to be a guilty plea. But there's another possibility: more charges.

I try Judi Riley. If there's a new victim, my hunch is that it's her missing brother, Jon. She gets back to me straightaway: she just landed in Toronto, she tells me. For an unrelated matter, she adds. She's as in the dark about the announcement as I am.

It's snowing outside. A huge system is moving in. What began as light flurries has turned into a wall of snow, flying sideways. As the streets turn white, and as traffic backs up around the city, the subject of Tuesday's announcement is becoming increasingly clear.

I check in with Tu Thanh Ha. He's already heard from Kayhan's family. They've been told to show up in court in the morning, they have no more information. I reach Karen—she and Ron will be there, too. Christie Blatchford, a longtime *National Post* columnist with an impressive network of cop sources, breaks the story first.

> Bruce McArthur expected to plead guilty to eight counts of first-degree murder.

I send the news to some friends of the victims.
Sarrah Becker gets back to me first: today would've been Skanda's birthday.

• • •

By the time I stepped out my front door the next morning, the whole city was blanketed in snow. Realizing quickly that public transit couldn't be relied on, I called an Uber. The SUV that picked me up, thankfully, had four-wheel drive. Even so, we slid through the streets.

On the sixth floor of the courthouse on University Avenue, a small cast of familiar faces was waiting outside the courtroom. Reporters, mostly. Sarrah Becker showed up. I saw Sean Cribbin, the man who believed he'd nearly been a victim of McArthur.

Inside the cavernous courtroom, the pews were starting to fill with a line-up of people impacted by McArthur's crimes. There were friends and family of the eight men, wearing expressions that ranged from bewilderment to steely resolve. A phalanx of cops, all of whom had contributed in some way to McArthur's eventual arrest. Haran Vijayanathan, who had helped bury the dead.

When McArthur was led in, wearing the same black sweater he'd worn for several of his previous appearances, he looked broken and ashen-faced. He looked thinner. Older. Meeker.

What followed was a choreographed affair.

"You understand you have a right to a fair trial?" Justice John McMahon asked.

"Yes," McArthur said, in a voice so soft that it was almost inaudible in the silent room.

"Is anyone pressuring you to plead guilty?"

"No."

The names were read. One by one, McArthur was asked if he, in a planned and deliberate fashion, had killed the men. He was asked how he pleaded to each count of first-degree murder. The names were in no particular order.

Majeed Kayhan.

"Guilty."

Soroush Mahmudi.

"Guilty."

Dean Lisowick.

"Guilty."

Selim Esen.

"Guilty."

Andrew Kinsman.

"Guilty."

Skandaraj Navaratnam.

"Guilty."

Kirushunakumar Kanagaratnam.

"Guilty."

Abdulbasir Faizi.

"Guilty."

• • •

Even as McArthur pleaded guilty for eight murder charges, speculation continued that he had killed others. Jon Riley, for one. Some wondered whether he had killed Sandy LeBlanc, or had been responsible for other cold cases.

All told, police had about a dozen names of other possible victims. By the time he pleaded guilty, investigators had come to a conclusion. "I have no evidence that there's more than eight. And I don't believe there's more than eight," says Detective Dave Dickinson.

Throughout the investigation, police were mum about what, exactly, McArthur said in the interrogation room, or whether he was even talking. Dickinson says the first time they sat across a table from each other, on January 18, 2018, "he lawyered up." But that doesn't mean he kept his mouth shut.

"He chatted with us for a long while. Did he provide us with any helpful information? No," he says. McArthur had evaded police twice before, and seemed to think he could do it again. The detective describes him as "deceitful and manipulative." He offered no information to investigators before his conviction, but seemed happy to chat.

"He was pleasant to everyone," Dickinson says. "That he didn't kill."

. . .

Courtrooms are naturally unhappy places. I'm not offering any grand cosmic insight when I say that, as the doors of the courtroom open after the wheels of justice have turned, there is never uniform joy. In criminal cases, an acquittal means a crime goes unsolved. A conviction means someone will soon face the state's unique brand of punishment. We know that.

What we often forget are the thousands of days of hearings that come before. The pretrial scheduling. Negotiations between prosecution and defence. The inane jousting over case law. The dispassionate entering of evidence into the record. The heart-crushing pain of listening to victim impact statements. In a normal case, those very different moments are spread over months. Years, sometimes.

McArthur's decision to plead guilty to those eight counts meant that the long, arduous process would come to a very quick end. But parts of the process still needed to be completed. Every step in the slow trot of the judicial system would need to be folded into just a handful of days.

And so we lined up outside the sixth floor courtroom again the following week, though most people chose to stay home. A nasty cold front had frozen the snow that had fallen the day of McArthur's guilty pleas. The city looked and felt barren and uninhabitable. The hearing was organized to schedule the next hearings for the following week and to ensure that both the Crown and defence were making progress in writing an agreed statement of facts—a chronological overview of McArthur's crimes.

The cold front passed and gave way to unseasonal warmth. Sunday was Groundhog Day, though it felt like an especially absurd tradition, as the temperature was already rising past freezing. As the sun rose on Monday morning, the thermometer hit six degrees. By the afternoon, people had shed their overcoats, and were walking through the overcast downtown as though it were already spring.

The courtroom, unlike the week before, was packed. Filling the seats were a new crowd of onlookers and journalists. I saw an old friend of McArthur, sitting next to Reza, the man who had unknowingly been dating a serial killer. There were scores of high school students, tasked by teachers with sitting in on some ongoing court case—many, it seems, jumped immediately to McArthur's hearing. And there was the array of cops, in dark suits, sitting in the front row, almost hovering over McArthur.

Before the hearing began that day, Crown Prosecutor Cantlon cleared his throat and made an announcement to the room that, he admitted right away, was extraordinary. The evidence, he warned, would be troubling.

"It could impact your appetite and ability to sleep," he told us. He strongly suggested that everyone "think carefully" about whether they needed to be here.

Cantlon took the unenviable job of reading the full facts of McArthur's case into the record. Standing to face the judge, back to the audience, he held the documents in both hands and read through the morning, into the early afternoon. The details were macabre, unsettling, and painful for many—but they were mercifully short on specifics.

In a normal criminal case, prosecutors leave few things to chance. Every bloodstain. Every photo of every item used in the commission of a crime. Every autopsy report. They would all be entered into evidence, over hours, days, maybe weeks of evidentiary proceedings. It is a process that is as slow as it is unflinching. In McArthur's case, an agreement between the Crown and defence counsel on what facts to enter spared the court many of those details. No photos of the victims were shown to the courtroom. Cantlon didn't dwell on the gory specifics. He stood in his requisite black gown, white bands dangling from his collar, and dutifully read every word on the page. He relayed the entry in Andrew Kinsman's calendar—"Bruce"—from the day he disappeared. He showed a photo of Selim Esen's notebook. He described the night Skandaraj Navaratnam left Zipperz. He detailed the photos found on McArthur's hard drive, a USB key, with a folder on it for each man. The clue that brought police to McArthur. The detail of the 2013 interview. The 2016 arrest. The 2018 arrest. "For years, members of the LGBTQ community believed that they were being targeted by a killer," he says. "They were right."

The statement of facts revealed that McArthur had been keeping tabs on the investigation. In a folder on his computer was a saved copy of a story I had written for VICE News in the days after Andrew Kinsman vanished. That sent a shiver down my spine.

Even without the horrible images, the thirty-six pages of evidence were stomach-churning. They still recounted the strangulation. The discoloration around the neck of Kirushnakumar Kanagaratnam. How McArthur had shaved Selim Esen's face after his death. We knew McArthur had taken photos of his victims, but the descriptions of those pictures still, I know, haunt the friends and families of these men.

Cantlon is perhaps the embodiment of what I expect from a Crown attorney. Serious, professional, pointed. His reading of the facts was necessarily dispassionate, for the most part. Until he reached page thirty-five.

"Finally, as previously noted, Mr. McArthur took photographs of Mr. Kinsman—"

It was there that Cantlon took a long, abrupt pause. He coughed out the next name, "Mr. Esen." He took a deep breath and continued through tears. "Mr. Mahmudi, Mr. Lisowick, Mr. Kayhan, and Mr. Kanagaratnam after killing them."

It was the first time I'd ever seen a Crown attorney cry in court. But, given the context, it was hard to imagine any other reaction.

As the court took a break, I stood up and wheeled around. Behind me was Reza. He was sobbing. A security guard moved in, tissues in hand. Reza sagged back down onto the bench.

• • •

By day two, any nervous energy that had buzzed through the courtroom had been dampened into exhaustion. When I walked into the courtroom, the benches reserved for the friends and family of the victims were lined with tissue boxes—one to every three seats. The pews weren't full for that second day. With no more evidence to come, some journalists and curious onlookers steered clear.

Friends and family of the men were given a chance to read victim impacts into the record, in hopes of swaying the judge's decision on sentencing.

The arguments then turned technical. The Crown wanted McArthur's murder convictions to stack—effectively cutting off his ability to ever qualify for parole. McArthur's lawyers asked that his sentences be given concurrently, leaving open the possibility of parole in twenty-five years. Eventually, both sides rested. The judge turned to McArthur, offering him a chance to speak.

"No, your honour, I've discussed it with my council. I don't want to say anything," McArthur said. It was the most he had said in court over the year-long legal process.

His voice was chillingly normal. Nasally. His voice didn't break or crack, and he didn't mumble.

With that, the court adjourned. It returned days later, on Friday, with the judge's decision:

Life in prison, with no possibility of parole for twenty-five years.

POSTSCRIPT

Along the solitary plain we went
As one who unto the lost road returns,
And till he finds it seems to go in vain.

—*Dante*, Purgatorio

IN the posters plastered around the city, Andrew Kinsman's face is lit up, grinning and bespectacled. Above his face is a small play on words. A sad turn of phrase.

MISSING: ANDREW KINSMAN, they read.

As Meaghan Marian put up those posters in the hours after Andrew's disappearance, the text served as a "play on his plight and on my sorrow," his friend and neighbour told the court. "I was, already, missing Andrew Kinsman."

Her voice was steely as she read through her statement—one part, a love letter to her missing friend; one part, an epic *fuck you* to the man sitting in the prisoner's box. She brought the courtroom into the early days of the terrifying realization that Andrew, her close friend and neighbour, was gone. "Sensing became knowing. With knowing Andrew was missing came an imperative to take action," she told the court in a slow, deliberate cadence. "Action birthed momentum, and momentum became commitment. Between the day Andrew vanished and this day, that commitment to standing up for Andrew has been unassailed. What has not been certain is, really, everything but that. We organized. We had posters up by the second day. We had hundreds of posters up by the fifth day. We had thousands of posters up within weeks. People that I have never met joined the work, conducting foot searches and doing outreach. Everyone was connected to Andrew, it seemed. He was everywhere, and wherever he was not yet, my mission was to project his image."

But Meaghan didn't fast-forward the tape. She didn't drag her cursor to the moment when she had found answers about what had happened to Andrew. She screened for the court, from start to finish, all the moments before that. She let play the agonizing in-between.

Meaghan used to hear Andrew through the wall. A permeable membrane, she called it. An acoustic window from her living room to his kitchen. He would drop a pan and curse, and Meaghan would sit and laugh. With his disappearance, with the police tape still sealing the door down the hall after months of silence, the wall between their apartments was no longer a membrane. "It was solid and lonely as marble. At night, I would press my palms against the wall, eyes closed, and listen, feel."

It's a comforting narrative to think of these friends and family, marching down Church Street, a stack of posters in one hand and a staple gun in another. Searching for their friend, searching for justice. Much of the coverage of this story, including this book, tells that story with the spotlight firmly trained on the investiga-tion. It's comforting because the alternative is just too dark. Too bleak. It's too uncomfortable to realize that there are limits to the searching. That narrative is not inaccurate, just incomplete.

Those are easily told snapshots—Andrew's friends, fanned out across the city, searching. Skanda's friends doing the same, seven years earlier. Basir's wife, walking down Church Street the day after his disappearance. Hamid's friends, sitting in a police station, trying to convey information to officers. Soroush's wife, so overcome by grief that she fainted on her living-room floor. Kirushnakumar's family, reaching out to contacts from Sri Lanka, trying to quietly learn of his whereabouts. Selim's partner, frantically calling his cell phone.

But those are just brief tableaus. They don't capture all the other minutes, hours, days, weeks, months, years before answers came. Meaghan had attempted to calculate it: "If Andrew was alive today, he would have baked approximately 340 loaves of bread, perhaps 30 birthday cakes, 450 healthy dinners, and 30 or so contributions to potlucks for friends. He would have done 110 shifts as a volunteer at the food bank, and contributed perhaps 500 hours of organizing skill to public health events. He would have exchanged something like 80,000 pithy, hilarious texts with his friends." Each of those units measured a "gesture of care."

There isn't much written about the sleepless nights these people faced. Or the terror that racked some when they tried to leave the house. Or the untouched dresser drawers, the padlocked storage lockers, the daily indignities of not knowing.

Many of them found some comfort in not knowing. "There was hope," Selim's friend Richard Kikot wrote to the court. "People who are marginalized can fall off the radar, for many reasons." Richard made a thousand little worlds, where Selim was doing better—or, at the very least, where he was safe. "Perhaps he found a more stable living arrangement and was regrouping, getting much-needed rest. It could be that he left town to seek out stability elsewhere. Of course there was a potential that he had been hospitalized or incarcerated. I fought the urge to assume the worst."

His three brothers wrote that losing Selim was "like part of our body is cut into pieces and will keep bleeding forever."

Jalil Kayhan, Hamid's brother, recognized the absurdity of trying to encapsulate those years of sorrow into the form provided by the court. "This statement, as long as I can try to put it into words, can never represent the true pain and suffering that I and my family members have suffered and will continue to suffer," he wrote. "This is merely a humble attempt to express a minute portion of it." Jalil represented a huge family, all bereft: Hamid's two children, three grandchildren, nieces, nephews, siblings, all of whom "will never be able to enjoy his presence again."

One of Selim's family members who the court did not hear from was Sammy, his former partner. Even if he had only been considered as a suspect in Selim's disappearance briefly, police and prosecutors continued to treat him coolly through the trial. He wasn't invited to deliver a statement. "These crimes were about eight victims, but that is not all," he told me. "It is about all the people who were attached to them." I spoke to him at length of his own struggle to come to terms with Selim's death. He recalled vividly the day after Selim had disappeared. "I woke up with a terrible anxiety," he wrote to me. "I have never felt so worried with bitterness. I reached out to call Selim, and his phone was off." He fell into a waking nightmare. Selim was at the bottom of a ravine. "Selim was saying my name, and trying to extend his hand to me." In this lucid dream, a figure attacks Selim. He watched as Selim was murdered, his body buried under a tree. His deep sense of foreboding was so similar to many who did read their statements that day.

As Bruce McArthur sat in the prisoner's box, those families, the other victims, finally got a chance to give the world a window into what he had done to their lives. What he had taken. Each person had a different style. Some read their statements defiantly to McArthur himself, while others ignored him entirely. For some, the grief was too much; their statements were read into the record by the Crown attorneys.

When it came time to hear from Umme Fareena, Soroush Mahmudi's wife, the judge called her: "Is Ms. Fareena in the court?"

She rose uncertainly in the back rows of the court benches. She wore a black dress, with a pink scarf wrapped tightly around her neck. She slowly slumped back into her seat, letting the Crown read her words to the court.

"My pain and suffering will always be there as long as I live. I will be constantly reminded of how my beloved and innocent husband was brutally murdered," the lawyer read aloud, channeling Umme. As he continued, a soft sob came from where she was sitting. "My life has turned upside down." As he went on, her sobs grew steadily louder.

Kareema Faizi lost her husband, too. "Every morning when I wake I have a headache and my whole body aches," she wrote in her statement. One of the Crown attorneys read her statement aloud to the court, pausing at times to regain his composure as the weight of her statement got too heavy. Kareema sat in the back of the court, listening to her own trauma being read into the record. In that statement, she talks about her daughters, about their memories of their father. "That's all they have left of him now." Kareema works double shifts to keep food on the table. When her daughters were old enough, they took on jobs to support their mother. Basir was ripped out of their lives in a day.

For other families, their loss was a distant fading.

Kirushnakumar Kanagaratanam disappeared slowly. That didn't make the loss any less painful. "When I sleep, I sleep with a sadness that fills my heart and always tears come to my eyes," his sister Kirushnaveny Yasotharan wrote to the court. "I have completely lost my harmony," she wrote. "I live with my mind on auto-destruction." Kirushnaveny's three children, still living a world away from where their uncle went missing, are incapable of grasping what had happened.

Piranavan Thangavel joined Kirushnakumar for those three months aboard the MV *Sun Sea* to, as he put it, "just seek the safety of our lives." He remembered the joy he and Kirushnakumar felt arriving on Canadian shores. "Many of our lives today have now been left in limbo, as the Government of Canada back then was not ready to welcome us with open arms." He wrote of the "uncertainty, insecurity and fear that we still live with here in Canada."

"Our friend Kirushnakumar's death itself has been a direct result of that."

Jean-Guy Cloutier, Skanda's close friend, recalled the day he finally had to accept that Skandaraj Navaratnam had disappeared. "I would constantly look for him on the subway, on the streets," he told the court. "I had emptied his place of residence and held on to his belongings."

The day finally came, more than seven years after the day he had last seen Skanda—he still remembers his friend, working on the roof at the cottage. "I received a call from Toronto Police advising me that Skanda had been identified as one of the victims," Jean-Guy said. Not everything is gone. Skanda's clothes still sit in the cabin. The spot where he would go outside to meditate is still there, too.

Emily Bourgeois addressed that court on a freezing day in January over the loss of someone she never really knew. She was robbed of the chance to know her biological father, Dean Lisowick. "Even though I never knew him, there was still a chance that maybe one day I would be able to meet him, bump into him downtown and talk to him, but now that is all gone," she told the court from the witness stand. Her children will never get to know their grandfather. Dean's cousin, Julie Pearo, cast aside the man sitting in the prisoner's box. "I will never speak his name," she told the courtroom. She likened referring to him to talking about the waiter at lunch. An afterthought. Julie, instead, focused on the man she lost.

"I struggle with the finality," Pearo said. "Acceptance of his death—of Dean being dead—is elusive. I know he is. I'm aware of the facts. But maybe science will make it untrue. There must be something logical, explained by science, discovered by CERN that will flip the universe or time so that Dean is still here and I will see his smile in front of me again. Where I can talk to him and he will speak back to me."

To sit in the courtroom and listen to these statements was to be faced with such a deluge of emotions. So many of the stories were so similar—not rote or familiar, but heartbreakingly kindred. Many of the victims spoke of the headaches, the physical pain of the trauma. Of being unable to sleep, of losing their jobs. Patricia Kinsman, Andrew's sister, explained how she has continued her social life with none of the same joy as before. "I am the sad clown." Others chose to challenge the man sitting in the prisoners' box. "Andrew outsmarted him," his friend Ted Healey said. "Andrew beat him. I can live with that."

For many, answers didn't come with a conviction. There may never really be answers.

"Selim spent his life asking why," his brothers wrote. "We will continue his quest and keep asking: Why?"

• • •

A postcard has followed me for the past three years. It is a small, black-and-white version of that poster: MISSING ANDREW KINSMAN. I was given the thick piece of paper in August 2017, at the town hall organized to address the disappearance of the missing men. I look at that card often.

I've been in journalism school twice. Both times, I dropped out. Wasn't for me, it turns out. But there's one assignment that I'll never forget. I've learned since that it's a trope in journalism schools. Many other budding journalists have been subjected to exactly this torture.

It was my first year. My professor walked into the room. Our assignment that week was to cover grief. We were tasked with going out into the world and finding someone who had recently experienced real, painful loss. The assignment wasn't to go and interview a long-time widower but instead to find someone who had lost a close partner or relative recently. Someone whose life had just been shattered by death. It was preparation, we were told, for the real world.

We were not, of course, in the real world. I left campus with my brow furrowed. *Why should I go poke someone's emotional wound for a grade?*

Sometimes journalists need to interview grieving parents. Or a recent widower. Or a traumatized survivor. But, in those situations, one hopes there's a greater good to be gained. Context, understanding, or comfort that could be relayed to the public through that interview. And that is a skill you gain over time. It can't be practised. At the very least, it shouldn't be practised *on someone*.

This assignment felt like a cruel prank. They'd speak to me, maybe over a glass of warm water with lemon and honey, a box of tissue within reach. I'd sit across their dining-room table, recorder between us, pen in hand. They'd spill their heart out, through sobs, in hopes that their loved one's memory might live on in my reporting. Or that their death could inspire someone else. Or right a wrong.

And instead, their grief would be translated into a rough eight-hundred-word story, rife with mixed metaphors and grammatical mistakes, to be read only by my professor. It would earn a B. Optimistically, a B+.

So I balked. I interviewed my boyfriend about his recently deceased goldfish. I got an F, marked in a big red scribble at the top of the paper, informing me I had ignored the purpose of the assignment.

I tell this story because I feel that far too many journalists took this infantile journalism school lesson to heart. The philosophy behind the assignment is still a pervasive guiding light for many in the industry. It rankles me every day. It's a philosophy that tells journalists we must chase and harangue people into speaking to us, and it is a toxic one. It's one I've only become more dead-set against since beginning this story.

I thought about that class assignment while sitting in the body of the court, as the victims read their statements. Many focused on the pernicious role the media played in magnifying their grief. Robin LeBlanc, a friend and neighbour of Andrew, really drove it home.

"A reporter put a microphone in my face and asked if I imagined all the 'gory details' of what had happened to him, and how I felt knowing now that there was no hope that the man we had been searching for all those months was still alive. Something burned out inside of me as I processed that and I began to fall apart."

Journalists can't pretend that our work doesn't harm the mental health of the people we cover. In trying to tell the tragedies we believe are important, we can harm the people already hurt by those stories in horrible ways. We can't absolve ourselves of that responsibility.

Over the course of my career, I have covered murders, terror attacks, sexual assault, and every colour of tragedy. I've sat in lockdown in Parliament as a gunman engaged in a firefight with security a few floors below, as I wondered if I would die. I've stood outside a hospital as dazed EMTs told us how they tried to save as many lives as possible after a van attack killed scores. I've sat in a courtroom while video of a sadistic murder played on every courtroom TV, focusing intently on the screen as reporters around me flinched and looked away.

There's a reason why you're taught robotic dispassion in journalism school, not empathy. Because empathy hurts. Empathy means crying into your hands, sitting in a café while you write this book. It means making professional relationships with friends of the victims that turn into friendships that become ethical landmines. It means being unable to get the quote that your competitor got, because you can't bring yourself to call the person you know is having a tough time.

But I think the future is in empathy.

Journalism can't exist as an industry that just sucks the emotional labour from people and walks away. At the same time, journalism can't be an industry that expects its workers to perform that emotional labour without support. A focus on mental health is only now entering the journalism school curriculum. Conversations about how to handle death and despair are only just beginning. We need to continue demystifying trauma, and empowering those in the media industry to stand up and admit that they're not okay.

But this is a lesson that needs to be heeded by the consumers of news, as well. A burgeoning true crime industry has turned murder into spectator sport. Investigations and prosecutions get derailed by media fanfare. Families get harassed and stalked by self-professed fans of the murder that ripped their life apart. Internet sleuths door-knock and bumble their way through an amateur investigation. The crime-entertainment industry is predatory and destructive.

Journalism needs to comfort these people in all those horrible hours before answers come, not descend like vultures once they arrive. Policing can't leave those families abandoned when their need is greatest. And community needs to rally around its missing and murdered, even when it feels like the rest of society has forgotten them.

I think all we can hope for, in this story, is that we have learned something more for next time. Because there will be a next time. There is, unfortunately, always a next time. What we can hope for is that, next time, we can all do a little better.

The time after that, a little bit better still.

Until we finally get it right.

NOTES AND ACKNOWLEDGEMENTS

Writing this book was a team effort—even if the rest of the team didn't know it at the time.

There were the people who had to deal with me as I worked on it, namely my partner and friends. And the staff and regulars of Food & Liquor, who kept me company as I occupied a spot at the bar, tapping away at this book for over a year.

I first started reporting this story while at VICE News. My editor, Natalie Alcoba, gave me both freedom and support to report out this story for more than two years. In the hours after the arrest was made, I rejoined the VICE team—Josh Visser, Manisha Krishnan, Rachel Browne, Mack Lamoureux, and Tamara Khandaker—to make sense of things.

At the *Globe and Mail*, enormous credit goes to Tu Thanh Ha and Nicole MacIntyre. So many of the interviews, insights, and revelations that I relied on for our reporting at the *Globe*, information that ultimately ended up in this book, came from Ha's diligent work. I literally could not have written it without him. Nicole, our editor, not only made my participation possible but gave us room to work, fought for our coverage, and provided an invaluable set of eyes while still, somehow, managing to keep the rest of the paper running.

Then there are the superhuman librarians, especially Rick Cash and Stephanie Chambers, who broke open leads that helped us understand the victims' lives. Other reporters and editors tagged in for help at various times, especially Molly Hayes and Marcus Gee, who helped keep the Toronto Police accountable. On the masthead, deputy editor Sinclair Stewart and editor-in-chief David Walmsley ensured there were always resources and space in the paper for the story we were telling. Even though we dealt with just about every ethical dilemma that could not have been imagined in journalism school, the *Globe* handled it perfectly.

The CBC asked me to produce a podcast about the murders and disappearances in the Village and gave me all the resources I needed to explore a history of violence and resistance going all the way back to the 1970s. So much of what I learned making that show informed my approach to this book. Arif Noorani and Tanya Springer made it happen; Jennifer Flower and Erin Byrnes produced, wrote, and researched the show with me; and David McDougall, Cesil Fernandes, and Mitch Stuart were all instrumental in putting it together.

And there's a myriad of others in the media that made these stories possible. There's Matt Gurney and Supriya Dwivedi, who first invited me on their radio show to talk about this story. Adrian Lee at *Maclean's* asked me to write about the police investigation.

There's Andrea Houston and Arshy Mann from *Xtra*. Andrea covered the disappearances in 2013, and Arshy covered them in 2017 and onward. A huge team at the *Toronto Star* managed to drive this story forward with humanity and a great dedication for uncovering the details of the case, especially Wendy Gillis, Kenyon Wallace, and Jayme Poisson.

This book also draws heavily on my own interviews with friends and family of the missing men and other members of the community, who sat and spoke to me, sometimes at great expense to their own emotional and mental state. Their contributions are invaluable, and I can't possibly name them all. I need to credit Meaghan Marian in particular, however, for her work in advocating for her friend, Andrew Kinsman; and for keeping me in line as I worked on this story. The victim impact statements submitted to the court were also incredible sources of information about these men's lives. I heavily relied on the meticulous documentation prepared for Project Prism and Project Houston, which recorded the facts of those investigations in great detail.

It would be impossible to properly credit and acknowledge every single person who contributed in some way to telling this story—so many came forward with information, helped bring humanity to the stories of these men, or otherwise swivelled the spotlight towards this issue.

It really does take a Village.

1: THE VILLAGE

Piecing together the backstory of Skanda Navaratnam, Basir Faizi, and Hamid Kayhan was no easy task. Tracking down those who knew these men took years and was an exhausting experience for many. My conversations with Sarrah Becker, Joel Walker, Kyle Andrews, and a handful of others were particularly helpful. The ITOs (informations to obtain) prepared by police under Project Houston also provided valuable insights into the backstories of these men.

8   **There was an actual throne** Phil Villeneuve, "Toronto Says Goodbye to Legendary Gay Bar Zipperz," BlogTO, August 3, 2016, https://www.blogto.com/city/2016/08/toronto_says_goodbye_to_ legendary_gay_bar_zipperz/.

14   **Jody spoke to queer newspaper** *Xtra* Brent Creelman, "Toronto Gay Man Missing Since Sept 6," *Xtra*, September 10, 2010, https:// www.dailyxtra.com/toronto-gay-man-missing-since-sept-6-9187.

2: THE VOID WHERE EACH MAN WAS

29   **A reporter stood on Church Street** Joshua Freeman, "Police Seek Info About Missing Men in Church and Wellesley Area," CP24, June 6, 2013, https://www.cp24.com/news/police-seek-info-about-missing-men-in-church-and-wellesley-area-1.1314394.

29   **An officer stood in the polished atrium of police headquarters** Frank Prendergast, "Is a Serial Killer Targeting Gay Men in Toronto?" *Xtra*, June 7, 2013, https://www.youtube.com/ watch?v=q3izFF3a6qU.

3: BRUCE MCARTHUR

The backstory of Bruce McArthur was a challenge to put together, in part because it was defined for so long by total normalcy. Much of the detail of his life comes from what McArthur himself told a forensic psychologist after his 2001 arrest and from the transcripts of his sentencing hearing. My conversations with those who know him and his family, including Karen Fraser, helped sketch out additional details.
    David is a pseudonym.

35   **McArthur's graduation yearbook** Richard Warnica and Jake Edmiston, "How Bruce McArthur Went From Small-Town Sock Salesman to Accused Serial Killer," *National Post*, February 3, 2018, https://nationalpost.com/feature/bruce-mcarthur-small-town-sock-salesman-to-accused-serial-killer.

4: REVIVING A COLD CASE

50   **The second hit is the story I'm thinking of** Andrea Houston, "Piecing Together the Story of Three Missing Men From Toronto's Gay Village," *Xtra*, June 8, 2013, https://www.dailyxtra.com/piecing-together-the-story-of-three-missing-men-from-torontos-gay-village-49400.

51   **Navaratnam was last seen leaving a bar on Church Street** Sarah Petz, "Police Investigating Link Between Three Missing Men Who Frequented Toronto's Gay Village," *National Post*, June 6, 2013, https://nationalpost.com/news/toronto/police-investigating-possible-link-between-three-missing-men.

51   *The South Bayview Bulldog* "Toronto Cops Suspect Pattern as Three Men Vanish," *South Bayview Bulldog*, June 6, 2013, https://bayview-news.com/2013/06/toronto-cops-suspect-pattern-as-three-men-vanish.html/.

51   **A local newspaper in Mississauga** Pam Douglas, "Police Seek New Lead on Brampton Man Who Disappeared After Leaving Work Five Years Ago," *Brampton Guardian*, December 15, 2015, https://www.bramptonguardian.com/news-story/6194630-police-seek-new-lead-on-brampton-man-who-disappeared-after-leaving-work-five-years-ago/.

52   **"Where have these men gone?"** Dotr, Re: "3 men missing in same Toronto ON neighborhood, 2010-2012," June 6, 2013, https://www.websleuths.com/forums/threads/3-men-missing-in-same-toronto-on-neighborhood-2010-2012.211457/page-3#post-11102176.

57   **There's Mohmud "Moe" Jiwani** David Lea, "Where Is Mohmud Jiwani?" *Burlington Post*, February 16, 2007, https://www.toronto.com/news-story/2961561-where-is-mohmud-jiwani-/.

58   **I look into Sahil Sharma** Jon Azpiri, "Crime Stoppers: What Happened to Sahil Sharma?" Global News, October 11, 2015, https://globalnews.ca/news/2271274/crime-stoppers-what-happened-to-sahil-sharma/.

5: ANDREW AND SELIM

Andrew's and Selim's friends were very proactive and collaborative through this whole ordeal. Every one of them deserves acknowledgement, but in particular I want to mention my conversations with Richard Harrop, Ted Healey, Meaghan Marian, and Earl Everett.

6: PARANOIA

Every reporter who worked on Alloura Wells's disappearance and the eventual discovery of her body, of which I am not one, deserves credit for this chapter. The same goes for those journalists who followed Tess Richey's murder and the eventual arrest and trial of her killer. In particular I want to credit Alyshah Hasham, whose coverage from the courtroom was thorough and dependable.

85   **They picked up the phone and called a prison** Denise Balkissoon and Tu Thanh Ha, "Death of Alloura Wells Tells a Story of a Vulnerable Community," *Globe and Mail*, December 15, 2017, https://www.theglobeandmail.com/news/toronto/death-of-alloura-wells-tells-a-story-of-a-vulnerablecommunity/article37356642/.

86   **Based on the state of the body** Muriel Draaisma, "Body Found in Ravine Undergoing DNA Tests to See if It Belongs to Missing Transgender Woman," CBC, November 28, 2017, https://www.cbc.ca/news/canada/toronto/body-rosedale-ravine-alloura-wells-1.4421448.

86   **I think he just couldn't wait to get me off the phone** Arshy Mann, "A Trans Woman Was Found Dead in Toronto. A Trans Woman Went Missing. Why Do We Still Not Have Answers?" *Xtra*, November 21, 2017, https://www.dailyxtra.com/a-trans-woman-was-found-dead-in-toronto-a-trans-woman-went-missing-why-do-we-still-not-have-answers-81381.

7: "WHO'S BASHING WHOM?"

I relied heavily on the *Globe and Mail*, *Toronto Star*, and *Toronto Sun* archives for the historical background in this chapter. I also drew heavily from the ArQuives, Canada's largest independent queer archives, whose fonds—especially the records of the *Body Politic*—were indispensable. Interviews with queer activists Peter Maloney, Dennis Finley, Brent Hawkes, Robin Rowland, and others were very illuminating, as were conversations with former homicide cops David Penny, Bernard Nadeau, and Julian Fantino.

    I relied on the city's main three newspapers in order to compile statistics on the annual homicide and solve rate for queer people in Toronto.

94 **They quoted Detective Julian Fantino** "Police Seek Leaders in Brutal Slaying of Gay Club Owner," *Body Politic*, October 1978.

94 **He was convicted of murder** "Boy of 16 Breaks Down When Sentenced to Life," *Toronto Star*, November 29, 1963.

95 **And there was the slaying of Bruno Seidel** Gwyn Thomas, "Crime —It's Soared 10% in a Year," *Toronto Star*, December 23, 1967.

95 **"Three faggots raped me: Teen"** Paul Bilodeau. *Toronto Sun*.

95 **"Who's bashing whom?"** Sean McCann. *Toronto Sun*, February 11, 1981.

96 **"The next thing you know there's like ten cops walking towards the table"** "#Hear Our Story—The Brunswick Four," March 19, 2018, YouTube, https://www.youtube.com/watch?v=Sinp1MDQbIo&feature=emb_title.

97 **"The chain of office for mayor is becoming a daisy chain"** Chris Bearchell and Ed Jackson, "Window on Sewell," *Body Politic*, February 1980.

98 **Some 190 men were arrested for "sexual offences"** "Every 46 Hours and Eight Minutes," *Body Politic*, March 1980.

101 **It took decades for the reports to be unsealed** Alan Cairns, "Toronto Police Eavesdropped on Chair of Review Board," *Globe and Mail*, May 18, 2007; updated April 25, 2018, https://www.theglobeandmail.com/news/national/toronto-police-eavesdropped-on-chair-of-review-board/article1076335/.

103 **"Lamonica's husband, Albert, had been shot to death by Toronto Police"** Warren Gerard, "To Serve and Protect and Sometimes Shoot to Kill," *Maclean's*, September 24, 1979, https://archive.macleans.ca/article/1979/9/24/to-serve-and-protect-and-sometimes-shoot-to-kill.

104 **In 1991, Toronto Police surveilled Peter Maloney all over again** "Toronto Police Illegally Bugged Ex-Chair: Tapes," CBC, November 19, 2010, https://www.cbc.ca/news/canada/toronto-police-illegally-bugged-ex-chair-tapes-1.969214.

106 **Penned an extensive story for the *Globe*** Gerald Hannon, "The Kiddie Porn Ring That Wasn't," March 11, 1995.

107 **When Blair showed up for a Pride brunch days later** Marcus McCann, Matt Mills. "Pride Toronto, Toronto Police Cocktail Party Turns Ugly," *Xtra*, June 29, 2010. Archived: https://web.archive.org/web/20120926134221/http://www.xtra.ca/blog/national/post/2010/06/29/Pride-Toronto-Toronto-Police-cocktail-party-turns-ugly.aspx.

8: SURVEILLANCE

This chapter in particular relies on Project Prism's investigative documents. I have read a lot of investigative records in my career, particularly search warrants; these were significantly more helpful than most. This chapter also relies on conversations with officers from the Toronto Police Service, both those who spoke on background and those who talked to me on the record, like Detective Dave Dickinson. Matt is a pseudonym.

115   **A tarp was laid out on the floor** "'I Knew He Was Going to Kill Me': Man Describes Escaping From Serial Killer's Van," Global News, March 25, 2019, https://www.youtube.com/watch?v=kDxTvMzbnL4.

9: THE ARREST

Conversations with Karen Fraser and Peter Sgromo were constructive in putting together the pieces of McArthur's life and figuring out his crimes. Details about McArthur's son's legal troubles come from court files.
    Reza is a pseudonym.

135   **McArthur's son had been charged with harassment for targeting a Waterloo woman** "Online Photos Led to Months of Obscene Telephone Calls," *Waterloo Region Record*, June 11, 2014, https://www.therecord.com/news/waterloo-region/2014/06/11/online-photos-led-to-months-of-obscene-telephone-calls.html.

10: DEAN AND SOROUSH

The researchers at the *Globe* were indispensable in so many parts of this story, but they really stepped up in finding Sarah. Her story told us so much about Soroush's past and revealed clues that could have helped the investigation, if only they had been fully investigated. Ha deserves all the credit when it comes to putting together the story of Dean's childhood, which he did with a tremendous amount of tact.

147   **Fareena later spoke to the *Toronto Star*** Victoria Gibson, "Murder Victim's Wife Tells of Love Story Turned Wrenching Tragedy," *Toronto Star*, February 23, 2018. https://www.thestar.com/news/crime/2018/02/23/in-the-apartment-they-once-shared-soroush-mahmudis-wife-fareena-is-surrounded-by-memories-of-a-man-with-a-good-heart.html.

11: INSIDE THE TORONTO POLICE SERVICE

Credit in this chapter goes to the reporters of both the *Toronto Star* and *Globe and Mail*. Their newsrooms have been holding the Toronto Police Service accountable for generations. I relied enormously on their reporting during this story.

My conversations with Mita Hans and Nicki Ward were enlightening, illuminating, and incredibly useful.

I also owe a debt of gratitude to the officers inside the Toronto Police Service who believe in accountability and who provided us with details about Project Houston, even as the service itself was stonewalling us.

166 **Nearly one-quarter of those entered into Versadex were Black** "Carding Analysis: Behind the Numbers," *Toronto Star*, July 25, 2014, https://www.thestar.com/news/insight/2014/07/25/carding_analysis_behind_the_numbers.html.

167 **The race ultimately came down to two candidates** Betsy Powell and Jennifer Pagliaro, "Two Deputies in Spotlight in Search for a Diverse Police Chief," *Toronto Star*, March 27, 2015, https://www.thestar.com/news/city_hall/2015/03/27/two-deputies-in-spotlight-in-search-for-a-diverse-police-chief.html.

167 **About forty-five minutes into the conversation** Tu Thanh Ha, "Toronto Police Chief Says Civilians Failed to Help Investigation Into Alleged Serial Killer," *Globe and Mail*, February 27, 2018, https://www.theglobeandmail.com/news/toronto/toronto-police-chief-says-civilians-failed-to-help-investigation-into-alleged-serial-killer/article38124737/.

171 **Only the *Toronto Sun* seemed totally deferential to the chief** Joe Warmington, "Chief Mark Saunders Has No Reason to Apologize," *Toronto Sun*, February 28, 2018, https://torontosun.com/news/local-news/warmington-chief-mark-saunders-has-no-reason-to-apologize.

175 **Days earlier, Idsinga had spoken to CTV News** Avery Haines, "The Missing," W5, CTV, February 27, 2018. Chris is a pseudonym.

179 **There was a link to a news story** Jayme Poisson and Kenyon Wallace, "Bruce McArthur Was Previously Questioned, Released by Police in Separate Incident," *Toronto Star*, March 6, 2018, https://www.thestar.com/news/gta/2018/03/06/bruce-mcarthur-was-previously-questioned-released-by-police-in-separate-incident.html.

12: A SWISS TIP

184 **Just a couple of years before** Chris Summers, "Man Reveals He Was Nearly Eaten by Mass Killer," *Daily Mail*, May 11, 2016, https://www.dailymail.co.uk/news/article-3584343/I-advertised-eat-alive-cannibal-said-d-meet-woods-chop-Man-reveals-nearly-eaten-killer.html.

13: RED FLAGS

192 **On March 6, two weeks after the editorial board meeting at the *Globe*** Wendy Gillis and Kenyon Wallace, "Man reported to Toronto police in 2016 that McArthur allegedly attempted to strangle him." *Toronto Star*, March 8, 2018, https://www.thestar.com/news/gta/2018/03/08/man-reported-to-toronto-police-in-2016-that-mcarthur-allegedly-attempted-to-strangle-him.html.

194 **Early that March, Sean Cribbin went public with his story** Catherine McDonald, "Bruce McArthur Had Me in a 'Kill Position,' Says Toronto Man Haunted by Date With Alleged Serial Killer," Global News, March 6, 2018, https://globalnews.ca/news/4063145/bruce-mcarthur-sean-cribbin-date-with-alleged-serial-killer/.

14: KIRUSHNAKUMAR

202 **The coast guard were keeping an eye on the ship** Marten Youssef, "Thai-Registered Asylum Ship May Be Headed to B.C.," *Globe and Mail*, July 23, 2010, https://www.theglobeandmail.com/news/british-columbia/thai-registered-asylum-ship-may-be-headed-to-bc/article1387982/.

211 **In late April 2018, Suthakaran sent me a poem** Suthakaran Thanigasalam, undated.

223 **Selim's service was held in a church but was distinctly secular** Victoria Gibson, "After Investigative Delays, Funerals Finally Under Way for Alleged Bruce McArthur Victims," *Globe and Mail*, November 1, 2018, https://www.theglobeandmail.com/canada/toronto/article-after-investigative-delays-funerals-finally-under-way-for-alleged/.

15: DUMPING GROUND

Of particular help in this chapter was Douglas Janoff, author of *Pink Blood: Homophobic Violence in Canada*. His insight on the scourge of anti-queer violence, especially on the gay/trans panic defence, was enlightening.

Once again, the reporting of Alyshah Hasham was instructive in reporting on Tess Richey's murder.

My conversation with Jack Peterson, a self-described ex-incel, also helped me more thoroughly understand the seedy, hateful world of the involuntary celibates.

16: KILLING WITH EASE

229 **By the time city supervisor Harvey Milk stood** Harvey Milk, "The Hope Speech." Gay Freedom Day, San Francisco City Hall, June 25, 1978.

231 **"My feeling is they don't want to be exposed"** "Man Suspected of 14 SF Slayings," Associated Press, July 8, 1977.

231 **Milk himself issued that call in a prophetic poem he penned before his murder** Harvey Milk, untitled poem.

232 **White was convicted of manslaughter** Carol Pogash, "Myth of the 'Twinkie Defense'," *San Francisco Chronicle*, November 23, 2003, https://www.sfgate.com/health/article/Myth-of-the-Twinkie-defense-The-verdict-in-2511152.php.

232 **Joseph Patrick Donoghue, found guilty of the lesser charge of manslaughter** "Manslaughter Verdict in Homosexual Killing," *Toronto Star*, March 25, 1977.

232 **When Paris Colin Rogers beat Gerald Douglas White to death in 1978** "2nd Killing Conviction Gets Man 6 Years," *Toronto Star*, February 20, 1979.

232 **William Richard Andes was sentenced to eight years for manslaughter** "Term Cut in Transsexual Slaying," *Globe and Mail*, April 18, 1980.

232 **Eric Swanson beat Edwin Kasdan to death in 1986** Patricia Sarjeant, "Jury Finds Teen-ager Not Guilty in '86 Killing of Toronto Lawyer," *Globe and Mail*, March 31, 1988.

232 **Bumping along in a car on a dirt road in rural Ontario** *R. v. Bouchard* (2014). 3 SCR 283. (Supreme Court of Canada.) https://scc-csc.lexum.com/scc-csc/scc-csc/en/item/14400/index.do.

233 **On the crowded dance floor of the Village's busiest gay bar** Alyshah Sanmati Hasham (@alysanmati), "This morning at Kalen Schlatter's trial for the first-degree murder of Tess Richey . . ." Twitter, February 5, 2020, 10:52 a.m., https://twitter.com/alysanmati/status/1225084825062854661; "UC-1 say he introduced himself as Mike," Twitter, February 5, 2020, 11:22 a.m. https://twitter.com/alysanmati/status/1225094939371020290.

233 **In New York, in 2016, James Dixon copped a plea deal for manslaughter** Julie Compton, "Alleged 'Gay Panic Defense' in Texas Murder Trial Stuns Advocates," NBC, November 2, 2018.

237 **That's what history teacher Kenneth Zeller discovered** Phillip Plews, "The Evil That Boys Do," *Globe and Mail*, April 25, 1986.

237 **Dandara dos Santos was the target** Trudy Ring, "Five Sentenced in Killing of Brazilian Transgender Woman," *The Advocate*, April 6, 2018.

238 **In Raleigh, police arrived** Carli Brosseau, Drew Jackson, Anna Johnson, "Wake Deputies Defend Force Used Against Owner of Raleigh LGBTQ Bar During Protest," *The News & Observer*, June 2, 2020, https://www.newsobserver.com/news/local/article243202416.html.

239 **A whole lot of shit happens to us because we don't resist** Andrew Kinsman, "On the murder of LGBTQ+ persons, after Orlando." Undated.

255 **Speaking to TVO before his departure** "Mark Saunders: Toronto's Police Chief Leaves His Post," *The Agenda with Steve Paikin*, June 25, 2020, https://www.tvo.org/transcript/2619324/mark-saunders-torontos-police-chief-leaves-his-post.

17: "THEY'VE ALL PURPORTED TO LISTEN"

My conversation with Wally Oppal, in particular, provided a lot of clarity on what the Toronto Police ought to be doing when it comes to missing persons cases. The report produced by his commission of inquiry is taxonomic for anyone looking to understand the intersection between policing and vulnerable communities.

My interview with Brent Hawkes also told me a lot about what it means to enact change in how the police operate. The records of the ArQuives were an enormous help in understanding the bathhouse raids.

18: GUILTY

262 **Christie Blatchford, a longtime *National Post* columnist with an impressive network of cop sources** Christie Blatchford, Nick Faris, "Bruce McArthur Expected to Plead Guilty to Eight Counts of First-Degree Murder: Source," *National Post*, January 28, 2019, https://nationalpost.com/news/canada/bruce-mcarthur-expected-to-plead-guilty-to-eight-counts-of-first-degree-murder-source.